African American Grief

The Series in Death, Dying, and Bereavement
Consulting Editor
Robert A. Neimeyer

Beder—Voices of Bereavement: A Casebook for Grief Counselors
Davies—Shadows in the Sun: The Experiences of Sibling Bereavement in Childhood
Harvey—Perspectives on Loss: A Sourcebook
Klass—The Spiritual Lives of Bereaved Parents
Jeffreys—Helping Grieving People – When Tears Are Not Enough: A Handbook for Care Providers
Leenaars—Lives and Deaths: Selections from the Works of Edwin S. Shneidman
Lester—Katie's Diary: Unlocking the Mystery of a Suicide
Martin, Doka—Men Don't Cry…Women Do: Transcending Gender Stereotypes of Grief
Nord—Multiple AIDS-Related Loss: A Handbook for Understanding and Surviving a Perpetual Fall
Roos—Chronic Sorrow: A Living Loss
Rosenblatt—Parent Grief: Narratives of Loss and Relationship
Rosenblatt & Wallace—African American Grief
Tedeschi & Calhoun—Helping Bereaved Parents: A Clinician's Guide
Silverman—Widow to Widow, Second Edition
Werth—Contemporary Perspectives on Rational Suicide

FORMERLY THE **SERIES IN DEATH EDUCATION, AGING, AND HEALTH CARE**
HANNELORE WASS, CONSULTING EDITOR

Bard—Medical Ethics in Practice
Benoliel—Death Education for the Health Professional
Bertman—Facing Death: Images, Insights, and Interventions
Brammer—How to Cope with Life Transitions: The Challenge of Personal Change
Cleiren—Bereavement and Adaptation: A Comparative Study of the Aftermath of Death
Corless, Pittman-Lindeman—AIDS: Principles, Practices, and Politics, Abridged Edition
Corless, Pittman-Lindeman—AIDS: Principles, Practices, and Politics, Reference Edition
Curran—Adolescent Suicidal Behavior
Davidson—The Hospice: Development and Administration. Second Edition
Davidson, Linnolla—Risk Factors in Youth Suicide
Degner, Beaton—Life-Death Decisions in Health Care
Doka—AIDS, Fear, and Society: Challenging the Dreaded Disease
Doty—Communication and Assertion Skills for Older Persons
Epting, Neimeyer—Personal Meanings of Death: Applications for Personal Construct Theory to Clinical Practice
Haber—Health Care for an Aging Society: Cost-Conscious Community Care and Self-Care Approaches
Hughes—Bereavement and Support: Healing in a Group Environment
Irish, Lundquist, Nelsen—Ethnic Variations in Dying, Death, and Grief: Diversity in Universality
Klass, Silverman, Nickman—Continuing Bonds: New Understanding of Grief
Lair—Counseling the Terminally Ill: Sharing the Journey
Leenaars, Maltsberger, Neimeyer—Treatment of Suicidal People
Leenaars, Wenckstern—Suicide Prevention in Schools
Leng—Psychological Care in Old Age
Leviton—Horrendous Death, Health, and Well-Being
Leviton—Horrendous Death and Health: Toward Action
Lindeman, Corby, Downing, Sanborn—Alzheimer's Day Care: A Basic Guide
Lund—Older Bereaved Spouses: Research with Practical Applications
Neimeyer—Death Anxiety Handbook: Research, Instrumentation, and Application
Papadatou, Papadatos—Children and Death
Prunkl, Berry—Death Week: Exploring the Dying Process
Ricker, Myers—Retirement Counseling: A Practical Guide for Action
Samarel—Caring for Life and Death
Sherron, Lumsden—Introduction to Educational Gerontology. Third Edition
Stillion—Death and Sexes: An Examination of Differential Longevity Attitudes, Behaviors, and Coping Skills
Stillion, McDowell, May—Suicide Across the Life Span—Premature Exits
Vachon—Occupational Stress in the Care of the Critically Ill, the Dying, and the Bereaved
Wass, Corr—Childhood and Death
Wass, Corr—Helping Children Cope with Death: Guidelines and Resource. Second Edition
Wass, Corr, Pacholski, Forfar—Death Education II: An Annotated Resource Guide
Wass, Neimeyer—Dying: Facing the Facts. Third Edition
Weenolsen—Transcendence of Loss over the Life Span
Werth—Rational Suicide? Implications for Mental Health Professionals

African American Grief

Paul C. Rosenblatt and Beverly R. Wallace

Routledge
Taylor & Francis Group

NEW YORK AND HOVE

Published in 2005 by
Routledge
Taylor & Francis Group
270 Madison Avenue
New York, NY 10016

Published in Great Britain by
Routledge
Taylor & Francis Group
27 Church Road
Hove, East Sussex BN3 2FA

Printed in the United States of America on acid-free paper
10 9 8 7 6 5 4 3 2 1

International Standard Book Number-10: 0-415-95151-8 (Hardcover) 0-415-95152-6 (Softcover)
International Standard Book Number-13: 978-0-415-95151-7 (Hardcover) 978-0-415-95152-4 (Softcover)
Library of Congress Card Number 2004022552

Library of Congress Cataloging-in-Publication Data

Rosenblatt, Paul C.
   African American grief / Paul C. Rosenblatt, Beverly R. Wallace.
         p. ; cm. -- (The series in death, dying, and bereavement)
   Includes bibliographical references and index.
   ISBN 0-415-95151-8 (hardcover : alk. paper) -- ISBN 0-415-95152-6 (pbk. : alk. paper)
   1. African Americans--Mental health. 2. African Americans--Psychology. 3. Grief--United States.
4. Bereavement--United States--Psychological aspects. 5. Loss (Psychology)
I. Wallace, Beverly R., 1954- . II. Title. III. Series.
   [DNLM: 1. Grief. 2. African Americans--psychology. 3. Attitude to Death--ethnology.
BF 575.G7 R813a 2005]

RC451.5.N4R67 2005
155.9'37'08996073--dc22   2004022552

Taylor & Francis Group
is the Academic Division of T&F Informa plc.

Visit the Taylor & Francis Web site at
http://www.taylorandfrancis.com

and the Routledge Web site at
http://www.routledgementalhealth.com

CONTENTS

SERIES EDITOR'S FOREWORD
Racism and Resilience

In its recently completed and comprehensive review of the literature on grief published over the last 20 years, the Center for the Advancement of Health (2004) attempted not only to summarize the best of contemporary scholarship on bereavement, but also to establish the research agenda for the next decade. Significantly, the first of these recommendations was to investigate the relatively neglected topic of diversity as it shapes the human encounter with loss, with a particular emphasis on such sociodemographic factors as race and ethnicity that are likely to moderate the impact of bereavement on critical health outcomes ranging from the psychological adjustment of survivors to their basic mortality. Indeed, of the over 4,000 studies published since 1984 on psychosocial issues at the end-of-life or during bereavement, only a small handful attempt to examine the potentially distinctive reactions to looming or actual loss for Americans who are not part of white majority culture. The result is a literature that tells us less than it might about the experience of other cultural and subcultural groups, thereby promoting a "one size fits all" conception of grieving of dubious relevance to any given community of bereaved persons, particularly those whose distinctive histories and social conditions depart significantly from those of the cultural mainstream. African Americans are one such cultural group, and redressing the inattention to this important population is the ambitious goal undertaken by Rosenblatt and Wallace in this groundbreaking volume.

The relatively few reports available that address the grief experiences of African Americans tend to follow a predictable pattern, taking the form of either thoughtful essays based on personal or professional experience, or incidental reports of racial or ethnic differences in a larger statistical study of types of loss or comparisons of grief outcomes for various subgroups. Building on this germinal literature, Rosenblatt and Wallace attempt something different: an in-depth qualitative study of the losses of dozens of African Americans, who generously volunteered hours of their time to discuss their encounter with the death of a loved one, in all of its psychological, social, and spiritual complexity. Using grounded theory analyses, the authors then extracted patterns from the welter of words, using extensive quotation of the men and women themselves to give voice to their unique experiences of loss and bereavement. The richness of the resulting report is hinted at by the sixteen chapters that comprise this book, focusing on topics ranging from various institutions, practices and beliefs that configure African American mourning to particular social processes and conditions that support or complicate grieving.

What can the reader expect to learn by immersion in this readable rendering of African American bereavement? In a phrase, a great deal. Concrete features of communal grieving come to light, from the significance of food made available following a service to the psychological and historical underpinnings of elaborate funeral ceremonies. Likewise, less tangible but no less important features of mourning and meaning are explored, such as the adaptation of African customs in the context of predominantly Christian rituals, resulting in distinctive practices of "praying a loved one into heaven" during "homegoing" celebrations. A *leitmotif* throughout much of the book is the resilience of the African American community in the face of centuries of racism, whose subtle and unsubtle influences can be discerned in both the lives and deaths of family members loved and lost. At times, this imparts an element of heroism to those lives, as stories of success against the odds form a source of pride for survivors. At other times, the injustice associated with, say, assignment to hazardous work that contributed to the death presents an additional challenge to the bereaved beyond the sundered attachment itself. The evenhandedness with which Rosenblatt and Wallace treat these themes is noteworthy, as when they illustrate the advantages and constraints associated with "being strong in grief," particularly for women who are pillars of their families and communities. Nor do they shy away from the hard realities of loss in African American families—families often marked by histories of division, conflict, splits, maltreatment, neglect, poor health, and substance abuse. But by situating these complicating factors in a broader cultural context, they both make them intelligible, and highlight the strength of people who have drawn on a fund of personal and collective resources to accommodate to loss in ways that are surprisingly resilient.

In short, Rosenblatt and Wallace have written a book that holds lessons for students and scholars, professionals and lay readers, lessons conveyed in the words of bereaved African Americans themselves. Drawing richly on the present day accounts of interviewees, it both illuminates a past experienced by members of this important cultural group, and offers a future take-off point for more sensitive studies of grief among African Americans. In short, by gathering, sifting, and interpreting these accounts, the authors have done a service for both the women and men who contributed their narratives of loss, and for those of us who need to be instructed by them.

ROBERT A. NEIMEYER, PH.D.
The University of Memphis
October, 2004

☐ Reference

Center for the Advancement of Health (2004). Report on bereavement and grief research. *Death Studies, 28*, 6.

ACKNOWLEDGMENTS

For funding that helped to supported the interviewing that underlies this book, we are grateful to the Agricultural Experiment Station of the University of Minnesota. For help with some of the transcribing, we thank Jessica Paulson.

Paul is grateful for stimulating conversations with Oliver J. Williams, Tawana Bandy, Roxanne Cohen Silver, and William Turner. For a home environment that supported the time commitments and involvements that led to this book, Paul is grateful to Sara Wright and Emily Wright-Rosenblatt.

Beverly is grateful to Dr. Carolyn McCrary and Dr. Ed Wimberly, professors at the Interdenominational Theological Center in Atlanta, for teaching her the art of care; the Emory Center for Pastoral Care, especially Theresa Snorton, Robert Morris, Osofo (Calvin) Banks, Janet Lutz, and Nancy Long, who gave her the opportunity to walk with those who grieve; and to Jacqui, who taught her about grief and loss on a personal level. Beverly is also grateful to Jaylen Samuel, William and Yolanda Silveri, her grandson, son, and daughter, who have endured her many travels, and to Richard Wallace, who supported her in all of her efforts.

We could not have written this book without the assistance of the 26 people who gave the interviews that are at the heart of this book. To them we say thank you, thank you.

INTRODUCTION

In the thousands of English language articles, essays, and books by researchers and practitioners writing about grief following a death, there is little about African American grief (Barrett, 1995). This is not to say that a small number of studies cannot be immensely important. We have benefited from reading the works that are in the literature and that we cite at a number of places in this book, for example, Barrett (1995), Brice (1999), Hines (1986, 1991), Kalish and Reynolds (1981), and Meagher and Bell (1993). But still there are so few works focused on African Americans that it seems to us that African American grief has been neglected to a remarkable extent. And the neglect is compounded in that, judging by what is reported in the *Social Science Citation Index*, the little that has been written is rarely cited in the wider grief literature.

Why the neglect of African American grief? One way to think about it is that many who write about grief may assume that African American grief is not different from that of Euro-Americans. In fact, we believe that the assumption is even broader than that. It is that grief is a basic human process. So just as all humans breathe in the same way, all humans grieve in the same way. Thinking along those lines, a person would believe that if we learn about anybody's grief we learn about everybody's grief.

It may be convenient to assume that everyone grieves in basically the same way. Then one will know about everyone just by knowing oneself and the few people one knows well or just by having studied grief in one ethnic group. One can define grief as though it is the same across all groups. One can theorize about grief without paying attention to all the ways that life experience, culture, and so on might make differences from one group to another. It certainly is attractive to entertain a simple, generalized view of grief. But there is no way to know if the assumption of commonality of grief processes across human groups is valid without actually having studied grief in many (most? all?) human groups. There is no way to know if African American grief is just like Euro-American grief without having studied it. In fact, there is considerable evidence that grief is not the same from one culture to another (Rosenblatt, 1993, 1997, 2001, 2003; Rosenblatt, Walsh, & Jackson, 1976).

One can wonder if theories and knowledge based on an oppressor group in an oppressive system apply to the people who are oppressed (Plumpp, 1972, ch. 8). One can also wonder if white ignorance or neglect of grief or any other aspect of African American life is connected to the larger system of racism and privilege that is almost impossible to escape in the United States. Most scholars who study grief are, like the first author of this book, white. Just as whites tend to ignore other areas of African American experience (e.g., Davis, 2000; hooks, 1992; Kincheloe & Steinberg, 1998; McIntosh, 1988) they may tend to ignore African American grief. Tuning out African American grief might occur for many reasons. Many white people live racially segregated lives, so they may have little to go on in thinking about African American grieving. And also, it may be that in some ways African American experience does not count as much as white experience for some white people. Moreover, African American grief may be aversive for some whites to study, because understanding African American grief could draw whites into understanding the pain and the premature deaths caused by white oppression and indifference to (or ignorance of) that oppression. (By "premature deaths" we mean deaths happening before they would be likely to occur if living conditions for African Americans were the same as they are for Euro-Americans.)

Perhaps these speculations are off base in general or for specific grief scholars, but even if they are, it is clear that there is not a lot written about African American grief and not a lot of attention in the scholarly literature to African American grief or even to the possibility that it differs in significant ways from white grief and is important to study in itself.

☐   The Aims and Limitations of this Book

As a contribution to furthering knowledge about African American grief and filling the gap in the literature, this book offers an analysis of grief as described by 26 African Americans who had experienced the death of someone important in their lives. Although the 26 people whose interviews inform this book constitute too small and too nonrepresentative a sample to provide a fully valid and comprehensive picture of African American grief, we intend for this book to offer an approximation to what will some day be that comprehensive picture of African American bereavement. Based on the 26 interviews, we describe, document, and analyze what seem to us to be key phenomena in African American grieving and key elements of difference between African American and Euro-American grieving. There is much that could conceivably be relevant to African American grief that the people who were interviewed did not talk about. For example, they had little or nothing to say about slavery or about matters related to health maintenance such as diet and exercise. Research may someday expose connections of slavery to contemporary African American bereavement. Research may someday explore how it is that grieving African Americans have so little to say about health maintenance activities that might conceivably be related to who dies of what disease when. But the present study, relying on the interviews we were given, remains focused on the domains those interviews opened up.

Although in many ways contemporary theories of grief may fit what can be observed in African American grieving, in some ways these theories are mute, misleading, or unhelpful. The standard views of grief do not speak at all to how African American grief might be shaped by and responsive to racism, economic disadvantage, the substantial difference in life expectancy between African Americans and Euro-Americans, the social class diversity of many African American families, and, for some African Americans, the powerful influence of drugs and community devastation. Nor do the standard views of bereavement speak to the possible influence of the African American church and African American culture(s). Although a great deal of grief literature is written as though one set of principles fits all, this book explores the ways those principles are and are not all we need to understand the grief of African Americans.

We have written this book for academics and professionals who focus on grief or on African American life.

☐ Beginning Assumptions

We began with the assumption that African American grief over the death of someone important in the person's life, in all its cultural, social class, and religious diversity, is like Euro-American grief, in all its cultural, social class, and religious diversity. And yet we also assumed that, despite the diversity of African Americans (Barrett, 1998, 2003), there would be major differences between African American and Euro-American grief because there is much that is different about the experiences and culture(s) of African Americans.

We assumed that African American grief might be like Euro-American grief in the core processes of dealing with loss, in grief feelings and their time course, the ways that individual grieving affects relationships, the spiritual issues, the ways a grieving person might have a continuing relationship with the person who died, and the events that set off renewed grieving. But we also assumed that African American grief would be different from Euro-American grief because the history and contemporary experiences of African Americans provide unique elements for meaning making about the death and because racism is often implicated in African American death and grief.

We assumed that the unique history of oppression would move African Americans to places that relatively few Euro-Americans are concerning emotional control, emotional expression, and perhaps the vital importance of one or a few close relationships. Then too, we assumed that the fact of difference in life expectancy would mean that more often for African

Americans than for Euro-Americans, losses would be experienced at a relatively young age. Also, because of how racism and economic oppression have affected and continue to affect African Americans, we assumed that proportionately more often for African Americans than for Euro-Americans, losses are occasions for marked difficulties and changes related to scarcity of economic resources. These may include, proportionately more often for African Americans than for Euro-Americans, having to move to a distant location following a death, having to assume parental responsibilities for siblings following a parent's death, and having to face long-term severe economic deprivation as a result of a death.

We assumed that many African Americans draw on religious and musical resources in dealing with a death that are to a degree different from what most Euro-Americans draw on. Much of it may have its roots in the time of slavery and in the century and a half of community life since then. Some African Americans talk about drawing on Afrocentric traditions, practices, and meaning systems in dealing with a loss, things that they believe may go back to the time before the Middle Passage. Len, for example, is quoted in chapter 15 as talking about:

> West African traditions that have been integrated into who we are as African Americans that are unspoken traditions that still happen, that still go on. There's that whole thing about (chuckling), for the brothers who ain't here, libations and so forth.

It is difficult for an observer to know whether there are historically African influences in how an individual, family, or community deals with death, but to the extent that what goes on in contemporary African American life has roots in Africa (Barrett, 1993, 1995, 1998, 2003), one can turn to the west and central Africa of the past for ideas about what to look for in African American grief. Judging by what has been written about the African roots of modern African American life (e.g., Barrett, 1995, 1998; Devore, 1990; Herskovits, 1958; Holloway, 2002; McIlwain, 2003, pp. 30–39), one might look for African influences in what might go on in connection with some, or even many, deaths in the African American community. The literature on the cultural roots of African Americans would point to possible African forms, emphases, and meanings in the practice of elaborate funerals, the sense of the importance of honoring the name of the deceased, emphasis on the crucial importance of links between mothers and children, the power of the spirit of the deceased, the importance of proper funeral rituals, the ways that losses are community losses and not just family losses, and the importance to the community of dealing properly with the death of a person of great spiritual power. Hines (1991) added that important elements of an Afrocentric view of grief include death not being an end but a progression to something else, death in old age being far superior to an untimely death, death may be willed by the individual who dies, death that may occur in conjunction with a birth, people who may delay dying until certain important days (holidays, birthdays), death is God's will, death is not to be feared, and life on earth is preparation for life beyond death. All this is by way of saying that there is plenty of reason to think that African American grief might differ from Euro-American grief.

☐ The Dilemma of Comparison

In comparing African Americans with Euro-Americans there is the risk of making Euro-Americans the standard to which African Americans cannot measure up. There is the risk of using Euro-American ways of understanding things to obscure the uniqueness and complexity of African American ways of understanding. And yet most social science and psychological theory about grief comes from studies of Euro-Americans, so if we are going to make use of theory in understanding African American grief and use what we learn from our interviews of African Americans to challenge that theory, we must compare.

We want this book to be not only about but for the benefit of African Americans. We want this book to focus on African Americans, rather than to define African Americans in relationship to Euro-Americans. We do not for a moment think that what is meaningful about African Americans is how African Americans compare with Euro-Americans. Still, comparison is useful in raising questions about theories that might be inappropriately applied to African Americans. Comparison is useful in illuminating the ways racism can create challenges for African Americans that are not present for Euro-Americans. For example, by comparing it is easier to understand how African American grieving may be entangled in African Americans relatively often receiving substandard medical services (e.g., Christian, Lapane, & Toppa, 2003; Dennis, 2001; Freeman & Payne, 2000; Smedley, Stith, & Nelson, 2003) and having a shorter life expectancy than Euro-Americans (e.g., Arias, 2002, 2004).

From another angle, comparison seems useful in that African Americans often compare their experiences with those of Euro-Americans. Many of the people who were interviewed did not hesitate to contrast African American with Euro-American grief or their experiences with employers, hospitals, and other societal institutions with the experiences of Euro-Americans. This suggests that in trying to represent African American realities, it is legitimate to compare African American and Euro-American experience.

The bottom line is that we write about African Americans in their own terms and we also compare African Americans with Euro-Americans where we think that is appropriate and useful.

☐ Knowledge and Generalization

Generalizing from a small sample of people is terribly risky. It is especially so when writing about African Americans, who have been and are the subject of many ignorant and harmful generalizations. We do not want to lose track of the limits of a small sample or of the individuality and diversity of the 36 million plus people in the United States who might think of themselves as African American. In fact, several of the people interviewed emphasized the individuality and diversity of African Americans.

Kenneth: All human beings need time to make adjustments to the loss of someone that they love, and I think that what it would be like would be as unique as each individual family structure and relationship. Because I don't believe that there's a monolith of black folk. (Chuckling) I think that we all have different traditions and celebrations as to how we celebrate life, as to how we grieve and mourn. . . . I think that you go to a funeral in New Orleans (*Beverly:* Yeah, they celebrate). You understand? (*Beverly:* I know). But if you go to one in Bronx, you go to one in Newport News, Virginia, or to one in Minneapolis or to one in L.A., and Atlanta, you understand? I think that there're certain things that will be a continuum in that process, but they're going to be very unique at the same time. Because the culture of black folk has been and is still being determined by many other factors other than their being black. So, yeah, I think it would look quite different. [Note: The names given to each interviewee and each person an interviewee mentioned are pseudonyms, but "Beverly" is the real name of the interviewer, Beverly Wallace.]

Because our sample is small and African Americans are diverse, the knowledge we offer in this book is not the knowledge of generalizations but rather the knowledge of perspectives and ideas that may or may not apply to any particular African American. We are not saying anything is true in general for African Americans, because we do not know and because we are skeptical that those kinds of generalizations can be meaningful. But we offer tentative hypotheses, suggestions, and explanations for what may occur as African Americans deal with the death of close family members.

☐ The Distinctiveness of African American Life

Every person interviewed for this book was clear that in identity, values, and life experiences they were African American.

Andrew: I can't be nothing but African American. I don't care how much that I'm ingrained into a multicultural society, I think, and this is me . . . that the greatest thing I do have is that I am an African American. An African American even to the point that, yeah, of African descent, but I'm African American. I really am.

The fact of distinctive identity would be one ingredient in thinking that perhaps there are clear differences between how African Americans and Euro-Americans grieve.

Every African American interviewed for this book mentioned organizations important in their life that were distinctively African American; for example, the National Council of Negro Women in the first of the following three quotes, the African Methodist Episcopal Church in the second, and the African American sorority Alpha Kappa Alpha, in the third quote.

Rosalyn: My life now it's centered around God. I work my job here, and I'm active in my church. I'm a church usher. And I spend my time with serving in my ushers' ministry. I work with our junior ushers at our church, and I'm the coordinator, leader for them. And I'm also with the United Church Ushers of Minnesota. And I've become an instructor. So I filled that void with things, worthwhile things, what I call worthwhile things. That's what I like to do. Render service to others. And (breathes out) work and then with the National Council of Negro Women.

Kenneth: My grandfather's Baptist too. This is my father's father who was an AME. All right? So on both sides of the family it's different tradition, but it's the same faith. Same God, all right? (laughs) And so these are the defining pillars and the shoulders that I stand on in understanding who I am and how I am in the world.

Willa: I buried her in a green dress. She was an AKA, so pink and green.

The fact of participation in distinctively African American organizations suggests that African American emotional life, meaning making, and social support takes place to a substantial extent in a culturally segregated environment. The separation of environments is another reason why it is easy for us to imagine that African American and Euro-American grief would differ in significant ways.

Nowadays for some people, and in the recent past for many who were interviewed for this book, the segregation of American society did not stop with death. Cemeteries for African Americans were often (and to some extent still are) separate (and unequal).

Willa: [My dad] was buried in the quote black cemetery, which means there was no upkeep or anything. . . . Couldn't even find all the people that owned property. It was some fraternal organization. They were scattered to the four winds. Most of them were dead. And if you wanted your people to be taken care of (chuckling) . . . I can remember many times, Mom would load the lawn mower up and her tool kit, and we'd go to the cemetery and cut Daddy's plot.

The separation of burial places means that African American burial ceremonies and cemetery visits are not necessarily shaped by the constraints and standards of Euro-American cemeteries. True, the influence of Euro-Americans can be seen in African American cemeteries, even in the names on tombstones. But that does not mean that white people could stop African Americans from knowing who they are.

Loretta: I went to our ancestral cemetery and showed my daughter the tombs from the 1700s. And when you can go back three generations and four generations, and say, "Here's your ancestors, and this is what they were about," and "Here's our last name, my last name was [misspelled]. They had six kids. The first three [had a last name spelled like mine]. The last three were [spelled differently], because the white people said we didn't know what we were doin' when we spelled our name. Okay? And that was one of my grandfather's siblings. His brother['s name was spelled like mine] and [my grandfather's name was spelled differently]. . . . Even though they did that to us, we still have that history, and we know who we are. And I know who I am. And we're not weak. We are strong.

The family life of African Americans, as described by the people we interviewed, includes uniquely African American elements. For example, children are reared in ways that are more characteristic of African American than Euro-American families.

Patricia: My grandmother never had to lift a hand on us. You know how African American women had the effect that just the voice (Beverly laughing) and the questions.

Relatively often grandmothers had an important role or the most central role in raising the people we interviewed.

And the relationship of the family to those outside the family was shaped by standards that were understood as different from the standards for Euro-Americans. That, too, may affect the ways people grieve. For example:

Gwen: In my culture you keep your business to yourself.

In explaining their reactions to loss and the reactions of other African Americans, some respondents framed things partly in terms of the effects of slavery on African American culture and psychology.

Kenneth: There's a process of conditioning, and people go through it when they live under adverse conditions. And I think that the institution of slavery that did so much to tear apart families did something . . . to have us make adjustments in how we deal with the separation from others. . . . Being taken away and brought to a different . . . land, under different circumstances and conditions, and being conditioned to live at the edges and the fringes of society, and having to survive does something in conditioning your psyche to deal with folk leaving. . . . In order for people to survive under these circumstances they must do some mighty psychological gymnastics to keep things intact. When you have your child sold to someone else, or when you have your husband sold somewhere else, you understand what I'm saying? And so this whole process, and still having to maintain and do what you're supposed to do. . . .

And so in understanding techniques of survival and grieving. A few framed things partly in terms of the carryover of West African traditions.

Clyde: I've been to some West African funerals, and it's a lot of similarities with us, a lot more so than I ever wanted to believe, that all this time, you know, I'm thinking I'm so Americanized. . . . It was like similar to the funerals that I've been to as a child growing up. (*Beverly:* Expressions) Expression, everything. The tone was a little different, but the emotion and the exhibition, as I called it before, all that. . . . There are people speaking in tongues and the whole nine yards. It was almost like a revival. I mean, it was a revival. In a lot of ways that's what it was, a revival. But it was a grieving revival.

Len: And then [one] of the neighbors came over . . . and he just wanted to sing. The Lord put it on his heart just to sing. . . . Beautiful voice. . . . So he sung for about two and a half to three hours, just singing the songs that came to his mind. And traditionally, I think, it's a custom for us to sing, you know, the voice, the old saying, "you sang somebody through," "singing through." Just like praying through, you sang them through, I guess, the old tradition. . . . It's an old African American tradition. Well I should say, it's probably regional. . . . As a person dies you sing their spirit through. And so he was there, and he did.

☐ The Importance of Researching African American Grief

African Americans need to be understood in their own terms, not ignored, not assumed to be just like Euro-Americans. The death of someone important to one can be a devastating experience. Grief for a major loss can affect every aspect of one's life and can last a lifetime. For counselors, therapists, psychologists, clergy, nurses, funeral directors, and other professionals who may be called on to help grieving African Americans, having a literature to turn to on African American grief may be enormously helpful.

At another level, we think one way to enrich the understanding of anything important in human life is to study it from the perspective of diversity. Everyone gains when we learn about the grief experiences of people in a group that has been neglected. The gains include increased understanding of the limits of theory, the importance of culture and context, and the influence of intergroup dynamics.

At another level, it is time for the social sciences to be for everyone, not for only certain people. We are not in the vanguard in studying African American experience. There are large and growing literatures about African Americans in a number of areas, but grief is one of those areas where there is still much to be learned about African American experience. We believe one of the great values of this book is that it gives voice to African Americans addressing a centrally important area of their lives.

☐ Narrative and Meaning-Making in Grief

Grieving people often develop narratives about the person who died, the dying, the death, and the aftermath of the death. For many people, grief involves constructing and voicing narratives (Gilbert, 2002; Harvey, 1996; Riches & Dawson, 1996a, 1996b).

> "Narrative" can be defined as a spoken or written connected description of a succession of events or experiences that includes a sense of something to be explained or of moving toward an end-state, markers of story beginning and of ending (or of reaching the present), coherence, characters, and settings. (Rosenblatt, 2000a, p. 1)

A narrative is a story, whether it comes out as a continuous flow or is voiced a bit at a time. The narrative of a grieving person develops over the years following the loss. The narrative gives meaning to the person who died, the dying, the death, the grieving, the family aftermath of the death, and much else connected to the death. Our intent in this study was for the interviews to tap into narratives, and we think they did. So what we offer in this book is not only people's records of the "facts," but their stories that contextualize and give meaning to their facts.

For grieving African Americans, narrative is often about the larger societal context for the loss and the grieving. For people who have been denied a voice in the larger society, denied their own voice, and denied the voices of other African Americans dealing with similar circumstances, there can be gratitude that someone is asking about their narratives. There is a sense that grief is at times not only about the specific loss but about slavery and about other forms of oppression that followed slavery and that, in many cases, have continued up into the present. Grieving is also about the collective loss from the ongoing oppression, and it is also about terrible things that have happened in the African American community as people try to cope with their many losses or, in a sense, give up on trying to cope. The following speaks to those broader issues and offers blessings for this study in ways that possibly one might never hear from a grieving Euro-American.

Toni: We got to reclaim our humanity. That's probably what racism has done. Human beings cry at deaths. We cry. We take time to remember. We don't have to suppress those memories. So that's part of what I think we need to redo in our community. . . . [I am] so happy that you're doing this work. It's important work. It's important for the life of our community as African Americans. We've got to reclaim our grief, and we've got to insist on it. Not only reclaiming, but we've got to insist this is a valuable legacy for us. And we've got to give ourselves permission to grieve being enslaved. That's gonna set us free. I think that's part of the reasons why reparations are so important too, is that they associated with our grief systems. And we also have to teach our young people how to grieve, 'cause so much of the addictions that we see are an attempt to repress grief. It's all bottled into that, so we won't get free until we revisit and reclaim our right to grieve. It is part of our humanity. . . . Our teaching of our boys not to grieve, not to cry, that is demonic. . . . It is vital, it is vital, I mean it's like for me on a list of one of the 10 things that black folk need to do to be free, it would either be one or two. It is that imperative. And we've got to grieve both individually and collectively. It can't be one or the other. It's got to be both/and. One of the things that I loved about [name of church] when we grew up around there is that I could come to [that church] and cry, and the ushers would let me. They'd give me a Kleenex, and they'd . . . let me sit there all day and cry. . . . Our churches have to be a place that invites grief and gives people, that's, we've got to recapture our wholeness. . . . Thank you for doing this. Beverly, God's blessings on your work. Thank you, thank you, thank you. And I'm just gonna pray, I'm gonna keep it in prayer because I'm gonna pray that you do turn it in a book, that you lecture, that you teach, that you do grief workshops, that you lay on hand. Whatever it takes and whatever we can do to help you we will do it, 'cause you are a vital piece of what's gonna help us to be whole and human again.

To be open to narratives like those this interviewee and the others could provide, Wallace had to ask questions that encouraged stories and had to be a good narratives listener. Being a good narratives listener means hearing the stories out, being alive to the narratives, not interrupting, but encouraging continuation of the narrative. It means asking follow-up questions. Wallace carried out what might be called "active" interviewing (Holstein & Gubrium, 1995) in that she worked at activating "narrative production." She encouraged interviewees with her interest, attentiveness, questions, encouragement to address matters from varying viewpoints and the ways she built throughout the interview on what the person had told her so far.

☐ The Research Process

This study is based on interviews with 26 African American adults who were residents of either a Midwestern metropolitan area of the United States or one in the Southeast. The knowledge we offer arises from what these people had to say, which was about their own experiences, observations, learning, thought, beliefs, speculation, and family life.

Recruiting People to Interview

Interviewees were recruited through announcements in newspapers and on a radio station serving the African American community, through announcements on bulletin boards in churches serving the African American community, and through word of mouth. We interviewed everyone who made contact with us and with whom an interview could be worked out. With this approach to recruiting, we have no way of knowing how many people heard or read the announcement of the study and decided not to participate. We are not in a position to say how many people or what sorts of people learned about the study but decided not to participate. But obviously the small sample has geographical and other limitations that reduce its generalizability to the vast and diverse African American population.

The Interviewer

The interviewer was Beverly Wallace, the second author of this book. Wallace is African American. At the time of the interviews she was a doctoral student in Family Social Science at the University of Minnesota, a Lutheran pastor, an experienced hospital chaplain, with a bachelor's degree in social work, a master's degree in child development and family relations that included extensive counseling training, and a master's degree in theology. She was also an experienced research interviewer.

We think an African American interviewer was crucial to recruiting people to interview, gaining rapport, eliciting stories, asking insightful follow-up questions, and, in the end, interpreting what people had to say. There are some matters, such as issues of racism that some interviewees said they would have been reluctant to voice to a white interviewer.

The Interview

The intensive qualitative interviews averaged slightly less than two hours. Interviews were usually carried out in the interviewee's home or office, or occasionally in a different location, chosen by the interviewee, that allowed reasonable auditory privacy. However, several people chose to be interviewed within earshot of a family member.

We asked each person who was interviewed to focus on one death, though three talked about two deaths, and one talked about three. The interviews were structured to some extent by an interview guide (see Appendix) that included questions about the interviewee, the interviewee's family, and the person who died. It asked for the interviewee's story of the death and included questions about the life of the person who died. There were many questions about grief experiences—including feelings and their time course, how the death affected relationships with others, how the interviewee had come to think about and make sense of the death, continuing relationships with the deceased, the connection of the focal loss to other losses, and spiritual and religious matters. There was a set of questions dealing with how the loss impacted family relationships, and how others in the family dealt with and made sense of the death. There were also several questions about what, if anything, might be unique about African American grief. All told, there were about 100 questions in the interview guide. But the interviews were only semistructured. Interviewees were encouraged to tell their stories as they chose, and the interviewer went with their stories. Eventually, in most interviews most questions that were relevant to the interviewee's life and loss were answered, but not necessarily with direct questions from the interviewer and never in the order laid out in the interview guide. Also, on many topics that came up, as the interviewees told their stories and brought up their issues, additional questions were asked to clarify things, to draw more out about the story, to provide a respectful and supportive listening, and to follow possible hunches about what had been going on in the situation being described.

The interviews seem to have tapped validly into interviewee experiences and feelings in that interviewees would speak at length and with intensity about their experiences and feelings. All offered substantial narratives. It is not as though they were fishing to give brief answers or to provide answers in which they were not confident. What they had to say was richly accessible to them. And each seemed to work hard to give honest, detailed, and accurate answers to the questions. On the other hand, the interviewees were generally talking about things that happened years ago, and they were only being interviewed at one point in time, in one context, by one interviewer. So it is possible that there is a lot they could have said were the situation, the time, or the interviewer different. Still, it seemed from how well developed the narratives were that most people had thought a lot about the issues they addressed. There is a validity in researching matters so significant in people's lives that they have thought about matters a great deal. That gives more stability, depth, and connectedness to what people have to say. They already knew most of it before the interviewer arrived, and what they knew was too important and too tightly linked to too much else to be easily changed by an interview.

Who Was Interviewed

Nineteen women and seven men were interviewed. One man and woman, a married couple, were interviewed together. Twelve of the 26 spent their early years in southern or "border" states or in the District of Columbia.

Interviewees ranged in age from 30 to 76 with a median of 50, and in formal education from 11 years to a Ph.D. Seventeen had at least a bachelor's degree. So in comparison to the general population of African Americans, the interviewees were older and better educated.

Of the focal deaths, 11 were of a mother, four were of a father or step-father, five were of a son, three were of a spouse. Other deaths talked about included a sibling, parents-in-law, grandparents, and an uncle. The time since the death the interview focused on the most ranged from 2 weeks to 39 years, with a median of 8 ½ years. The first page of the Appendix lists the names we assigned to the 26 interviewees, along with the age and focal death or deaths for each.

Analyzing the Data

Audiotapes of the interviews were transcribed verbatim, which means every word, every sound, everything audible—laughter, throat clearing, pauses, re-starts, slurs, whispers. . . .

Rosenblatt transcribed most interviews and thoroughly checked the few transcriptions made by someone else. In a sense, the data analysis was well along during the transcription phase, because it became clear during the transcribing that a narrative analysis that focused on racism, African American culture, and the grief process would capture a lot of what was central to what people said. After the transcriptions were complete, we separately coded several transcriptions in detail and discussed our coding, while not forgetting all the other interviews, because Wallace had carried out every interview and Rosenblatt had transcribed or thoroughly checked the transcription of every interview. We found we were in good agreement on the initial coding, and so we worked up a tentative book outline that would also be a tentative guide to coding. Then Rosenblatt coded all transcriptions with that outline in mind, generating chapters and chapter sections. Wallace checked Rosenblatt's work by reading the drafts of chapters and challenging coding that seemed inappropriate. Where there have been disagreements or differences of opinion about coding, we have talked things over. If we did not agree or if it was not clear that we agreed, we dropped the relevant material. We went through several cycles of coding, writing, challenging, and rewriting before we arrived at the book you hold in your hands.

We have tried to write in a way that enables readers to check coding validity. At most places where we make assertions, we provide illustrative quotes—typically what we think are the best quotes we have on the point being made. The quotes enable the reader to decide whether our assertions have support in the interview data. We do not provide all the relevant quotes for an asser-tion, but the reader can still see whether a quote that we thought was a good illustration of the assertion fits the assertion.

Interview Quotes

All the verbal complexity of the transcripts was used in coding and making sense of the interviews. But in quoting people we have omitted most uh's, er's, and other nonlexical sounds, restarts, many instances of words and phrases like *okay, you know, I mean, like, whatever,* and so on. We have deleted quite a few repetitions of the same word, phrase, or sentences. But we have also kept some repetitions, because for many people who were interviewed repetition seemed to be part of the message. That is, in repeating they were emphasizing, focusing the listener, making a statement about the importance of what they were repeating (see Snead, 1990, for a view of the importance and place of repetition in African American oral expression). We also have edited many quotes to make the point we are making clearer, to simplify, and to make this a book of manageable length for readers. The places in quotes where we have edited out material are indicated by ellipsis dots (. . .).

☐ "African American" versus "Black": A Note on Terminology

Everyone interviewed for this study was African American. Some of the sources we cite and some of the people who were interviewed use the term *black*, rather than the term *African American.* In quoting those sources, we maintain their usage, but in textual material that is original with us we draw a distinction between "African American" and "black." We use the term *African American* to refer to people who have grown up in the United States, who have African ancestors, and who identify themselves as part of a community that is distinctively rooted in the culture of people of African descent who have lived in the United States for many generations. We use the term *black* to refer to all people who have African ancestors, including those who are from the Caribbean and from West Africa and have cultural roots in those regions.

Grief and Life Span

African American grief occurs in the context of a substantially shorter life expectancy than is true for whites (Barrett, 1997, 1998; Freeman & Payne, 2000; Lamb, 2003; Meagher & Bell, 1993; Moore & Bryant, 2003). In recent mortality data (Arias, 2002, 2004; Levine et al., 2001), African Americans averaged a 5.6-year shorter life expectancy at birth than whites, with the difference greater for men (6.4 years) than for women (4.7 years). Although since the late 1990s, the disparity between African Americans and European Americans in life expectancy has decreased somewhat, the long-term trend has been toward increasing disparity (Levine et al., 2001). African Americans experience pregnancy and infant loss at double the rate experienced by whites (Guyer, Freedman, Strobino, & Sondik, 2000; Hillemeier, Geronimus, & Bound, 2001; Papacek,Collins, Schulte, Goergen, & Drolet, 2002; Van, 2001), and African American women are several times more likely to die in childbirth than are Euro-American women (U.S. Centers for Disease Control, 1995). As Barrett (1997, 1998) and others (e.g., Krakauer, Crenner, & Fox, 2002; Krieger, 2003) have observed, the differences in life expectancy are to a substantial extent about things that racism does. Racism leads directly or indirectly to greater poverty, a less healthful environment, poorer health, fewer physician visits, poorer pregnancy care, poorer nutrition, and poorer access to health care. Presumably racism is also the key to understanding why African Americans are more likely to lack health insurance than are whites (22.2% vs. 15% for whites—U.S. Bureau of the Census, 1999).

☐ Early Loss of Parent

The shorter life expectancy for African Americans means that proportionately more African Americans than Euro-Americans will not be adults when a parent dies. If there is a surviving parent or grandparent who is taking care of the newly grieving young person, that adult is also likely to be grieving intensely. We know from studies of Euro-Americans that grieving parents are often inattentive, neglectful, and emotionally unavailable to surviving children for quite a while following the death of a child (Rosenblatt, 2000a).

Among the people we interviewed, in some cases the early loss of a parent meant that a person had no parent left who was able and willing to provide care. The result was, that as teenagers or preteens, some of the people who were interviewed experienced not only the devastating death of a parent but also the devastating loss of a surviving parental figure's nurturance. Barbara was one of several people who, while still a minor, had to move to a distant household to receive adequate nurturing.

Barbara: I am 56 years old. . . .

Beverly: What brought you here to this part of the coutnry?

Barbara: The death of my mother. . . .

Beverly: How old were you at the time?

Barbara: Mama was buried on my 17th birthday, exactly.

Several interviewees had personal experience or stories of other family members taking on parenting responsibilities for young children when the mother of those children had died at a comparatively young age.

Franklin: [My sister] was in her early 30s [when she was killed]. She had three children. . . . The youngest was only four months old. . . . My sister who survived is another one of strength. (crying) She took those children (pause). She raised them. Along with her own two, with all five of those kids she took 'em, and their father didn't give them not one solitary dime. . . . She raised them. And they're all grown. . . . [My] oldest sister is the one who was killed. The middle [sister], she's the one who did the rearing.

Among many possible consequences of losing parents when one is young, is that such a loss might make it less likely that one will know well how to parent one's own children. One will not have had the experience of observing one's parent do what parents do. That can add an element of grieving to one's own parenting.

Charlotte: It impacted every step of my life. . . . When I recognized that I had that missing in my mothering, parenting, I was parenting my teenage daughter. . . . I remember saying to her . . . , "This is the best I can be." But just as I said that to her, I remember thinking, "I didn't even have a mother as a teenager," so I didn't have it to go on.

Early loss of a parent also means that one will have fewer memories of how parents deal with the challenges in life. And relatively early in life one no longer can turn to memories of how parents dealt with the milestones of life. For example, not having a parent who went through menopause or who lived long enough to retire, one will not have parental models of how to deal with menopause or retirement.

The fact that there are so many deaths of parents at an early age in the African American community can make it seem to an African American to be quite a blessing for a parent to survive well into a son or daughter's adulthood.

Calvin: Our family has been blessed. [When] my mother died, I was 36 years old. I was grown. Grown. And that's just not true about a lot of families, that that chain is not broken for that many years. And so. . . . We've been blessed. We've been blessed. Really. We really don't have a complaint when we look at the big picture.

☐ Early Loss of Spouse

In data from 1940, 1950, and 1960, Lopata (1973, pp. 22–23) showed that at least for ages beginning at 45 or 50, African American women were more likely to be widowed than white women. The differences were especially great at the early ages, when a substantial difference in life expectancy might show up most clearly. In more recent years, the census data continue to show substantial racial differences in widowhood. For example, according to U.S. Bureau of the Census (1990) statistics (cited in Hobbs & Danon, 1993), among people age 65 or older, 55.5% of black women were widowed, versus 46.7% of white women, and 23.3% of black men were widowed versus 13.2% of white men. Although some have argued that at advanced ages, African American life expectancy is greater than Euro-American life expectancy, the evidence now seems to be that the earlier research finding was an artifact of erroneous age data for elderly African Americans (Preston, Elo, Rosenwaike, & Hill, 1996; Shrestha, 1997). The current view in the demographic literature seems to be that the life expectancy of African Americans at any age is less than it is for whites, so at any age a married African American is more likely to become widowed than a married person who is white. Among many consequences of the early death of a spouse is that one may find oneself as the sole parent at a relatively early age.

Elsa: [My son's] dad died when he was 6. He was killed in a motorcycle accident.

If parenting a child one has shared in raising since birth can be difficult when one becomes widowed, the problems may even be greater when it is a stepchild that one must raise. The problems may not only be with the child but also with the deceased spouse's family of origin, who may want the child to live with somebody in their family. When Len's wife Camille died, there were difficulties with her family of origin about where Len's 15-year-old step-daughter, Janet, should live.

Len: Camille's family initially had a question about what would happen to Janet. And so there was some tension that Janet was supposed to come live with one of them. Because of me; I'm a stepdad. I'm not a biological father. And so there was just that uneasiness, but it got resolved very quickly, because Camille had made it very clear that Janet was gonna stay with me. And so once the family really knew that and it was communicated clearly, then there was no more pressure there.

☐ Early Loss of Sibling

Given the shorter life expectancy of African Americans (Arias, 2002, 2004; Levine et al., 2001), we can infer that sibling losses, are, on average, experienced at a relatively young age by African Americans.

Franklin: My sister was killed in a car accident along with my fiancée and her mother. . . . [My sister] was in her 30s, early 30s.

Among the interviewees, some sibling deaths were attributed to the use of alcohol or other chemicals. In any group of Americans, some people die prematurely from using alcohol and other chemicals. African Americans may disproportionately experience such deaths, presumably in part because some are strongly motivated to numb the pain and frustration of racism, the blocks to opportunity, the economic marginalization, and the daily insults of racism. For example, according to the National Institute on Alcohol Abuse and Alcoholism (2003), the death rate for cirrhosis of the liver is higher for African Americans than for Euro-Americans, with the difference being especially great for men. Barbara talked about her brother's death at an early age from an overdose of alcohol.

Barbara: In between Mama and Daddy, the knee baby Pierre, the wild child, passed. And he didn't just pass. He went home one weekend. He was living in New York by this time, him and his family. But he came home for the weekend. When you come home for the weekend, the cousins get together. And basically he had an overdose of alcohol, at 33.

Sibling deaths at a young age may, like parental deaths at a young age, be especially challenging. The first death one experiences of somebody important in one's life is often unusually difficult (Rosenblatt, 1983, p. 158). And the first death may be even more difficult if one is relatively young. One lacks the life experience, maturity, social supports, knowledge, economic, and other resources to deal with the death as well as one might. The experience of a sibling death, that is one's first death of someone close, and that is experienced at a relatively young age, can be especially devastating. And a grieving parent may not be much help in that situation.

Evelyn: My sister older than I passed on, and this was something that I couldn't understand. I couldn't handle this. I just couldn't understand it, and it really, really clouded my thinking. I couldn't think; I couldn't do nothing, and it just, this girl we were very close, but she was, let's see, a year older than I was. And she died all of a sudden. And I just couldn't understand this, and then I was just telling myself, "God, why couldn't it have been me instead of her? Why, why, why?" And I just couldn't understand that, and I went on day by day and I was just in a daze. I just couldn't think. I couldn't do nothing, and so gradually just started easing up, easing up, and I would go and I would try to understand. . . . I would try to talk to my mother, and she didn't understand how to talk to the children like they do today or get you some help or something. And I just drifted along and tried to understand, but . . . it was very, very difficult for me.

Beverly: How old were you?

Evelyn: I was 16.

☐ Death of Child

African American children are much more likely that Euro-American children to die at birth or soon after (Guyer et al., 2000; Hillemeier, Geronimus, & Bound, 2001; Papacek et al., 2002; Van, 2001), and such losses are reflected in our data. Several parents talked about their continuing struggles, many years later, to deal with an infant or child's death. For Maya, for example, the still-born death of a son, who she never saw, continued to hurt many years later.

Beverly: Did you ever see the baby?

Maya: Nope, they had already disposed of him. Did away with him. I don't know what they did to him, or even how they disposed of him, and that bothered me. . . . Every year [on his birthday] I go through a depression, and no matter how I try to fight it off or pray it off, it's always there. And, I don't know, for a long time I blamed God, and I didn't realize that I was blaming Him. . . . I think his birthday is the hardest for me, and I don't know if I'll ever, I might never get to the point where there's a complete healing of my desire to have him with me.

☐ Conclusion

The African American interviewees in this study, like African Americans in general, were relatively likely to experience major deaths at an early age–the death of parent, spouse, sibling, or child. We cannot say that these premature deaths produced qualitatively different grief than what might be observed in Euro-Americans experiencing losses of similarly close family members at similarly early ages. But we can say that experiencing premature deaths means that African Americans relatively often experience the additional challenges of grieving that come with early bereavement. These include, for loss of a parent, being moved elsewhere to be parented, or being parented by someone who is grieving intensely. For loss of a spouse, the additional challenges include the likelihood of taking over single parenting of a child or stepchild at a time when one is grieving. All early losses can include the additional challenges of grieving a first death of someone important to one at a relatively young age. Among other things, early losses may involve grieving when one is rather short on experiential, cognitive, emotional, financial, social, spiritual, and other resources for dealing with a loss, understanding one's own grief and the grief of others, facing the mortality of loved ones, and facing personal mortality.

For an African American who is aware of the shorter life expectancy, there may be a heavy burden of anger and resentment entangled in grief. Almost any death may seem to be an injustice, and not only a cause for grief but also a continuing, painful reminder of how much racism has disadvantaged the deceased, oneself, and all African Americans. Hence, if one's brother or husband died at 50, one's grief can be complicated by anger, resentment, anguish, and other feelings that might arise from realizing that if he had been white the expectation would be that he would have had four more years of life. If one's mother or wife dies at 65, one's grief can be complicated by feelings that arise from realizing that if she had been white the probability would have been that she would have had almost two more years of life (U.S. Bureau of the Census, 2002, Table 97). A critic (possibly white) might say that differences in life expectancy are unimportant in a practical sense when considering how long a middle-aged or elderly person lives, but many people seek advanced medical help and go to great effort and expense to keep a loved one alive and well for a matter of days, weeks, and months, let alone the substantial number of years between the life expectancy for African Americans and the life expectancy for Euro-Americans.

2

Racism as a Cause of Death

Judging by what interviewees had to say, in order to understand African American grief it is important to understand how an African American death may have been caused in whole or in part by racism. Many deaths in the United States are premature in the sense that they occur at a time prior to what is the average for the general population. Premature death can happen to anybody, regardless of race or ethnicity. But, as was indicated in chapter 1, premature death happens relatively often to African Americans. Why do these premature deaths occur? There are, we think, myriad reasons, many of which have to do with the direct or indirect effects of racism.

Direct experiences of racism and such indirect effects of racism as housing deficiencies, lack of jobs, and poverty may so stress the cardiovascular system, the immune system, and other bodily systems as to jeopardize health (Clark, Anderson, Clark, & Williams, 1999; Din-Dzietham, Nembhard, Collins, & Davis, 2004; Ellison et al., 2001; Steffen, McNeilly, Anderson, & Sherwood, 2003; Williams, 1999). Racism in health care may mean that African Americans are given less than the best and most prompt treatment. This is true, for example, in the case of breast cancer (Mandelblatt et al., 2002), cardiovascular disease (Ofili, 2001), and prenatal care (Sims & Rainge, 2002). Toxic waste dumps and chemical plants that emit hazardous chemicals into the air and the water table are located in places where a relatively high percentage of the people living in the nearby danger zone are African American (Bullard, 1990; Bullard & Wright, 1989–1990; Dorsey, 1998; Pine, Marx, & Lakshmanan, 2002; Rosen, 1994). Unemployment, underemployment, and employment in

7

economically marginal jobs are part of why African Americans are less likely to have health insurance (U.S. Bureau of the Census, 1999) and that may be one reason why African Americans are less likely to receive early treatment for diseases that become life threatening when treatment is delayed (e.g., prostate cancer; Horner, 1998). Residential segregation by race is an important factor underlying racial differences in socioeconomic status, because higher socioeconomic status provides an important foundation of resources for good health (Cooper, 2001; Williams & Collins, 2001). A continuing pattern of economic discrimination pushes African Americans toward more dangerous jobs and work environments and less safe homes and communities. Racism can also operate quite directly to produce premature death. For example, as will be laid out in narratives presented in this chapter, because someone is African American, he or she may be channeled into a dangerous job or be denied access to the best available medical care by people acting in a racist fashion.

When economic discrimination or direct racism seems to a grieving African American to be partly or fully responsible for a death, it may add elements of anger, rage, and indignation to the grief. It may draw on the feelings and memories associated with other deaths the person has experienced personally or has heard about from others, that seem to have been caused, in whole or in part, by discrimination and racism. It may draw on the feelings and memories associated with personal experiences of discrimination and racism that were not fatal but still stung and harmed. It can add feelings of hopelessness, vengefulness, inadequacy, and desperation that can come up at anytime an African American faces, remembers, or thinks about discrimination or racism.

There are also matters of meaning making. People make meanings about a death as a part of the grief process. In making meaning, they come to a story about the person who died, what happened that brought about the death, and what feelings are appropriate. As they develop their narrative, they frame things in terms that make sense to them, drawing on religious, medical, psychological, and other cultural bases of meaning. With deaths seemingly caused in part or entirely by discrimination or racism, there is the template of stories of discrimination and racism, drawn from experience and African American culture that can provide part of the meaning and story pattern for a death.

We cannot say that things for African Americans are entirely different from the way they are for Euro-Americans, because Euro-Americans certainly have stories of preventable, avoidable deaths, and the feelings that go along with those stories. They even have their stories of deaths caused by someone else's malevolence. But they would not be likely to have stories and meanings coming from centuries of being victimized by racism and from ongoing personal, familial, and community experiences of discrimination and racism.

☐ Death by Racist Assignment of Hazardous Work

Some African American deaths are understood to have been caused by racist assignment of hazardous work. Franklin, who at the time of the interview was 58 and whose stepfather had been in the military during the Vietnam War, thought his stepfather, who had died about a year prior to the interview, died from an illness contracted as a result of a racist assignment in the military that involved exposure to cancer-causing chemicals. With a death that did not have to happen when it did and in the way it did, the pain of grief was very intense and included feelings of anger and rage.

Franklin: He had had a confrontation with his commanding officer (crying). . . . The guy made these comments. [My stepfather] then . . . asked him, "Sir, may I have permission to speak man-to-man?" Which is that military request for, "Let's forget about rank now. We can take these chevrons off my sleeves, and we can take . . . that bird off your shoulder," because it was a full bird colonel. "And I'll tell you about black folks, and what you're calling 'spooks'" and some of those other terms that they use, which I'm still not going to use, the 'n' word. . . . The commander did give him permission to speak. He said, "We can go outside . . . and I'll whoop your (laughing) ass right now." Which, of course, the colonel did not do. And he was calling to tell me that he had had this confrontation. "I told that (chuckling) so-and-so that, too. And I'm serious. . . ." The Vietnam conflict was on at this time. . . . He already served a tour of duty there. . . . When he told me on the phone, I said, "Dad, I wish you hadn't done that. . . ." Because here's a dude who could control your life. They'll send you right back to Vietnam. . . . I didn't know how prophetic that that was. . . . He called me back less than two weeks later to say, "Son, you're right. I got my orders. . . ." He did go back to Nam. . . .

Beverly: You talked earlier about his illness and the relationship of this illness and his death and the military. Would you say that racism affected or caused or had an impact on his death?

Franklin: (chuckling) An explicit statement? Of course. There's absolutely no, no way *not* to say that racism played this role. This man wound up twice having to deal with Agent Orange. They were the ones who were loading it. He was in the group that was loading Agent Orange. One time they got sprayed. . . . How is this not, when you know all of the folks, or the vast majority of the people who have to deal with this war, [were] black folk. Who were the ones that were so much in the filling up the body bags in out*rage*ous numbers? Black folk. Who were the ones who had all of this hazardous duty crap . . . ? It was black folk. Who was he commanding? A whole black group (laughs). I think he had two white boys in the outfit under him in Nam. . . . Ah! (crying) A rage is what I feel (laughs).

Beverly: Why a rage?

Franklin: (pause) . . . This is racism, and racism is racism.

☐ Death by Medical Racism

It is no secret that racism is a big barrier to African Americans getting adequate health care in the United States (Barrett, 2003; Feagin & McKinney, 2003, pp. 184–194; Freeman & Payne, 2000; Smedley, Stith, & Nelson, 2003).

Kenneth: believe that institutional racism has many effects, and the most direct would be health, health care, and access to that health care. There's an article in *Jet* magazine that shows that African Americans who are in Veterans Administration hospitals outlive whites, because they have access to health care. . . . So I think that institutionalized racism plays a role in that respect, by denying health care and quality health care services to the folk.

Approximately 40% of the people who were interviewed talked of a death that they felt resulted at least in part from medical racism. In these cases, the meaning making of the grief process of necessity includes making meanings concerning medical racism. And feelings of pain, anger, and rage can easily come to the fore as one thinks about the racism, feels that both oneself and the person one is grieving for were helpless to counteract it, thinks about other instances of racism, and feels the injustice of the death.

One version of medical racism that people talked about was the denial of services. The hospital would not treat someone African American; the ambulance would not come to pick up someone African American. Some of the examples people gave were from decades ago; some were more recent. As the literature cited earlier in this chapter indicates, medical racism is not only a thing of the past.

Franklin: The racism that . . . was in play in my sister's death because across the bridge, where their car had the accident, they had to take her 22 miles away to a hospital that took black folks, because the one on *this* side of the bridge in the town in which we lived didn't take [us], which was only seven miles away.

Beverly: Do you think racism or discrimination was in any way connected to [your son's] death?

Gwen: Yes. When he got the meningitis, of course I didn't know what it was. . . . It was a Sabbath. I went to church, and he had this fever. I could do nothing about this fever. . . . We were down in [name of town]. . . . That's where our church was. So there was a little white hospital there, and I took him there, and they wouldn't even do anything. And they would not really treat him. They didn't know what it was. They didn't have facilities to deal with him. . . . They did not give him anything. And I don't know what the delay might have done. I do feel that the delay probably was detrimental, but that was because we were black.

Toni: When my grandfather had a stroke, he was taken to the poorest hospital in [the city] . . . where you basically go to die.

Beverly: And he went there because?

Toni: Because that's where the poor black people went . . . unless you were the elite of the elite. And so that's where they called with the ambulance, and later on what we found out, I want to thank you for this time, because I had forgotten all this stuff. . . . Where he was doing the plumbing [when he had his stroke] was in a very poor, poor area, and the ambulance wouldn't come and get him. They had to call a cab to take him to the hospital, and they had insurance. And the doctors, my grandmother did have a white doctor friend (she was working in a nursing home), that examined my grandfather, and they said if they would have gotten him to a better hospital in a better time that they would have been able to start treatment earlier. Now it may still have resulted in the same result, but then the other piece was they stopped giving him physical therapy.

Beverly: Because?

Toni: Poor. "Oh your insurance doesn't cover it." That may very well, may have [been so], but who was there to advocate for [it]?

Another version of medical racism that people talked about was the carrying out of a high- risk procedure on someone who was African American, without adequately informing the family members, who consented to the procedure, of the risks.

Beverly: Do you think that racism or discrimination was connected to your mom's death.

Calvin: (takes deep breath) Could very well be. If [my father, who gave consent for the procedure] had been an older white man, maybe they would not have been so quick to do [a high-risk procedure]. Maybe they would have waited a little while. That's possible. That's very possible.

Freeman and Payne (2000) and Barrett (2003) summarized a medical literature showing that African Americans are less likely than whites with early-stage lung, colon, or breast cancer to receive potentially curative surgery, and also showing that African Americans with chronic kidney failure or the potential for coronary artery disease are less likely than whites to receive appropriate medical referral or diagnostic procedures. Perhaps the definitive analysis of the medical racism is from the Institute of Medicine of the National Academy of Sciences (Smedley et al, 2003). It reviews an enormous number of studies showing that whites on the average receive better medical care for a wide range of health problems—coronary vascular problems, HIV infections, diabetes, end-stage renal disease, pediatric care, mental health care, rehabilitative services, and so on. There are a few areas where African Americans are more likely to receive certain medical procedures, but arguably receiving these procedures is a symptom of failure of more desirable treatments (e.g., amputation; Smedly et al., 2003, p. 6). So it is not surprising that one version of medical racism that interviewees talked about was that a family member was given minimal or token care, rather than extensive and careful examination and state-of-the-art treatment.

Beverly: Do you think that racism or discrimination was connected in any way to your mother's death?

Clyde: . . . Had she been European I think there were other tests and other things that I'm sure . . . could have happened. I just believe that. I mean from just the way that she was uh, I could see how the doctor was, and the doctor would come in and see her, and how he reacted to her. No one touched her. He never touched her, touched her that much that I could see. I always wondered. I always felt, "Wow," you know, but what he didn't know was I knew about bedside manner . . . and I would just look at this person and think for some reason my folks, they don't believe that a doctor could be a racist bigot. They just don't see a doctor as a racist. [But] he's a person first and a doctor second, so he can be a racist, and he can withhold certain services or medications. . . . If he don't give it to you, you won't know anything about it. And the encounters I had with them was always . . . he just felt that I was one of them that went north, and just was a smart ass.

Beverly: So he gave you a hard time.

Clyde: Probably the other way around. He always felt that I was hostile. Probably was. But I just felt that uh, 'cause it didn't mean anything to him. She was just another person that he was gonna see. He was going through his motions. I just felt that they look at African- American lives differently. That's all. That's what I felt. And I'm gonna go with my gut feeling. I won't change it.

Beverly: Do you think racism or discrimination was connected to your grandmother's death?

Toni: Umhm, oh yes I do, because one, even in terms of the quality of care that they got, even though this was still in California, California is still one of the most racist places. It's just the southern west. That's it. And so I'm sure that there's care she did not receive. And the other piece of it was that a couple of the nurses aides told my mom, "You need to sue them. You need to sue. . . ." My mother wouldn't do it. She wouldn't do it, 'cause she is still afraid of bucking Mr. Charlie. And if she sued them, then she wouldn't fit in.

Beverly: Do you think racism or discrimination was connected at all with [your mother's] death?

Cynthia: . . . My family, they did mention some concerns, and they felt that she was not as attended to as well as what she could have been. And my father was concerned about some issues, but he never was that specific.

Medical racism might mean that a person was limited to being seen by physicians who did not have the resources that might be available to physicians a white patient might see. Toni talked about the care her grandmother received.

Toni: They went to a black doctor, but his office was no larger than this room, and he didn't have the up-to-date equipment.

Beyond the roughly 40% of deaths where it was clear to interviewees that medical racism had a part in the death, there were a few deaths where there was suspicion of medical racism but the interviewee and other family members chose not to investigate whether it had occurred. They chose not to fight that battle for themselves or for the family member who might not have received the treatment a white patient would have received. Patricia talked about family suspicions that racism was involved in the treatment and death of her mother, who had died seven years prior to the interview. But Patricia and her family chose not to explore the matter.

Patricia: I think the fact that when it really started we didn't know. You could've attributed a lot of things in terms of how well were we really viewed and screened when we went in for checkups and so forth. You never know whether things were taken lightly or overlooked or not taken as seriously because of our race. . . . So some of us wondered, there was something where we thought we might try to look into, the doctors and the hospital and see if they had done this or checked this and checked that. My mom would be the type where she would not want to make more of a scene about things. It wasn't that she didn't feel like she could stand up for her rights, because she would. So there would be some things she would think . . . let God handle whatever. . . . But there's nothing that we would be able to really document per se. Unun. We just make certain assumptions . . . about it. . . . So healthwise, we would consider that resolved, because there's some things you can carry so long that you won't want to be able to let go and still not get, but there was nothing there that we felt like we needed to do for the sake of her integrity or ours.

☐ Not All Deaths Were Seen as Caused by Racism

We do not mean to imply that everyone who was interviewed thought racism played a direct part in a death they talked about.

Beverly: Do you think racism or discrimination was connected to her death?

Andrew: No! Mama just died.

Beverly: Do you think that [your son's] death was related in any way to racism or discrimination?

Evelyn: Ah, no I don't think so. . . . I just think that he was just ill. Just got this terrible, terrible disease. Had nothing to do with that racial . . . stuff.

But some people, just saying that they did not think that racism caused a death, told a lot about the racism of the medical system, which leads many African Americans to mistrust the system (Barrett, 1998, 2003; Smedley et al., 2003, pp. 135–136, 174–175). For example, Kenneth said his grandfather received good medical treatment, but only because his grandfather was treated in a hospital run by and for African Americans, a hospital where his grandfather had been chairman of the board.

Beverly: Do you think his death was related to issues of racism or discrimination?

Kenneth: I don't think so. . . . The hospital that he died in was run by African Americans. And he was chairman of the board. . . . The guys who worked on him knew him well, and he trusted them. And he got the best of help for an African American man....

Beverly: So he chose to go to an African American hospital.

Kenneth: Exactly. . . . Probably because it was three blocks from his house. (chuckles) And he knew all the doctors who worked there. He knew their credentials. And like I said, he trusted them. He would rather deal with them than deal with folk he didn't trust. . . . He knew (chuckling) that we had qualified doctors to do the same things, and even better. And so that was one of the issues, that he wasn't going to go to another hospital if he had it right three blocks from his home, with doctors who were qualified to do better than most whites.

Len talked about how, even though medical racism happened often to African American patients, his wife, who had died six years prior to the interview, had the strength of personality to motivate her white doctor to provide her with the best treatment possible.

Beverly: Do you think racism or discrimination had an effect or impacted her death at all? Or her illness?

Len: For anybody else I would say "Definitely," because the way the health insurance is. . . . I almost got the feeling that the insurance company writes people off. . . . There was pressure on the doctor that . . . basically . . . he was . . . told to quit . . . giving certain treatments. . . . This is a terminal person, and you need to start taking some other means. . . . [But she] was such a fighter, and because of her personality, 'cause she could win you over. I think she won the doctor to her side. I think they probably did a lot of things to extend her life that the insurance company was not pleased with. . . . I do know that there was definitely some conflict between him and the HMO around treatment and prescriptions, 'cause the prescriptions were very costly. . . . I think some of the medication was like, just for a small pill, I think it was like $500 a pill, $600 a pill. She had to take it three, four times a day. And so I know that . . . there were some issues there: Who's gettin' this and why? Like . . . the president of Norwest Bank, and there's that status thing. Okay, we'll give into it, but "You're givin' it to who?" And I have nothing concrete to point at, but you just get that gut feelin' and sense. . . . During the latter part of [her] life, he was removed from the case. . . . I didn't fight, because I thought it maybe was because he was just havin' a hard time with it. He got really attached to the family. . . . But I think that definitely, if it wasn't for [her] personality and determination to fight, that racism would've played a bigger part in that for her not to get adequate treatment. But because she fought with the insurance company, because she was so outspoken about what she knew was going on in her body, they had to give in. Or somebody heard the voices speaking to them. But for the average sister or brother who maybe's not as clear and articulate and forceful with issues . . . and the knowledge of the medical field itself, then it would be a real . . . pushing people to the side. And even in the latter days, the doctor that took the [first doctor's]place was not, there was just a atmosphere and tone, and it was more, "We're gonna put her in hospice. . . . We're gonna stop basically treatin' for life. We're treatin' for death."

Jo-Ellen talked about a situation where she was sure there was discrimination in denying her son adequate diagnostic services, and she was inclined to think that it was racial discrimination but, as she said, the discrimination could have been about something other than race.

Jo-Ellen: When [my son] was 18 months old, he became *very* ill. And I took him to the doctor, and they said he had a bad cold, and they gave me medication for him. And I remember giving him his medication for a couple of weeks, and he wouldn't improve. And I took him to a hospital emergency room, and they ran a bunch of tests, and they said he just had a bad cold. I took him home again and waited about a week, and by this time he was extremely lethargic. And I knew something was wrong, more than a cold. And I took him to another hospital's emergency room, and I got in an argument with the nurses and doctors there, because I told them something was wrong. . . . This just was not normal, and they said, "No, all the tests came back," that he just had a bad cold. And I said I was leaving him at the hospital, that I was not taking him home. And they explained to me that that was illegal, that if I did that they would have to turn it over to the courts, and I'd be charged with abandoning my child. But I chose to do it. . . . I was 19 going on 20. And I made the choice to do it, and I ran out of the hospital. They had my name and everything, but I did run out. I didn't get a call that night, but I did get a call the next morning. And they said tests had come back, and that they needed me to come to the hospital right away. And I asked them what were the tests. . . . They told me that he had leukemia. . . .

Beverly: Do you think that what happened at the hospital with him had anything to do with discrimination?

Jo-Ellen: I think it did. . . . I think it had a lot to do with me being a welfare mother. I think definitely the emergency rooms did, because there is no way, there is no way that as lethargic as my child was that they should have sent him home. There is not. And it's sad to say that I had to have went to the extremes that I did, as a young mother, not even yet a legal adult, to leave my child in a hospital emergency room and run the risk of going to jail, literally. And so that had to have reasons other than them just saying, "We can't find anything wrong." And so I don't know what the discrimination was. If it was because I was black. If it was because I was a welfare mother. I don't know what it is. But whatever it was, something was wrong. There were no other children that I ever met that had leukemia that were black. All of the children at the hospital were white children.

Loretta's mother had died seven years prior to the interview. Loretta said that she did not think there was racism in the medical treatment of her mother, who had been suffering from dementia, but there was in the admission to the geriatric center where her ailing mother could have received the best support possible.

Beverly: Do you think that racism or discrimination was connected at all to her death or her illness?

Loretta: (breathes out loudly) That's hard to say. We have a former President in Ronald Reagan who had Alzheimer's and there's nothing they can do about it, so it's a disease that [defies] social status, wealth, economic conditions, or anything. It would be easy to say if she had cancer, that she didn't get proper treatment, but Alzheimer's in the '70s, and '80s, there was so little known about it, it didn't matter if you were African American or if you were white or Hispanic. And they still don't know that much about the disease. . . . I think being black or an African American prevented her from being admitted into [the] Geriatric Center.

☐ Death by Poverty

Another angle on racism is that some people told stories in which it seemed that poverty was a cause of death, a poverty that resulted in whole or in part from racial discrimination. Some stories were from the Jim Crow era, stories of not being able to afford a phone with which they could have called for emergency help or not having access to an ambulance because the family was African American. Barbara, talking about her mother's death more than 30 years prior to the interview, told about the long delay in getting her mother, who had a stroke, to an emergency hospital because of those factors.

Barbara: We were sharecroppers. So life was pretty hard. It didn't *seem* exceptionally hard, but it's when you look back on it you know that it was tough work. . . . What happened was . . . we came home from school one day, and Mama was not in the house. . . . I ran upstairs, calling her name, to see if she was upstairs, and also to change my clothes at the same time, 'cause back then you changed your school clothes, and you had work clothes. So anyway, but I looked out my window and I saw that my mother was sitting down by the woodpile. And it didn't make sense. So I ran back down the stairs. By this time my niece who lived with us and was raised with us like, well, she is like my sister, she was outside by this time, and she's calling to Mama, but Mama's not answering. So I'm calling. She's not answering. She's not turning her head. So I come around in front of her to see what's going on, and no matter what we say, it's not registering. And she is busy trying to remove something from her dress. And her eyes are just very, very red and glazed over. So the way that we get attention out on the farm, if you can't yell loud enough, if you don't have the wind at the back of you, then you have a bell. So we rang the bell, so that Daddy could come in from the fields, 'cause he was out in the fields with a cousin. So they came home, and we got Mama inside. Now we didn't have a telephone, so that meant that our cousin had to run down the lane to Mrs. Scott's house, to have them call the doctor. . . . In order for her to go to the hospital, what he had to do was go back [to the neighbors' house] and call the undertaker's office. Yeah. The black undertaker's, so that they can send their wagon out to pick her up and take her to the hospital.

Other stories about racism as a cause of death could also be understood as being about poverty resulting in part or entirely from a racist system. In a country where money buys access to medical care, people with less money, without health insurance, or with limited health insurance will receive poorer care. So some of the stories quoted earlier in this chapter about denial of medical services or poor medical services may be about lack of economic resources. And in the United States, the past and current racist system means that, on the average, African Americans have lower income (U.S. Bureau of the Census, 2004), less in economic assets (U.S. Bureau of the Census, 2003), and are less likely to have health insurance than whites (Mills & Bhandari, 2003). This means they bring fewer economic resources to medical situations. Economic resources buy health care and, at times, an extension of life.

☐ Conclusion

Racism and discrimination were often involved in interviewee understanding of how a death came to be or how it could have come to be if someone had not been unusually resourceful. Because of that, emotions associated with racism and discrimination may be entangled in feelings of grief. These feelings may include anger, rage, moral indignation, despair, and vengefulness. Also, with grieving African Americans, meaning making and narrative development may often have to deal with discrimination and racism. The cognitive and social processes of meaning making and narrative development might in a fundamental way be the same for African Americans and Euro-Americans, but the contents may often be different in important ways. African Americans will be much more likely to be making meanings and developing narratives that deal in part with discrimination and racism.

Racism and Discrimination in the Life of the Deceased

The narratives people come to in the grief process typically include a great deal about the person who died (Rosenblatt, 2000a). They talk about the qualities of the person, particularly the good qualities, as they define who the person was and is for them and how much they have lost. This is certainly true for the narratives of the African Americans interviewed for this study. However, one thing that was different from Euro-American narratives about a person who died is that many of the African American interviewees talked about how the person who died had faced racism.

On one level, racism is so much a part of life for African Americans that it makes sense that it would be a significant part of a narrative about the deceased. Racism could be entangled in any story about African American life. But at another level, talking about the person's encounters with racism helps to define who the person was and is. It could be a way of saying how much the person suffered or lost. It could be a way of saying how, despite the person's great capacities, the person did not accomplish what she or he could have done had there been no barriers of racism. From another angle, it is a way of saying that even though the person was, say, a nurse's aide or a cleaning woman, the person had the capacity to be much more than that, if they had not been pushed down by racism. Another piece of it might be to say how staunchly and effectively the person struggled against racism.

☐ **Racism Deprived Him or Her of So Much**

Some narratives spoke about racism causing enormous deprivations in the life of the person who died, and of affecting life chances, economic well-being, status, education, personal growth, and advancement.

Beverly: In what way do you think your stepfather's life was affected by racism or discrimination?

Franklin: In every way possible. He would have been, if he had gone in just a straight military route, he should have been a four-star general, because of what he was able to accomplish, and what he had done, and how well he was able to get things done. General Mays was someone that he was proud of. He was proud of the fact that it was a black man who was a general. . . . He always *knew* that it was possible. He was in during the Korean conflict, and as a result, remember, that's [after] Truman integrated the troops. He knew before, because he was a part of it before they were ever integrated. He wasn't integrated into troop things. It was an all black group. . . . He loved being in an all black group, [though] he didn't like what that meant, being in an all black group, because it meant everything you get is going to be the last of anything, the worst of everything. . . . And you're going to be looked down on at all points in time. So you have to battle both the declared enemy, as well as the one who is supposedly your ally.

Charlotte: [My mother] graduated from a business school, which was still not the norm in that era. . . . She went to high school. . . . There weren't many schools for you to go to if you were black. . . . they all went beyond what your average black person did at that time, those three girls did. . . . They grew up in a home their father had purchased for them. That was unheard of. My grandfather was a postman. That was not the norm. And so that tells you why she [mother] might have been someone who wasn't fulfilled. Because of what was expected. . . . Yeah, she could have had anxieties about possibly not achieving.

Willa: [Mother] had very few choices as a young woman as to what she could do with her life. (chuckles) She used to tell, "We could only be nurses, social workers, or teachers, if you wanted to be a professional person." And of course secretaries, but there's no need to have a college degree to be a secretary. You can go to business school, or you could back then anyway. So she lamented the fact that she had few choices. And she did two of them (laughs). She was a social worker and then she went into teaching.

Clyde: [Mother] was a maid for these rich people. And she would see how things were wasted. And how she wasn't able to get certain jobs, because she was black . . . The only school they could go to at that time was Florida A & M University.

Toni: [Grandmother] was not allowed to go to college. And she always wanted to go to college, and she was brilliant. My grandmother, I mean truly, and I'm not making her a hero, my grandmother was absolutely brilliant.

Loretta: [My mother] went to junior college. But we were talking back in the '30s, and us black folks didn't have a whole lot of opportunities. . . . We're from [a city where] . . . racism abounds. It's just . . . blatant. . . . She went to school with people who became the doctors, the lawyers, the judges. . . . Back in those days, the '30s and the '40s, black women should only aspire to be domestics. Either you were a cook or you were somebody's maid, and my mom didn't want either one of those. And because she couldn't pursue the things that she wanted to, she became a lifetime member of the NAACP, and worked to effect a change in the status quo. I can remember when we had death threats, because of my parents' activeness. They went crazy, but they effected a lot of changes.

The six instances cited above deal with denial of promotion or opportunity in the military, denial of education or of a high level of education, and denial of access to the full range of employment opportunities. The person who died was seen as interested in moving up and fully capable of doing so, but racism denied the person the opportunity for upward mobility and access to better education and to higher status, more fulfilling jobs. All of these six instances refer to a time several decades in the past, but that does not mean that racism has ended. We believe that many people who will someday mourn African Americans who are alive now will still be able to talk about how racism deprived them, affecting life chances, economic well-being, status, education, personal growth, and advancement. Racism and discrimination have not ended, though clearly some things are better than they once were. Quite a few of the interviewees had much more formal education than people of their parents' and grandparents' generation, and quite a few had middle-class jobs in terms of status and, we presume, income.

The narratives talked about deprivation, loss, and humiliation in the life of the deceased, but some also talked about the ways the deceased had not been devastated by racist deprivation. Despite the losses and difficulties, some people were able to transcend the problems and achieved productive and rewarding lives.

Beverly: As [your mother] would look back over her life, would she feel good about her life or mixed or not-so-good?

Calvin: I think she'd feel real good. Yeah, I think she'd be real happy with her life, because she impacted the lives of people, which is really what life is about. And you can do that in many arenas. You got the classroom; you got the home; you got the church; you have the work place. There are many arenas. And the arena that God placed her in, she [did] well. I think she'd be happy.Coming up in the era in which she lived, of course she knew about the "colored" signs and all that type of thing. And had to do day work and that type of work. Had seen as a youth . . . blacks get shot or whatever for no reason. Mistreated. But she did not allow that to dictate to her the principles that she would teach us. She always taught us, "Hey, you do what's right, whatever's right, even though this is wrong, you still do what's right. This is the system, and you can maintain your integrity and thrive in this system. . . ." She didn't allow it to keep her from doing what she had to do, and I don't know if she was ever turned down for any schools or anything like that.But we came up and had a rich home. I look all the way back, and my dad always had a new car. And they always had Sears and Montgomery Wards credit cards. . . . We never went to school raggedy.

☐ How the Deceased Challenged Racism

Some narratives spoke of how the deceased challenged racism. The person who was now dead was not always passive when faced with a racist attack or barrier. That was a strength of the person and something the person taught others to do. One example in the narratives was the woman described above in this chapter who was active in the NAACP and who received death threats because of her effective work to bring about change. She and some others who had experienced major deprivations because of racism were characterized as strongly standing up to racism.

Beverly: Do you think that discrimination or racism played a part in [your mother's] life?

Andrew: Definitely. Yes definitely, but Mama was the one that taught me to talk to white folks. And when they do you wrong, you have to tell them, and not allow them to, you know, I got that from her. Every time I [deal] with one, when I'm faced with it, she was the one that taught me, "You tell them. They don't always tell you. . . . " Something be wrong . . . she'd get loud, kind of so loud. But I see she would talk to the white folk.

Franklin: [My stepfather] didn't take back seat. He didn't back seat. He would battle. He stood up.

Barbara: Mama did some day work for [white families]. . . . She was at this house, and she was doing work, and this child not only was disrespectful, called her by her first name and, you know, she had told the child to stop doing something. The child kept right on. And Mama grabbed that child and pinched. . . . And the child was being disrespectful racially, too. And Mama didn't then agree with that, and she wasn't going to take it from the child. So then she told them she wouldn't be working for them anymore.

Verna: [My father] would say . . . that they don't give black men chances. So he was a victim. I didn't know what that meant. I was too young to really get it. When he bought the land in [the suburb], they went out to look at this land in a white community. Another couple was there, and they said to this Jewish man, "Whatever they're offering you, we'll pay double, because we don't feel that niggers should be out here. . . ." The next day [the Jewish man] came over to Mother and Dad's house and said, "You offered me the least on the land, but I'm going to give it to you because of the racism." And he repeated what the couple had said. And Dad saw that as a gift from God, that God's transcending any racism. Now once the house was built, we've had crosses burned on our lawn. And that was the first time we ever heard him getting a gun. Up until that time we didn't have a gun in our house. We called the police. They didn't do anything. . . . I was ready to move out. "Get me back to the city. We don't want to be out here anyway. . . ." And we're going to a white school. But he says, "No, we're staying. God gave it to us, and we're keeping it. We're not going to be run off our land." He was a . . . tiny man . . . and he was abused on the job. . . . They would tease him, or they would some days have the . . . conveyor go faster than it would normally go. So that they could either make him hurt himself or make him quit. But he said, "I started singing my songs and glorifying God, and I made it." And that's why education was his way of saying, "If you have an education, racism would disappear." When I was in school . . . [a foundation] hired me to do some antiracism programs. And I says, "I'll do them under one agreement, that you hire my father with me. And he gets to tell his story." And that was the best thing I could ever have given him, for him to sit in a circle . . . and tell his story, how he has been mistreated and how that was real for him, racism. And then to have white people process with him the pain, and apologize. We did five of those, and he was like, without an education; he's still somebody. He's still pretty powerful. So once in a while I look at those pictures, and I think, "That did change him," that as a black man he got respect for the first time.

Beverly: Do you think that racism or discrimination impacted [your wife's] life?

Len: Yes, definitely, in a lot of ways. I think because she was the type of fighter she was, she would take those challenges on with a sense of excitement. . . . Being an African American woman who was very outgoing, outspoken, and also very large in terms of her height and her size, and had a deeper voice. When she talked, she had a real powerful . . . she had a tenor voice. And so a lot of people got intimidated, even when she didn't mean to intimidate, quote, and I say "white America." "White America," especially white males, got very intimidated by her, and so on the job she faced a lot of unjust persecution and judgments, simply because they were intimidated. . . . I remember one situation where this happened to be a older white woman. . . . And these crazy allegations coming down from, and partly because she was just intimidated. And partly jealousy, because [my wife] did move up through the ranks, and probably surpassed her. You know, in our day and age all that stuff that comes up with that. "You got it because of affirmative . . . and da-da-da." But [my wife] was very skilled at maneuvering and working through that . . . and the individuals that got so crazy with some of the stuff, allegations that the company knew was crazy. And the company ended up settling with the woman . . . just to keep her mouth shut. . . . [My wife] was very upset, because she thought that was giving in to a very unjust portrayal, who not only she was, but who the company was, simply because this woman was intimidated by who [my wife was] as an African American woman. And it came out in the statement that the woman had made that it was clearly that, "You're big and you're black, and when you come into a room I just feel uncomfortable with you. . . ." . . . That was an incident I seen her work through. . . . I know many others, in terms of just even being a African American woman in the reservists. It tends to be white males, and white males who have inadequacy for whatever reason that they couldn't actually become a police officer, so they want to play police officer on the weekend (laughs). So bein' in the midst of that, and basically rising up through the ranks to be a sergeant over them, and to have to deal with attitudes and perceptions. I think it says a lot about her character and her determination.

☐ Intergenerational Relationships and Reactions to Racism

It is possible to understand many of the accounts of how a person who died dealt with racism as, in a sense, an explanation of intergenerational differences and of the struggles between the deceased and the interviewee. For example, in the quote that follows, of all the things that could possibly explain how stepfather and stepson got along or had their difficulties, it is striking that a key basis for explaining the difference is how they thought about racism.

Racism is so big in African American life that it can be a central ingredient for a narrative that illuminates the relationship between an older person who died and a younger person who is grieving because of that death.

Franklin: It was late in the night, where the radio went off, and as it went off it played "Star Spangled Banner." And I reached over and turned it off. . . . I had been in the . . . Air Force. . . . He was still in the Air Force. Very patriotic man, in spite of all the things that he kinda understood he'd gone through . . . he'd suffered through. He joined the Air Force at an early age. . . . So he was very, very patriotic, very proud of it. And I mean, very proud. . . . The conversation then kind of got heated, 'cause I'm pointing out the facts of it. . . . It made no sense to me to talk about fighting for the American flag. It made no sense about this red, white, and blue stuff, when it does not embrace us. And he was saying, "But I fought for it." So I'm challenging and condemning . . . , "But, Dad, wait, wait. I've been there. I was there. I'm not condemning you. It's not your fault. . . ." And . . . he did not recognize . . . that thesis.

☐ Racism Was There, Even if the Deceased Did Not Talk about It

Not every narrative addressed problems of racism in the life of the deceased family member. Some narratives said in one way or another that the interviewee had no direct information about problems the deceased had with racism. But in saying that, these narratives could still indicate that racism was significant in the world in which the deceased lived. For example, in the first of the two accounts quoted immediately below, Vickie talks about her father's skill in protecting his wife (the deceased) and his children from racism, and apparently part of that was not telling them anything about his experiences with and knowledge of racism. In the second narrative Jane, a widow, seems to be saying that her husband was hired, despite racist resistance to the hiring, because the government demanded that his employer hire some black people. Neither narrative speaks directly to how the deceased was affected by racism, but both speak about how the deceased lived in a world that was racist.

Beverly: Were there any issues of racial discrimination that affected your mom's life?

Vickie: I don't think so. I think my father did a very good job of protecting . . . us. My sisters, and they're right about this, and I have always said, Daddy always taught us what people should be like. . . . I think part of it was my father sold carpets . . . and he was actually the first black person they ever let go into those houses . . . in that part of the country. (*Beverly:* So they trusted your dad.) Uh huh. And even now, and now we grew up in Memphis, and I'm 40, so he was there when Martin Luther King was assassinated. He had to have seen a lot of things. I have never heard my father talk about it once.

Beverly: In what ways do you think [your husband's] life was affected by racism or discrimination?

Jane: I don't think it was. It might have been back in the days when he was coming up, because he was so much older than I am, and I'm pretty sure back there in those days it was rough. But . . . the only thing I know [is] his job. . . . They didn't have no blacks on the job. They all white. And the government stepped in and told them that they had to hire some blacks. And he was the first minority to get that job. They did not want to hire no minority, because the job paid a lot. He made like 60 some thousand dollars a year, and they didn't want to pay minority that kind of money.

One way to understand the racism that is hidden from view in these two narrative examples is that in some African American families people do not talk about racism or about certain experiences of racism (St. Jean & Feagin, 1998). In some families, people try to avoid spreading the pain, fear, and anger concerning racism to other family members. Sometimes a person wants to leave the pain behind rather than talk about it. And for many people there have been so many experiences of racism that they do not want to start describing what could be an interminably long list of unpleasant experiences. This may be particularly so for family elders like Vickie's father. There would be too much to talk about. Nonetheless, our inclination is to think that when African Americans have little to say about the experience of a deceased family member with racism, they still may have some idea about those experiences. Their lack of knowledge of specifics represents dynamics that are common in African American families, dynamics that block or minimize talk about racism or that omit mention of most of a person's experiences with racism, but in no way deny the pervasiveness of racism.

☐ Conclusion

If part of meaning making in dealing with a death is to develop a narrative about the person who died, African Americans often differ from Euro-Americans by including in their narratives accounts of racism and discrimination in the life of the deceased. These aspects of the narrative make it possible to talk about how much the deceased suffered because of racism. They make it possible to talk about the special abilities and strengths of the deceased, while accounting for how it came to be that the deceased did not have great status in the larger society. These aspects of the narrative make it possible to frame and explain the deceased's bravery and capacity to overcome great disadvantage. They help to link the deceased to the grieving person to the extent that they help to explain aspects of the relationship of the two; for example, the efforts of the deceased to teach the person who is now grieving to cope with racism.

Even when the deceased did not talk much about his or her experiences with racism, narratives about the deceased often make clear that the deceased still had to face racism and discrimination. The fact of not talking about racism and discrimination can be understood to say something about how the deceased and the deceased's family chose to communicate about experiences of racism and discrimination, not that they lacked such experiences.

CHAPTER

Visitations, Wakes, and Funerals

African Americans may put relatively great resources of money and time into providing a proper funeral and into attending funerals (Barrett, 1998; Boyd-Franklin & Lockwood, 1999; Hill, 1983–1984; Hines, 1986, 1991; Pleck, 2000). Perhaps an important aspect of such a heavy investment in funerals is that, as Barrett (1993) wrote, "African American funerals . . . represent a posthumous attempt for dignity and esteem denied and limited by the dominant culture" (p. 226).

All but one of the interview narratives included accounts of a visitation or wake and then a funeral for the person whose death the interviewee focused on. (The one exception concerned a stillborn child, whose body was unceremoniously disposed of by hospital authorities.) Typically, the body was displayed in an open casket, often with photographs of the deceased nearby. Family members came, even from far away, and young children from the family might be present too. There were always friends and acquaintances from the African American community present. All the funerals described were carried out in a Christian tradition. The funerals typically included gospel music, at least one eulogy that painted a positive picture of the deceased (Moore & Bryant, 2003), and a sense of religious meaning for life and death, whether the ritual was done at a church or a funeral home. In almost every case the body was then buried in a cemetery. (There was one cremation, and several people who were interviewed suggested that more people in the younger generation in the African American community are open to cremation.)

Some interviewees did not have much to say about the wake or visitation and the funeral. They had been too numb or felt too much pain to pay attention to what was happening. But others had extensive narratives of the events.

The rituals they described seemed to us to be similar in structure and under-lying motivation to the death rituals of various Euro-American Christian groups in the United States, but it was clear in the narratives that there were, as well, distinctive African American cultural elements. Here are two examples. Franklin, in talking about the funeral of his stepfather, who had been in the military, refers to somebody wearing "full African attire." Clyde, talking about the funeral of his mother, refers to the presence of "play family," fictive kin, people in the African American community who are counted as kin although they are not kin by blood, marriage, or adoption.

Franklin: Nice funeral. He was a member of a . . . little small church that he and my mother belonged [to]. And they had the military folks and my mother. . . . Quite a few of the military folks who were old friends . . . and a number of folks from the . . . Disabled American Vet organizations, of which they were a part too. My side of the family, meaning my sister and my nieces...we were there as a group. . . . I spoke as the head child, the eldest child. His two sisters were there. . . . I tried to be encompassing. I tried to, in terms of family, since I also tried to speak about the strength of the man, and how much he meant, and I tried to understand and re-spect what his wishes would have been to, "Okay, now, make it brief (laughing) and to the point. Deal with it. Sit down." And I was in full African attire.

Clyde: There was a woman that was sort of like her play daughter, if you want to call it that. She had met her, she was working at the hospital, and she was a teacher now. And she worked there with my mom, and my mom was the one that encouraged her to get on the evening shift and go to school. And that's what she did. She did finish that. . . . She became a play daughter.

☐ People Helped Me/Us

Many of the narratives about funerals and the other rituals immediately after the death talked about the help others had provided. Friends, relatives, mem-bers of the church, coworkers, and others came through in ways that sup-ported the interviewee and others who were closest to the deceased and that helped them do the right thing for the deceased. In the narratives of many interviewees, the help that others provided was important and valued. Help like that at the time of a death is not unique to the African American commun-ity. But the interviewee narratives are important in providing an understanding of the experiences and expectations at the time of a death in the African American community.

Different narratives emphasized different kinds of help. Andrew's friends helped him with funeral expenses. Jane's narrative described a wider range of help, including emotional support, funeral participation, and the bringing of food.

Beverly: You helped plan the funeral.

Andrew: Oh, I did it all. I didn't help. I did it. My brothers and sisters, they know me, and when I got to [where mother died], and I had a nice little bit of money with me, and then I called back here. . . . "Hey . . . I need it." My friends are like that. They didn't hesitate. One call. I said that in my prayers. Said, "God, I've made one call, just one of these, and I'm thinking," and that's all I would say. "Send me $2000 today. I need it now." And I made that one call, and one of my friends...and they know I've never asked for nothing. He didn't hesitate. . . . Mama was going to . . . some little church, and she had a few close friends, just a few of them. So it was our family, and a few of her close friends. . . . And [the preacher] did the eulogy, and I wrote a poem. A lady sang. We picked a nice casket, and we buried her out there.

Jane: [My husband's] funeral . . . was at my church, and my church was very supportive of me, and they helped me a whole lot to go through the thing. And it was nice. They sung some of his favorite songs. . . . His sister-in-law sung, *One of These Old Mornin'*, and his cousin sung, *Precious Lord Take My Hand.* And one other hymn was *Blessed Assurance.* Our choir director, she sung, *Goin' Up Yonder* . . . then we had a dinner. He was buried at [the military cemetery], and we came back from there. We had a dinner at the church, in the fellowship hall. It was a pot luck. Everybody brought stuff, and that's something really nice.

Echoing what Jane said, many narratives of funerals, wakes, and visitations indicated that people in the community brought things to help with the ritual and to support those who were grieving and others in attendance—flowers, food, folding chairs, donations of money, and so on. It was a way of saying that the person who died and those who were grieving were not alone; others cared about them. What was mentioned most often was the food, which was brought to feed those who were grieving and to relieve them from responsibilities for preparing food. In fact, food seemed an essential part of postfuneral gatherings of family, friends, and community members. At one level the food is about something like communion. At another level, it is a way to be sure that people who are preoccupied with their grief or who have come from far away have something to eat. None of this is unique to the African American community, but the prominence of accounts in many narratives of people bringing things, makes it clear that one has to grasp the importance of bringing things if one wants to understand African American experiences and expectations early in bereavement.

Willa: Small town, people came to the house. They brought food. . . . Didn't have to worry about cooking, 'cause people were bringing ham and chicken, and I never want to see another piece of fried chicken.

Verna: Everybody was really encouraging, real supportive, really food conscious. . . . I believe I've never seen so much food brought over to my mother's house, over to my sister's house. . . . Eight days of food, just constantly brought. And I thought, "This has to be cultural."

☐ Honoring the Dead

Visitations, wakes, and funerals are partly for the living, supporting their initial struggles with the loss and helping them to define the death and their feelings. Visitations, wakes, and funerals are also to honor the dead.

An Appropriate Service

Interviewees talked about trying to honor their deceased family member by providing a good send off, which might include eulogies, poems, and music that connected with, spoke about, and honored the good attributes of the person who died.

Jane: The pastor said to me, "What kind of music did [your husband] like?" I said, "He liked blues. He liked gospel." And he go, "Whatever was his favorite song, we can play 'em." So we did. We played blues for the first half hour of the wake. . . . It may have sounded strange (laughing), but we did. I said, "That's what he liked; that's what I'm gonna do."

For some, an appropriate service was one in which family members had an active role.

Patricia: We have an uncle who's a pastor. He does all of our weddings and funerals...and so he obviously was doing a eulogy, and [we] three sisters did something too. . . . My older sister, who didn't want to get in front of people that much, said, "You are not gonna leave me out. . . . I'm . . . gonna do this for my mom." So the three of us did that. . . . We did sort of a dedication. . . . We did some things that reflected on her as a person and talking about us as babies.

The active participation of family members can be taken as their expression of caring, and it can also be taken as meaning that the funeral rituals are for them as well as the dead. Or, from another angle, it can be taken as family members feeling that they best know the person who died and so the appropriate way to honor that person is for them to have their say about her or him.

Another characteristic of an appropriate service was that religious words were spoken and, as Franklin said, the deceased was in a sense prayed into heaven.

Franklin: It's very strongly religious . . . in almost all cases. Even when the individual was not religious . . . the religion just takes over . . . 'cause batches of folks in their family are religious. That boy may not be a church funeral, it may be at the funeral parlor, but some preacher somewhere somehow is going to be there to speak for him, gonna say some kind of words over him. It's almost like he gonna pray him into heaven.

Respecting the Wishes of the Deceased

In accord with Sullivan (1995), who wrote about African American funerals, some people spoke about trying to carry out rituals that respected the wishes of the deceased. They felt they owed it to the deceased to do what he or she asked to have done. And sometimes what the deceased had asked for was seen as reflecting the teaching and moral lessons the person had tried to impart to others.

Patricia: My mom . . . planned the funeral. The pastor said some things that were offensive about my nephew, and some other things that kind of didn't put the pastor in the best light in my mom's eyes. . . . [But] when she planned the funeral, she still put the pastor as a part of the program to give him the respect that he needed. . . . My mother was the type of person who encouraged you to do the right thing. . . . Even in her departing she's still teaching and setting examples. . . . I would have said, "You're not gonna be a part of my service. . . ." But she acknowledged the pastor, gave him a role.

A Large Attendance Honors the Deceased and the Family

Many in the African American community, feel that it is important to attend funerals and value heavy attendance at their own family funerals (Barrett, 1998). In fact, the attendance at a funeral is ordinarily seen as a measure of the status (importance, influence, esteem, power, reputation) of the person who died and of the grieving family (Sullivan, 1995). The deceased and the family have higher status if more people attend. Perhaps things are no different in many other ethnic groups, but in order to understand experiences and expectations of many grieving African Americans, it is important to be aware of the issue of funeral attendance.

Franklin: The funeral is more of a public expression. It's a public sharing. It's an opening up and invitation to the public. It's a process that also allows for me to demonstrate that I know the right things to do (laughs). . . . It's also a thing that is a count; it's a measurement of status within a community. Funerals play that role of saying, okay, look, "Wasn't nobody at that funeral. *Everybody* shows up at this one." There is status attached to that. You gotta ha' that (chuckles).

If a funeral is well attended, that can be taken to mean that the deceased was a good person who touched the lives of many people and that many people care about the grieving family.

Barbara: Many people respected my mom and loved her, so the funeral was big as far as people coming to pay their respect to her. . . . There was nobody like Mama. . . . She had touched a lot of people.

Rosalyn: I had a visitation at the church. . . . There were hundreds of people. I never realized [my husband] had touched so many people's lives, neighbors, coworkers passing his body. And it was really nice. . . . We shipped his body the next morning to [our home town]. . . . And they had a motorcade. I never seen so many friends and relatives. It was over 500 people. It really warmed us huge. . . . The church was packed.

Willa: It was amazing how many people came. I'd say a good half the town showed up to pay [mother their] respects, because she had taught for so many years. And she was on the city council after she retired from teaching. And teachers that she had taught with [came].

Verna: I think he would feel wonderful about his life. . . . He told my sister . . . that you could tell the way a man lived by the way people respect him when he dies. . . . In the church . . . was different people, choirs, in and out, to honor him. And then the day of the funeral there was a winter storm. There was nowhere to sit. We had people everywhere. We had put people upstairs in the kitchen. . . . It's a large church. We moved into the parlor, and there was the sanctuary that's large, and then windows open that you can add on to the sanctuary from another room. And we had chairs in there, and that was packed. And then we had people sitting in the parlor that could not see. . . . In the choir stand were ministers from all over, white and black, the community that knew him. And from out of town too. They came to honor him. . . . I could hardly get a seat. So his life was good.

As the four quotes immediately above indicate, the people who come to a funeral not only mark the importance of the deceased, they often represent the deceased's place in society, perhaps particularly the place in the world of work and of organizations. That gives meaning to the deceased person's identity and also says that the deceased had a valued place in society.

From another perspective, not attending a funeral can be a shirking of responsibility to the dead and the living. Angela, who was 28 when her father died, was stung when several of her friends from high school failed to attend the funeral.

Beverly: Was there anyone who let you down during the time of your dad's illness and death?

Angela: Yeah, some friends that I went to high school with. . . . They didn't come to the funeral, and they didn't stop by. One called, and I think both of them sent cards. But when my one friend's father. . . . died, I did go to his funeral, to show support, and I guess I kind of felt let down or disappointed that they weren't there for me when my dad passed.

Having Many Clergy Participate Honors the Deceased

In the narratives of funerals, one of the markers of status is when a funeral is attended by many members of the clergy.

Calvin: It was a great homegoing celebration. My mom was quite a lady and well-respected. . . . So she had great homegoing. It was at [the] church where my sister belongs, and me and my other pastor brother had the opportunity of doing a eulogy, in two parts. . . . And the Lord blessed (he's crying). . . . A lot of pastors were there. All of her former pastors.

Attendance by White People

Some narratives mentioned the attendance of white people at wake, visitation, or funeral. That might be a marker of status of the deceased or of family members of the deceased, though it might merely mean that the person who died or members of the immediate family worked with white people, or otherwise had contact with them. At the very least, the mention of white people can be taken as a sign that racial awareness is a factor in at least some African American narratives about funerals.

Evelyn: We had the wake and the funeral and . . . lots of people had been there and gone when we got there, but it was still a whole bunch of people, and it was mixed with white, we had a lot of white people there.

☐ Social Status Diversity and African American Funeral Rituals

The people in attendance at a funeral ritual represent the social world of the deceased and the grieving family. For some African Americans there is an enormous diversity of social status among family, friends, and acquaintances, ranging from wealthy and powerful members of the elite to people living in the most devastated areas of the inner city. One thing that is striking in some of the narratives is how some of the interviewees had connections across that range of social status. In Rosenblatt's experience interviewing dozens of grieving white people, he never heard an account like the following, in which a mother who had recently left the streets to be a Christian talked about her young son's funeral being attended by people from both her old and her new social world.

Jo-Ellen: I was a new Christian at that time. I had come basically out of the streets, so all my old friends were drug addicts and drug dealers and prostitutes and pimps, and all my new friends were Christians. . . . I grew up in [the community], so they closed down a lot of businesses the day of [his] funeral. And people called to volunteer to be pall bearers. I had pall bearers that were Christians and that were pimps (laughs).

In the typical narrative that referred to social status diversity, a person who was now middle class in terms of education, ongoing employment, income, occupation, place of residence, or law-abidingness mentioned funeral participation by people like them, but also mentioned people who were not. For example, two people talked about alcoholic, drug-using, ne'er-do-well siblings. Another mentioned a brother who was in prison. Some talked about the person who died or themselves living in low income neighborhoods (sometimes called "the projects") at the time of the death or having grown up in such a neighborhood, so the neighbors and friends who attended included people who were from "the projects" as well as people who were middle class.

☐ Family Hassles Regarding Visitations, Wakes, and Funerals

In interview narratives, death rituals were not necessarily smooth running. Families with ongoing power battles, strong differences of opinion, or long festering divisions or resentments may find it difficult to work harmoniously in putting on a ritual. There are certainly stories of family hassles around funeral rituals in the narratives of grieving white people, but perhaps there are issues that make for family hassles relatively often at African American funerals. Knowing what we know about the family situations of the three people quoted immediately below it may be that comparatively often African American families bring to funerals not just differences of opinion from the past but real splits in relationships and allegiances. Franklin was raised by nonrelatives for quite a while, then came to live with his mother and the man who became his stepfather. The key family hassle at his stepfather's death involved a young man who allegedly had been "adopted" by his mother and stepfather but may have been the stepfather's biological son with another woman. So Franklin had no relationship with the "brother," whose relationship to Franklin and Franklin's stepfather remained ambiguous. Toni was conceived in marital rape, rejected and maltreated by her mother, raised for a while by a lover of her mother, and eventually rescued and nurtured by her grandmother, whose death she was grieving. So the split between Toni and her mother began even before Toni was born. Loretta's brother had abandoned their mother, whose death was the focus of the interview with Loretta, in every sense except that he continued to receive financial support from the mother. As the mother declined and became demented, it was Loretta who was responsible for her care. Her brother had not visited their mother for many years. With their mother newly deceased, her brother failed to do the most basic things that most people would do, and that he seemed to have agreed to do, when a mother died, notify a few close relatives who lived near him and far from Loretta.

Franklin: More dysfunctions come out in black families during funerals. . . . If there is even a slight degree of dysfunctionalism, it comes out full storm. And ours was no exception.

Toni: There was a wake [for my grandmother], and all the little dignitaries and all that . . . came to the wake, and my mother sat up there like the queen. She refused to cry, because she's [The Queen], and so she sat. "This is your mama." Okay, she's sitting in the chair. She's [The Queen] entertaining, and putting her hand out (laughing uncontrollably). And that's bad. . . . Oh God, she just gets on my nerves.

Loretta: I assumed my sibling would help me with funeral arrangements, but considering he had not told anyone that she was dead, he couldn't deal with it. He was just panic-stricken. Got to [the distant city where her brother lived and where their mother was to be buried], took care of my brother. Yeah, I had to take him a suit. Got his hair cut. Got him together enough to attend the funeral. I thought he would be part of the arrangement-making process. He didn't do that. So my daughter and I did that. . . . It was a family funeral, and when you deal with my family, someone had to be the pillar of the strength, so emotionally I couldn't be involved. . . . I had to take care of what I had to take care of, and had no room for emotion. . . . Family rifts and things like that, I instructed family how things were gonna go, how they were gonna be, and if anybody didn't like it, please meet me at the door. . . . You doing one funeral, you might as well get a discount for two.

☐ God May Speak to Those Who Are Grieving

In some narratives, death rituals were not only occasions to honor the dead and to be reminded of ongoing family issues, they might also be a time when God speaks to a grieving person. Rosalyn talked about God communicating to her about which gospel music would be most appropriate at her husband's funeral.

Rosalyn: My cousin had come over, and she says, "We got to plan the funeral. We got to plan songs and things we need to have done." And I say, "Right now, I can't even think of any song. . . . I want to be alone." So I went up . . . I took the Bible out and . . . I began to pray. And I said, "Lord, (sighs) please fill the void in our lives with Your work. . . . You're going to have to help us through it. . . . We don't even know what songs to sing." It was revealed to me, "God never fails." So at that point I jumps up and I run..downstairs, and . . . I said, "I prayed, and the Lord has given me a song, 'God never fails.'" So my cousin said, "Do you have a song book?" My sister say, "Yes, I have a song book." We opened the book. There was the song, *God Never Fails*. We read the words, and my cousin said, "This says it all." So that was one of the songs we had sung at his funeral.

☐ We Didn't Break Her Heart

In a racist world with limited opportunity and considerable pain for African Americans, and a legal system that is tilted toward jailing them, it is not surprising that many African Americans have been in jail, have turned to crime as a way to earn a living, or have overused drugs and alcohol in order to numb their pain. That means that at a parent's funeral, some of the parent's children may be missing and some may be in terrible physical and emotional health. In some narratives it was a measure of how well a parent did if the offspring were all present, in relatively good shape, and doing well economically and in other ways.

Calvin: We were able to hold our heads up, because we didn't break Mom's heart. Of course, like all children, we made her cry, but we didn't ultimately make her regret that we were her children. So she was blessed by that, and I thank God that she lived long enough to see all of her children doing well. She lived long enough to see all of us well established in life, and serving the Lord.

☐ Speak Well of the Dead

Every narrative spoke well of the deceased, and also talked about others speaking well of the deceased. That can be understood in many ways, including the point that speaking well is a measure of the loss (the person lost was a good person who was valued), a way of honoring the dead, and a way of supporting those who are grieving.

Jane: I didn't even know half the people that [my husband] knew that came to his funeral, and they all came up to me and had good things to say about him.

Angela: A lot of [my father's] co-workers said some really nice things about him. And our cousin, who I think was like a sister to him.

☐ Wailing, Weeping, and Passing Out

Some people said they or other close family members of the deceased were numb during the death rituals (more on this in chapter 7). But it was not uncommon for narratives about what went on during death rituals to describe very strong expressions of emotion—wailing, intense weeping, passing out. That is another aspect of interviewee narratives that differs from the narratives Rosenblatt has gathered from grieving white people in recent years. Moreover, the strong expressions of emotion can be taken as consistent with the findings of Owen, Goode, and Haley (2001) that African Americans are less likely than whites to experience the death of a family member, even after a long and debilitating illness, as a relief.

The intense expressions of emotion can be taken as cathartic release (Holloway, 2002, p. 152; Moore & Bryant, 2003). One can also take the narrative descriptions of intense expression of emotion as statements about how great was the loss and how important the person who died had been to the survivors. The narratives about strong emotional expression are also, in a sense, about social support, because they always talk about others coming to the aid of the person who expresses such intense feeling.

Jane: When the limo got to the church, I heard [my daughter crying]. . . . She was just like crying, crying, and crying. I said, "Oh, my God," 'cause we could hear her crying (laughs) while we were [still far away]. . . . Her and my husband was so close. They was so close. And he was just her stepfather. And she just broke, so I go, "Oh, my God," and so I went in there, and they took her out, because they thought she was going to make herself sick. And I went in there. And I hadn't seen [my husband's body]. I didn't go up to [the funeral home] to look at him when they dressed him. . . . I hadn't seen him since they took him out of here. . . . I went up to the casket, and all of a sudden I passed out. . . . I remember they puttin' cold towels on me, fannin' me, waking me up.

Evelyn: My granddaughter, she kind of broke down . . . so my nieces they took care of her, and that was good.

Some narratives referred to the intense expression of emotion at African American funerals as "whooping and hollering." Sometimes people said that to explain how their family was like other African American families who "whoop and holler," but some people contrasted their family's more subdued emotional expression with "whooping and hollering."

Gwen: My family . . . don't whoop and holler. They sobbed, but wasn't any whooping and hollering . . . going on. . . . I think I cried. I cried. I'm sure I did, 'cause I was cryin' all the time anyway, so I'm sure that I did.

Not whooping and hollering could be a way of placing oneself and one's family at a more educated, more urbane, more northern, more-like-whites' status in the community. That may be part of why, in the quote immediately below, the interviewee's mother was so uncomfortable when others who were grieving her mother (the interviewee's grandmother) at a funeral in a white church were whooping and hollering.

Toni: My grandmother was a foster mother for 60 some odd children, and so some of the kids came, and they were kids from all over, so they whooped and hollered in this all white church, and of course my mother wanted to kill 'em.

But not whooping and hollering also could be about the person who died having gone through a long illness and decline.

Evelyn: It was sad. It was. But it wasn't one of those that would just kind of tear you up inside, 'cause you're already tore up, but going through this long sickness . . . I had done my crying, and done my heart aching, and somehow when that came I had strength to go on with it.

☐ Alcohol and Drugs

As with some Euro-Americans who are grieving (Rosenblatt, 2000b), a few narratives referred to alcohol and drugs as a way some family members medicated their grief at the time of the death and perhaps took a kind of communion with one another.

Beverly: Did people start drinking more (chuckle) after [your son] died?

Evelyn: Tell you the truth I couldn't tell the difference (laughs). I couldn't tell the difference, I'm telling you. . . . After the funeral . . . they had their celebrations. . . . They went out and they drank; they partied, and they drank and drank. . . . I got away from them. When they start doing all that drinking, I get away from them. I can't associate with them.

☐ Reminiscing

With alcohol or without there might be reminiscing about the deceased and the good and bad things of the past, along with words about getting together more often and at other times than funerals.

Franklin: Depending upon the type of family structure that it is, there's likely to be some alcohol or something like that. That's also been a portion of it and wherein guys will tend to drink a bit more than women do. . . . The women join in with the drinking too, and the I-remembers come out of that. And talking about the ol' family fetes and the reminiscences about not having come together other than at this particular time . . . , "The only time we ever see so-and-so, that so-and-so is maybe over there. Don' see each other until it gets to be, we got to do somethin' about that. We got to do these things," and there are these proclamations of what might be done, and expressed desires to do something.

☐ Amusement and Laughter

In some narratives there were accounts of amusing and funny stories being told at the wake, visitation, funeral, or burial. With some African American deaths, not only is the deceased cried into the grave, the deceased is also laughed into the grave. The amusement and laughter may represent many different processes, but what may be most dominant is that the amusing things said about the deceased offer a tenderness and honesty about the deceased that can be taken as an expression of caring and love.

Willa: Everybody was telling stories about [Mother]. Merry stories (laughs). So it wasn't gloom and doom . . . even though I was just dying a little bit inside myself. It was nice to hear all these funny stories about her. And people just sat around and it was just a time to visit basically. I know some wakes are kind of morbid, but this one wasn't.

Whites, by contrast, are seen by some African American interviewees as not being able to get to the African American level of laughter and amusement at a funeral.

Marcia: I did go to a wake of a sister of a [white] colleague, and she died of breast cancer. And there was some chitchat . . . but not the laughter like it is in African American folk.

☐ Conclusion

The interviews suggest that African American death rituals are like and unlike Euro-American death rituals. They are like Euro-American rituals in that there is typically a Christian ideology, religious music, the quoting of scripture, and religious meaning given to the death. Family, friends, coworkers, neighbors, and others will be present and offer support, not only emotional and spiritual support but also help with the substantial work and expense of proper funeral rituals. There will be eulogies, condolences paid, feelings expressed, and eventually there is a burial.

But there are differences. African attire might be worn. Play family [fictive kin] might be present, and even if fictive kin are common in other ethnic groups, there is arguably an African American flavor to play family relationships in the African American community (see also, in this regard, a quote from Gwen in chapter 15). Attendance by white people will be noticed and included in a narrative (whereas, in Rosenblatt's experience, Euro-American narratives about funerals do not mention the attendance of African Americans). Reflecting the social class diversity of many African American families, and the modest economic origins of many African Americans who are now middle class, there will often be considerable social class diversity among those who attend African American funeral rituals. Perhaps relatively often there will be intense family hassles reflected in what goes on at the rituals, and these hassles may often have their origins in relationship difficulties of long standing that are rooted in the difficult circumstances that many African American families have had to face. In addition, because of the ways racism and discrimination affect African Americans, it is not uncommon for African Americans, particularly African American men, to be in legal, chemical dependency, and related trouble. Therefore, it seems relatively likely that at the death of a parent, it will be noticed and mentioned if none of the parent's children had "broken her or his heart." Expressions of emotion may be more intense at African American funerals (including, perhaps, "whooping and hollering"), but even if the emotional expression is relatively constrained people will be aware that they differ from what is common at African American funerals. Finally, it may be that relatively often at African American funerals, the deceased is not only prayed and cried into the grave but also "laughed" into the grave, with amusing stories about the deceased a topic of conversation that is loving and that acknowledges the humanity of the deceased.

African American Institutions for Dealing with Death

Many interview narratives dealt with one or more of four African American institutions that can help people deal with a death: the African American church, gospel music as it is in African American culture(s), African American funeral directors, and African American cemeteries. These cultural institutions had a role for a number of interviewees in defining and dealing with the death.

☐ The African American Church and Clergy

Historically, the African American church has been of vital importance in meeting the spiritual needs of African Americans and in helping to deal with difficulty (Billingsley, 1999; Lincoln & Mamiya, 1990; Meagher & Bell, 1993; Raider & Pauline-Morand, 1998, pp. 57–63; Staples & Johnson, 1993, pp. 211–218). Reflecting the diversity of African Americans along religious and spiritual lines (Barrett, 1995), a few interviewees were minimally or not at all connected with a church. But a substantial majority provided narratives of how they were church connected. Some African Americans attend what could be called "Eurocentric" churches (Bolling, 1995), but most of the people interviewed for this book attended a church that they might call "black" and that might also be called "black" by scholars such as Lincoln and Mamiya (1990). That is, the churches most interviewees talked about attending were clearly African American in the sense that the clergy and many or even all of the members of the congregation were African American. So the church rituals, social relationships, community linkages, and symbols had elements that were distinctively African American.

Some narratives spanned several African American churches. This was so because some people moved from one part of the country to another, and some changed churches within their community (see Baer & Singer, 1992, pp. 30–31, on the multiplicity of churches and denominations in some African American communities). Also, if the person who had died had lived in another part of the country, there might be church-connected death rituals both in the grieving person's home church and at a church where the funeral and perhaps the burial occurred.

Sometimes the church that the grieving person or the deceased belonged to when the death occurred, was particularly supportive and helpful because the members of the church knew the person who died and the whole family. That does not mean the church members helped directly with matters of grief. Their caring mattered, but paradoxically their caring might stay away from the most central problem of all, the grief of a surviving family member.

Charlotte: There's five generations of us in the same church. . . . It was comforting from the standpoint uh those people, what my mother meant to [them] we meant to them. So we were surrounded. They were still looking out for us, still caring for us, still supporting us. But there was no one who said, "Let me help you with this problem. Let me help you with your sadness. Let me help you with your grief. . . ." Nobody at church ever said anything.

One way to understand how churches and church congregations might not be of help with grief is that the primary involvement of many churches after a death is in the few days immediately following the death when there are the rituals of visitation, wake, and funeral. Also, the members of a church congregation are human, and in their humanity some may say things that a grieving person would not find helpful. In fact, some interviewees distanced themselves from members of their congregation because they knew they were likely to hear words meant to be supportive that would offend rather than help. Maya, for example, was careful not to discuss the stillbirth of her son with members of her congregation.

Maya: People are so judgmental. And if they don't understand, you know, "Oh girl, you got other kids, what you trippin off of that?" I hate to hear that. I don't deal very well with that. "You don't understand. I lost something very precious to me." "Well, you didn't even get to see it!" Oh, fightin' words, see, so it was just better that I just kept it to myself.

Some people had trouble with the theology (and hence the expectations, truths, and meanings) they thought they would hear from a clergyperson or a member of their congregation regarding a death. A piece of theology that some resisted was the notion of a hell for sinners. One way to think about that is that in some parts of the African American community there are many people who sin by various standards but are still seen as good. Some interviewees were clear that they did not want to think that most of the people in their family and community were going to hell, or that the people they knew, who had sinned by some standards but also seemed good, would end up in hell.

Ron: I believe our soul lives on. . . . I do not believe in the conception of a heaven and hell. I think that it'd be an evil God that'd throw somebody in hell forever and ever. A man thought that shit up. . . . God did not say he was gonna do that. God loves us. . . . Our souls continue to live on. And our souls continue to support us. And at some point our soul will move on. . . . The religious belief system about the final day of judgments, and that you're gonna be punished, which then makes you afraid of death, I reject that. I will not accept that. And I know for a fact that it's not real, because of my experience. . . . The religious belief system has all this judgment and condemnation and fear, unless you're saved and you're one of them chosen few. . . . I think all of us is God's children, and that God loves us.

For some people the clergy in an African American church may be especially helpful in dealing with the first shock of the death, whereas for others the greatest help may come later on, as a person struggles with grief or with spiritual issues connected to the death (Taylor, Chatters, & Levin, 2004, p. 125).

Willa: I think under the best of circumstances people talk with their religious leader or pastor. That's the best thing to do.

☐ Gospel Music, Spirituals, and Popular Sacred Music

Religious sacred music and popular sacred music are not unique to the African American church, but there are distinctive African American spirituals (Thomas, 1988, p. 5), and most African American churches may be distinctive in how the music of their rituals is learned, sung, used, and interpreted.

Traditional African American spirituals can be understood to have many levels of meaning (Costen, 1993, pp. 96–98; Jackson, 1972; Lincoln & Mamiya, 1990, pp. 356–359, 369–373; Spencer, 1996, pp. 52–55; Thomas, 1988; Walker, 1979, pp. 45–48, 141–145). Rooted in the dreadful time of slavery, when death by murder, whipping, overwork, mutilation, rape, poor sanitation, psychological attack, depression, and much else was common, many spirituals could be understood as saying that death freed a person to go to a better place (Jackson, 1972; Thomas, 1988, p. 12). So spirituals speaking of people's relationship with God, which offer solace and hope for those in pain, and offer life meaning, were historically important to African Americans, and come to the fore when African Americans deal with death. In fact, spirituals often speak quite directly to death and grief (Holloway, 2002) and can be seen as a means to bring pain to the surface and channel it (Martin & Martin, 1995, p. 93). African American spirituals can be understood as "depicting the process of healing through collective empathy, collective support, and hope" (Martin & Martin, 1995, p. 94). In fact, consistent with what others have written (e.g., hooks, 1993a; Moore & Bryant, 2003), some interviewees said that gospel music was good for them in their grief. It inspired them and helped them to see the joy and hopefulness in life and death.

Beverly: Is there any music that has been particularly important to you as you have dealt with your husband's death?

Rosalyn: Gospel music. Spirituals. Inspirational.

Beverly: Is there any music that was particularly important to you during that time?

Jane: Oh, gospel music. Always listen to gospel music. I listen to gospel music all the time, and that helped me a lot, 'cause I would turn the radio on, put a tape on, and just listen to gospel songs. And the words in the song just really helped me a whole lot.

Beverly: Was there any other music that had particular importance to you as you dealt with [your son's] death?

Gwen: A barrage of songs. Because that is where I do get my strength, in the music. And I choose music because of the message that it has. And at the time there were so many songs. One was a song called *Keep Looking Up.* And it says, "Life has its joys and sorrows too. Sometimes the mist will hide our view. If we would hope and faith renew. There's just one thing to do. Keep looking up. Thy God is still the same today. Keep looking up. He will not fail thee, come what may. Keep looking up. The darkest clouds will roll away, so do not doubt, but keep on looking up."

Like Gwen, others talked about specific gospel, spiritual, or popular sacred songs that supported them in their grief. They would listen to those songs at home, play them, sing them, hum them, imagine them, and be especially moved and supported by them when hearing them in church. In some narratives, a key to the support found in such music was the reassurance that there is a heaven or that the person who died is in heaven.

Beverly: Is there any music in particular that was important to you as you dealt with your mom's [death]?

Andrew: My gospel, *I'm Going Up Yonder* . . . "Going Up Yonder." And see, that song is real for me, going up yonder. Whoo! Mmm.

With some religious music the support is that the music speaks to the feelings of the bereaved person and what they are missing as a result of the death.

Beverly: Is there any music that has been particularly important to you as you dealt with your mama's death?

Barbara: Right afterwards the song *Sometimes I Feel Like a Motherless Child,* was *most* prevalent in my mind, because I did feel that way. I felt that there was nobody . . . here to take on the nurturing, to fill that void. . . . Folks made me feel at home, feel like family. That's kind of the void that they filled. They were nurturing. But that was the song, and I guess after I kind of got over things, there's a song that came up, *The Wind Beneath My Wings,* and that reminds me of her, because she was the cheerleader for us to go ahead and to do things and to be the best.

With a few people, religious music was a support in part because the music was meaningful to the person who had died.

Beverly: Is there any music that has been particularly important to you as you have dealt with your dad's death?

Verna: Gospel. I told my sister the other day . . . I came home and I went through a box of Dad's old tapes, and I put them on, and I says, "Did I ever tell you that I took his box of tapes?" She says, "No, and I don't care. . . . Dad is gone." And so I says, "I'm going to [keep them], because the musical tapes of the gospel choir and the gospel workshops comfort me, because they were his kind of music.

☐ African American Funeral Directors

There was a time when African American communities generally had their own funeral directors. White funeral directors would not serve them, and African Americans would not necessarily trust white funeral directors. African American funeral directors would understand how to do African American hair and makeup, understand the religious norms of the African American community, and know what was proper in the community.

In interviewee narratives, some funerals were described as being conducted by African American funeral directors. Many African Americans may still prefer to use an African American funeral director (Moore & Bryant, 2003), but especially in small towns in the south that no longer can support an African American funeral director, the funeral director was likely to be white.

Some people who were interviewed felt bad about that, for all sorts of reasons, including missing the many ways an African American funeral director could be important to the community.

Willa: Things have changed. And the (laughs) woman who used to be our black funeral director . . . Miss B., by this time Miss B. had died. . . . We used to have bake sales at the funeral home (laughs). . . . At Miss B.'s, we'd have, people'd come by, buy slices of pie and stuff, 'cause she rarely had a body. So you use the place for something (chuckling). And she belonged to our church, so we would have church bake sales and stuff at Miss B.'s. Sometimes we would sneak off . . . and scare ourselves to death and look in her coffin room. . . . By this time things had changed. . . . There was only one [funeral home], and it was the *white* funeral home. . . . The woman who runs the funeral home with her husband is also a hair stylist. And she said, "I will do my best with her hair," because she had a fresh perm. No problem, just curl it. And even though nobody was going to see her, I still wanted it to look nice. And she said, "Yeah, I'll do my best with it," and I believed her. . . . But back then (chuckles) if they put water on [permed hair] (she screams in mock horror). . . . It also has to do with makeup. . . . I think probably . . . black funeral directors were better with makeup for black people. They knew how to choose the right colors to complement, so that you didn't look orange or pink or gray.

People who talked about using an African American funeral director generally seemed to see that as a positive part of dealing with the death. The African American funeral director might know the family and definitely understood the community and what the community standards were. However, in that knowing, there could be problems. For example, the African American funeral director might have known the deceased well and so would be a mourner, perhaps grieving so intensely as to find it difficult to carry out the duties of funeral director. But still, there seemed generally a sense of comfort and that things were right when people talked about using an African American funeral director.

☐ African American Cemeteries

Some people talked about their loved one being buried in a distinctly African American cemetery. The African American cemetery was, and in some African American communities still is, a significant cultural institution. For some people, it is a place where many loved ones are together. Although it might be a place where the relatively poor economic situation of many African Americans can be seen in the neglect of the grounds, even in neglect there can be joy.

Willa: [My mother] could find humor in everything. And here's how bad some of those graves were kept. After we finished mowing the lawn and trimming around [Daddy's grave], we would get out our buckets and pick blackberries off some of these graves. It's a lot of brambles when you grow blackberries. And some of these people (laugh), poor things, I mean they'd been long forgotten, probably their relatives are all gone, and these brambles had grown up over their graves, and Mom (chuckles) would make blackberry jam and cobblers and she'd call it "graveyard jam." (both laugh) She'd say, "Go down to the basement and get me a jar of that graveyard jam." (both laugh) She had a sense of humor about death.

☐ Conclusion

There were four African American institutions mentioned by a number of interviewees that often were important in helping deal with a death: the African American church; gospel, spiritual, and popular sacred music with forms and meanings that are distinctively part of African American religious and cultural traditions; African American funeral directors; and African American cemeteries. Each of these institutions resembles institutions in the Euro-American community, but they have forms or flavors that are distinctively African American and address in various ways issues that are distinctively African American. For example, the African American church provides a community and leaders who can better understand what might be especially challenging about being African American and about African American grief. Religious music in the African American community might encourage hope in a time of pain with music that has meanings drawn from the time of slavery, the Jim Crow era, and more recent experiences with oppression. The African American funeral director will understand African American cultural standards and meanings concerning open coffins, makeup, hair styling, body disposal, and so on. African American cemeteries provide a resting place among the dead of the African American community, including perhaps many of the loved ones of the deceased and the survivors.

6
CHAPTER

How People Talked about Grief

As interviewees talked about grief, their ways of defining it seemed to us to be like grief would be defined by many Euro-Americans. For the African American interviewees, as for many Euro-Americans, grief is a personal, painful, long-term, largely private response to missing the person who died.

Franklin: Grief is personal and internal. . . . While . . . public expression may allow one to do some outpouring . . . grief is an ongoing thing that is there until you get through it. (*Beverly:* No matter how long it takes.) No matter how long it takes. You will get through it, maybe (chuckles).

Kenneth: Grieving [is] a mourning and a sorrowfulness [about] . . . having [lost] physical access to engage in dialogue and to recall memories and to use as a resource for guidance, and so that is no longer there, as being able to call them up on the phone, to stop in to their house, because it's not available to us in this realm that we live in, so that's the sorrowful part. Not that they [haven't] gone to be with the Lord. It's just that we (laughing) don't have 'em anymore. The things that we cling to and that we have grown comfortable with are those who have nurtured us. We don't have them anymore. And so that's the sorrowful part. That's why I grieve, because they aren't there.

Verna: Grief [is] a longing for, a missing, a hurting, an aching, a pain, a [sorrow for] love that's gone. A wishing, and a hopefulness, for that person. . . . Never ending (pause), sad, funny.

Beverly: How do you define grieving?

Cynthia: It's a sadness in the loss of someone.

☐ Acknowledging and Accepting the Feelings of Grief

For the interviewees, grief involves many different feelings, and many of them said that a key to the process of grieving is to let oneself have whatever feelings one has, to acknowledge and accept them.

Calvin: My advice would be to let your feelings flow, let your feelings flow. You're not strange for your emotions, almost weird emotions, clamoring within you, without any sense of direction. From hopelessness to stability, all these different emotions come at you from time to time. But you're not strange. Just let it flow. Go through each stage, and then hopefully you'll have the foundation of your faith in God to bear the cross.

Maya: There are so many feelings that you're gonna feel with this, and it doesn't happen at one time. It all happens in a period of time. When you think you've gotten over it, wrong answer. It comes back.

Pain

If there is a single word that encompasses the core of feelings of grief that interviewees talked about, that word is *pain*. For them, the grief process is almost always at its core a pain process. As they talked about their grief they again and again referred to pain.

Andrew: When I talk about it, when I really think about it . . . yeah, it's painful, because Mom is dead. . . . It's . . . ifficult.

Franklin: If you're revisiting the pain from grief, the pain of separation is what that is to me. It's the pain of loss of not being able to, in an absolute way, redo, undo, recapture, revisit, other than by memory. There's nothing else you can go and do to talk to that person or to two-way talk. . . . It's not there. It's not available. If I need to have something else for the additional strength that I need, it's not now. So that pain, that pain of separation.

Gwen: I was hurting a lot . . . when [my son] died.

Typically there is an aching intensity to the pain the interviewees talked about, and with it frequent, for some at times even constant, crying. Jane talked about her husband's death from heart disease four years prior to the interview.

Jane: At first when [my husband] died I cried a lot. I cried constantly. . . . I was just crying, crying, crying, especially the second week. . . . My family was here for a week with me. And the second week . . . (breathes out), I cried a whole lot here in the house, because I missed him, I missed him a whole lot. I still miss him, but during that time I really, really missed him. . . . We're all so used to seeing him all the time. We did things together. . . . I prayed a whole lot for God to give me strength to go on.

Distancing the pain, putting it aside for a while, occurs more often and for longer durations as the grief process goes on. People know they are putting the pain aside temporarily, but they can also know the pain is still somewhere inside of them or is likely to return.

Franklin: I don't talk about [the pain]. I don't deal with that like that. I submerge. . . . Is [the grieving process] an acceptance of the absence and the loss? . . . Is it enduring . . . the pain of the loss and getting out of the pain? I'm at that place where that pain is back over here, and I only deal with it when I go visit it. . . . Or if something else hurts that then triggers that piece, then I may visit it. But other than that . . . I choose not to. And it's a conscious choice. . . . Is that where I want to be? No, I don't know that. I would think that where I want to be is "not to have to do it." (chuckles) Not to have to deal with it, not to have it.

People distance the pain for many reasons. If the pain cannot be avoided, it may be debilitating and distracting, overwhelm one, and get in the way of anything else one might want to do. However, it seems that often a key reason for distancing pain is that it hurts too much.

Patricia: I just sort of feel like I didn't totally deal with it. That's what I've always felt. . . .

Beverly: Do you have a sense of why you haven't dealt with it?

Patricia: Well, yeah, because there's some pain there . . . that I know it's going to involve.

Religious Faith and Pain

In the religious communities of some who were interviewed, people are encouraged not to grieve but to celebrate that the person who died has "transitioned" into heaven. Along with that there seems to be the idea that if a person has a strong enough faith there will be no need to grieve. Despite those messages (and despite what grieving people may tell themselves), religiously observant people still reported grieving.

Rosalyn: Even though I'm a Christian, I hurt. That's what I told people. When my husband passed, people were saying, "You're a Christian. You should be able to cope with it." I says, "I am a Christian, but I hurt. I go through pain."

Some talked about how they dealt with the discrepancy between the religious value that deaths should be celebrated and their powerful feelings of loss that were definitely not celebratory. Patricia seemed to resolve the discrepancy by saying that if one accepts that the deceased person has transitioned to heaven and that's good, that one will still feel pain, but one's religious understanding will put limits on the pain one feels and expresses.

Patricia: You can't describe the void. . . . God in His grace . . . gives you what you need to go on, but then it's funny, because void, I used to almost think of "void" as some of the negative, like a person's absence. That's a negative. So even though I would view my mom not being around as not positive, in one sense, 'cause of the selfishness [of] wanting her around, I try to accept why that is, but in God's wisdom, in His purpose and all that, and so then it's almost, to me, to say that that void is not good is almost like saying that what's God's will is not good. So this starts bringing in some of that unresolved stuff. . . . We're not supposed to grieve anyway. . . . We're supposed to celebrate homegoings to heaven. . . . I hear people saying all the time, "We're supposed to be happy for where they're going." And it's almost like even when what we consider bad things happen, we're supposed to trust in God. Let go, not carry, not deal with, not feel. . . .

Beverly: Do you think that God would want you to feel though?

Patricia: Yeah. You have to feel. But I guess it's what you do with those feelings afterwards. And how far do the feelings go when you let go.

Expressing Pain Publicly

How people show their pain to others, if at all, varies. Some people keep the pain to themselves, perhaps because of what they believe to be the standards of their community or perhaps because of their own inclination to be strong (see chapter 12). Some may at times express their feelings without reservation, particularly in the first days after the death (see chapters 4 and 7). Those who express feelings publicly after the first few days may be rather subdued. For example, some may moan and sigh, which has the potential to communicate about their pain to others but is still understated.

Kenneth: I've never been a person who cries a lot. I hurt, but the tears don't come. . . . I guess I'm a moaner. . . . I moaned. And I sighed. But I don't cry with tears. . . . I don't think I've ever seen any of the men in my family cry, with the exception of my brother. . . . [My grandfather's death] was painful in the sense of a loss, of not having access to him, and being denied any parting words. . . . That's always painful when someone is gone.

☐ Anger

The word *pain* does not encompass all the feelings of grief that people generally talked about. Often pain was blended with other feelings, and often in that blend was the feeling of anger.

Ron: When you talk about the grief process you keep talking about grief. I like to talk about [it] in terms of pain. Because, see, you feel pain that's emotional or psychological or, in their pain is this sense of loss. That [person] is irreplaceable. You cannot replace this person, their presence, anymore, is not there. And it's gone. So you feel pain. And sometimes you, like sometimes I would, in my journey with it, I would be angry about having to go through that much pain.

Pain blended with anger and perhaps feelings of betrayal and guilt can also arise from feeling that one did not have the opportunity to say a proper goodbye.

Clyde: I talked to her on the phone a few times, and I woulda came right now, but I was bein' told that, "No, she's gonna be okay."

Beverly: Who told you that?

Clyde: She said that, but also my brother. . . . And my dad, especially my dad. "Ah, you don't need to come down here now. She's gonna be okay." She was in the hospital . . . but it seemed as though she was gonna be gettin' out. . . . I felt sort of . . . a betrayal. But you feel all those kinds of things when you don't have any control over what's going on, so all kinds of stuff can come into play. . . . You look at movies, TV, and . . . people always have the last, they always say some things then leave this world. And they have a conversation, you know, an opportunity. In my mom's circumstances that didn't happen.

Another kind of anger that might occur early in grief is anger at people who are like the person who died but who are still alive. Sometimes the anger comes simply because they are alive, but sometimes the anger seems focused on the injustice in their being alive though seeming to live a life of less value than that of the person who died. Rosalyn talked about such feelings following the death of her husband in an automobile accident.

Rosalyn: After it happened, when I'd see every young man around, I'd get bitter. I'd get mad. "They're here, and he's not. . . . See those men walking around. Don't want to be nothing, on the street. And here he is working. Trying to be a family man."

The pain that is blended with anger can also be connected to additional burdens acquired as a result of the death. Loretta's additional burdens included acquiring responsibility for the blind and retarded foster child her mother had been caring for up to the time her mother was institutionalized for the dementia that was part of her mother's dying.

Loretta: I have a lot of questions. I have a lot of concerns, but how to verbalize them, I don't know. . . . To open myself up to all of that would be to open myself up to a tremendous amount of pain. And I don't do pain well. . . .

Beverly: You were talking about being angry with (*Loretta:* The world). . . .

Loretta: And maybe the resentment was a result of hurting, and channeling it somewhere else, a transferral of emotion, that instead of feeling the hurt of my mother's demise, that I could transfer that into being angry. And I'm still angry. I'm still angry with [my brother].

Beverly: What would it take for you to let go of that anger and to grieve the loss of your mother?

Loretta: I don't know. . . . I still resent having to take care of [her foster child]. . . . That's a responsibility I will have no matter what's going on in my life.

Franklin said that he wanted an excuse to be angry, and so he welcomed barriers that arose to his grieving.

Franklin: For me it was necessary for those [barriers to grieving] to get in the way. Because then I can take out a portion of my anger, which is a part to me of grief is anger. They're mixed in, I don't know if [in] equal parts, but it is so intermixed.

Some people talked about anger at God, anger for taking a good person, anger for their loss, anger for a death so sudden that one could not say goodbye. Also, some people talked about anger at family members who might have made different choices that would have prevented the death or who behaved inappropriately prior to or after the death. Anger may even be at the heart of the grief process for some people. Barbara, whose mother had died when Barbara was a teenager, almost 40 years before the time of the interview, talked about her anger at her father and at God. And she also talked about her anger with the family poverty that seemed to have led to her mother exerting herself in a way that caused her fatal stroke.

Barbara: I was angry. And I was angry at God. And I was angry at Daddy, 'cause what I thought was if we had lived in the city, if Daddy had worked for the pulp mill, that her life wouldn't have been so hard, 'cause what had happened was she was out chopping kindling, to start a fire in a wood stove. Even though she had a gas stove, she had to have that wood stove going. And so I was mad at him. I was angry at both of them. If I could've gotten to God I would've boxed him for sure, 'cause He had taken the wrong person. He could have taken any of us, but not her. And it took a long time, a long time not to be angry (crying), or to even work it out in my head. So that was the thing. And that Daddy was sad, and that I was gone, and he was left all by himself (crying). And, oh, that didn't even sadden me, really. At first he lost a lot of weight, but (weeping) that didn't sadden me, because I was still angry at him. She was the best of all of us, and it wasn't fair. Any one of us could have gone. That would have been the right thing to do (sobbing), and He didn't do that. (sniffles) (pause) So that was it. I was real angry. It took me six years, six years to be able to cope with. . . . I couldn't say, "She passed," without crying.

And then there was the anger that some people had at the racist situation that seemed to have contributed to the death. In chapter 2, Franklin is quoted as he talks about his rage at the racist situation that led to his stepfather being assigned to extremely dangerous duty in the military.

☐ Conclusion

The ways in which interviewees defined grief, and the feelings they talked about, seem to us to be like what one would hear from Euro-Americans. There seems to be a core sense of grief that is shared across the two groups. But still there were subtle differences, particularly in the area of anger. Rosalyn's anger at young men who continued to live when her husband died was directed at young men who, in the devastation of poor, urban African American communities, are something like predators or ne'er-do-wells, not responsible young men. Loretta's anger at her brother was about him being like the young men Rosalyn was also angry at, a drug user who was not acting responsibly. Barbara's anger was in part about a poverty so deep and extreme that it may have led to her mother's death. So even if the feelings referred to in African American accounts of grief are like the feelings in Euro-American accounts, there may be important differences in the issues underlying the anger of grief.

Grief Soon after the Death

Early in grieving, a person may deny or question the reality of the death. One may need time to assimilate the information, and also the full emotional intensity of the grief may be delayed as one deals with pressing responsibilities that cannot be dealt with if grieving intensely.

☐ Numbness, Denial, and Delayed Grief

Statements like the following fit this idea of delayed onset of intense grieving and, we think, could be heard from white interviewees just as much as African Americans.

Kenneth: I think [it was] three weeks after I had gotten back from the burial and the funeral before I actually broke down and cried. . . . Every day I would go out and [hunt pheasants]. I didn't see a bird for three weeks. . . . [My grandfather] was always in the back of my mind, and it just seemed like when I came to grips with it, and I finally realized it, and I broke down and cried. . . . I was out less than five minutes . . . shot two birds, and it was over, hunting was over. That was the limit. . . . It was one of those surrealistic type of experiences . . . so I think that having to deal with something that he had taught me to do distracted me from dealing with the issue that this . . . person is no longer there. . . . After I had a successful hunt, I realized that there was something missing. . . .

Beverly: It sounds like you were numb for the three weeks.

Kenneth: To a degree. I don't know if it was so much a numbness or an absence or void of some kind in my consciousness and understanding the finality of death . . . and what I really had with my grandfather . . . the things that he had taught me.

Verna: I spent two days shopping. . . . I was trying to decide what I wanted, and so I called home to tell him I needed a credit card, and he wasn't there, and mother said, "Your dad is dead. I'm not giving you these credit cards, girl. Are you losing your mind?" And I says, "Mother, really!" She says, "No, your dad is dead. I need money to live. . . ." So that was my first reality. "My life is changing. I don't have his credit cards . . . 'cause she ain't giving them up." So I whimpered about that for a while, and I bought what my money (laughing) would get me. . . . It took three weeks before I cried, and when I cried I didn't know where it came from. . . . I bent doubled over and thought that I would die myself. I couldn't catch my breath. . . . I was grieving so I could not go back to work. I didn't want anybody to ask anything about it. I just stayed in the house for two days and cried, and couldn't even get it together enough to tell my mother I needed help, that this is really painful.

Willa: [Mother] named us coexecutors, but [my brother] doesn't have a business bone in his body. So I had to take care of all the estate business, so I didn't really get to grieve until a long time later . . . about a year later. I guess I must 've started it before then, 'cause I always found myself crying on the way to work, for no good reason. But there were things that had to be done, and I had to do 'em. And . . . about this time I developed irritable bowel syndrome. . . . It's triggered by stress. And I feel like I should own stock in Imodium.

In another example of what seems to be delayed onset of intense grieving, Vickie talked about the day she learned her mother had died.

Vickie: This is when you go into autopilot, because that was the day I went to pick up my friend's children. And my boss said to me, "Your mom just died. Where are you going?" I said, "I have to go get [my friends' children]." And she said, "Can't you find their parents?" I said, "They're both at meetings, and I don't know where the meetings are. So I can't call to tell them. . . . I don't mind going. . . ." And I had a workshop the next day, and I kept saying over and over again, "Oh, I don't know if I'll be able to make my workshop tomorrow." And my boss kept saying, "Why do you care?" I said, "You spent money." She said, "I spent $40. I don't really care. If you want to go, fine. You don't have to go for my benefit. . . . . . . " So I said, "Okay." So then I had to get in my car and go pick up [the children]. . . . But at this point I'm thinking, "Oh, dear. I have to go to a funeral." 'Cause I never thought my mother would die.

Not before my father. . . . I don't think I even shed a tear. I was just floored. . . . We had a wake on Sunday, funeral on Monday. . . . I was really nervous about seeing my mother dead. And you know something? I still didn't believe she was really dead. . . . It was so surreal to me.

Some instances of delay in grieving or what might be denial can be attributed to what some people experience as an initial shock of the loss. And this too seems to us as likely to occur among African American interviewees as it would for white interviewees. Evelyn talked about the death of her 2-year-old son.

Evelyn: It was just such a shock to me. . . . I just would sit here. . . . "I just can't believe this. I can't believe he's gone." And it was a long time before I would even, well I still don't have, I have his picture but I wouldn't even put it up (laughs). . . . It's just a shock. But I'm getting better. Through prayer, I'm getting better.

Ordinarily, what seems like denial or delayed grief is not totally separated from full awareness of the death. Some people seem simultaneously to know the person is dead and not to know or not to believe it fully. Or they seem to alternate, fully aware of the death at one point, then acting like the death is not so real, then fully aware again, and so on. And this too seems to us to be as likely to occur for the African Americans who were interviewed as for white people in the research we are familiar with.

Maya: I said, "Man, why don't you stop lying to me. I don't know why you all want to play games. I've had a baby. Where my baby? Bring my baby to my room. . . ." [The doctor] said, "I'm sorry." And I was like, "You lying." I think it was starting to register but I didn't want it to register. And I got a little out of hand, and he got (chuckling) out of the room because I threw a chair at him because I told him he killed my baby. And they took my baby and sold my baby. Oh I got to talking real crazy. And my mom was trying to talk to him, and I said, "You're my mother. . . . How in the world you gonna let them take my baby from me?" And she said, "Honey, it wasn't like that." And I said, "Well, did you see my baby?" She said, "No." I said, "See I told you [you] was in on it."

Toni: I was headed out the door, and my older sister called and said, "Granny's gone." And my grandmother was so feisty that I said, "Oh, my God." 'Cause she would have walked out the nursing home, so I said, "Oh Lord, let me go get her." And I could have talked her into coming back. And she said, "No, because she's dead." And, you know, I don't get it, I mean I still don't understand that.

Beverly: What did you say? What did you do?

Toni: I was just numb. I just couldn't understand. I just could not understand it. I still don't think I get it really. I know she's dead. There's still a part of me that I just don't understand how my grandmother could have left. I just don't understand it.

Jo-Ellen: The day of [my son's] funeral is when I started falling out, because I had purchased him a ring, and I went to put it on his finger, and his finger wouldn't bend. The reality (*Beverly:* That he was gone) that he was gone just was overwhelming. . . . I remember standing there and I felt like passing out, and it was like my brain was like, "Wait, wait, wait." And then everything pulled back together again. And then I was like, "Oh, he's deceased. He's not in his body. That's why you can't put the ring on him, so why don't you put it on a chain and put it over his head?" And then his shoes, [the mortician] had told me, "He doesn't need to have shoes on. His body doesn't need shoes." And I remember struggling with, "Wait a minute. But his feet," so I think I went in and out of still being a mother that feels like, "Well, yeah, but his body needs to be well covered." And then the reality, "Wait, he's dead. It doesn't make any difference." But I still went out and bought him some house shoes to put on. So I kinda went in between knowing he was dead. . . . There was a part of my intellect, a part of my psyche, that wanted to just pretend that he was gone for a while. . . . I remember the funeral, and I remember everybody's . . . support. I had a excellent community support system, but I was still numb.

Another version of what might be denial is that Patricia had trouble using the word *death* when thinking about her mother, who had died. But it could also be seen as something other than denial, a product of religious belief and an acknowledgment of the real memories a grieving person still has of the person who died.

Patricia: I can refer to *death* as a word, a concept. But . . . I don't associate it with my mother. . . . The reason I don't like the word *death* is because when I think of "death," it's like an ending. . . . I knew people could say, "Her life here on earth ended," but it sounds like it doesn't exist anymore. And that doesn't work for me, 'cause it has not ended. Her life is still here in me. It has not ended, and so what I think of is, oh, so unresolved. I'm trying to deal with. . . . I struggled with her no longer being there for me, or for us, or for me to share stuff with, just to not be there.

Patricia was one of four interviewees who used the word *transition* to apply to the change for the deceased from being on earth to being in heaven. Death was not an ending but a "transition." For example, Patricia started out the interview by saying, "It won't be a story about [my mother's] death at all. It'll be a story about her transition from earth to heaven."

At an extreme in terms of something resembling delayed grief was Maya, who said she did not grieve the death of her stillborn son until many years had passed.

Maya: I didn't start dealing with his death, his not being a part of my life or any of that until this year when I just recently like, I think I've been going now since July.

But Maya's delayed grieving seemed not only about her own psychological processes but about what the hospital staff did when her baby was stillborn. They did not let her see the baby, disposing of him without ceremony. So she missed the reality of seeing the body and the social processes in funeral rituals that help to move a person along at the onset of the grief process.

Nobody said they thought it was appropriate not to grieve or that it was even possible not to grieve. Some people, in fact, said that grief is in a person and demands that one enter into the grief process.

Charlotte: The grief is in you, and in your life. If you don't go through that process, it's festering.

So it seems that among the African American interviewees there was a sense of grief that cannot be denied fully or for long or stopped. A person might be numb or not fully convinced of the reality of a death, particularly in the days and weeks immediately after a death, but the reality is there and grieving will go on.

☐ I Lost My Mind

In their narratives some interviewees, sounding to us like some white interviewees would sound, said that early in grieving they felt as though they were losing their mind or that their world had turned upside down. Their pain, the loss of a person who was central to giving their life direction and anchoring their sense of self, the disorganization that comes with all the changes and demands immediately following a significant death, all pushed them to act in ways that in retrospect they felt were not quite sane.

Beverly: In what ways have you grieved his loss?

Verna: I bought clothes. Dad died, I left the hospital twisted and crazy.

In talking about feelings of losing one's mind, some people said that they only were able to cope because of the help of family members or God.

Franklin: I lost my mind, the little bit that I had (chuckles), with my sister's death. And took other family members to kind of like help me get around then.

Jane: God's the One that's going to give you the strength, and He's the one that's going to keep you going. And that's what happened to me. . . . If I hadn't God on my side . . . I'd probably be crazy, in a nuthouse somewhere, because that hurted me. It really hurt me when [my husband] died.

☐ I Lost My Sense of Direction

Sometimes, particularly early in grief, one can feel a loss of sense of direction. The person who died was crucial in giving one's life direction. Losing the direction a parent (spouse, or someone else) provided, one can feel rudderless. There may be nobody who helps with important decisions, acknowledges successes, assuages pain, and provides support. We believe that statements like the following can also be heard from grieving white people. However, it may be that in proportionately more African American families, the loss of an important family member is experienced as a loss of direction because deaths occur at a younger age (for survivors and for the deceased), and because the deprivations of racism are more likely to mean that the support of a close family member is extraordinarily important.

Willa: I can't tell you how many times I picked up the phone to call her, and even dialed the number, and then realized, "Oh. . . . " When your remaining parent dies, especially if it's your mother, you're sort of feeling rudderless. . . . I don't care how old you get, you still need your mom. . . . When the happy things have happened, I want to tell her. When I was upset about something, I'd want to tell her.

Parent figures are, for many people, key in providing direction. So the loss of the direction provided by a parent figure can be extremely difficult and can even feel like an abandonment.

Beverly: You feel like she left you?

Toni: Yeah, I do. And I know she didn't mean to, and I know she didn't want to. And my grandmother was very aware of the place that she had in my life. . . . It was just horrible. I never really had to live without my grandmother [and] make decision without her.

☐ Feeling Alone or Lonely

Another aspect of grief that seems to be primarily a phenomenon soon after the loss, and this is one that might be reported as often by African Americans who are grieving as by whites, is that some people said that at times they felt alone or lonely with the deceased no longer an active presence in their life.

Jane: It was hard for me when [my husband] died. All of my relatives was here, and the hardest part for me was when everybody left, and I was in this house by myself. I went back to work early, 'cause I did not want to be home by myself, and the hardest part for me was coming home from work, because he would usually pick me up at work.

Even people who had not been living with the person who died could feel lonely at times when, if the deceased were still alive, they would be in contact.

Cynthia: It did feel lonely because she always called me on the Saturday morning, about 9 or 10 o'clock, when she got up and was having her morning coffee. And for the first month after she died it seems like to me that any minute the phone was gonna ring on Saturday morning and it would be her, so I missed that for a while.

☐ Keeping Busy

For some people, part of the grief process, particularly in the first weeks or months after the loss, is wrestling with emotional and physical inertia. Grief can knock one down so far that one might not feel able or willing to get out of bed in the morning. But some people resist the inertia. They get going and keep busy. The following are, we think, things one might hear from white people as well as African Americans.

Beverly: How was it during those two to three years [after your wife died]?

Len: For me, I get busy. I took on another job. I was working. . . . That kept me goin'.

Rosalyn: I came right back to work. I felt I didn't want to be at home . . . because my husband was not there. So I felt that work was the best place. . . . You're busy when you have to work. Your mind is on . . . your work. And you don't have time to think about those things until you get home again. When you get home . . . you're so tired.

Although there are indications in the bereavement literature that keeping busy in grief might be more common for men than for women (e.g., Martin & Doka, 2000, ch. 7), we saw no clear gender pattern in that regard in our interview data.

☐ Legal, Financial, and Estate Hassles and Grief

For anybody in the United States, a challenge to the grief process, particularly soon after the death, is dealing with legal, financial, and property matters attendant on the death, all the practical things about estates, personal possessions, insurance policies, death certificates, and bills.

Norma: I got a book that was just wonderful. . . . It was called, *Prayer Starters,* and it would just say, "For today, I'm going to," and you could fill it in. And it was a really good way to get focus[ed] on not runnin' all over. . . . There're . . . many, many business things that have to be taken care of, that linger on and on. It's like, "Will this ever be done?" We had problems with the death certificate. There's just lots of things that months later you want to be done with.

Although dealing with all those details is partly a distraction from the grief process it also can be entangled in the grief process. In particular the personal possessions of the deceased and the home in which the deceased lived are powerful reminders of the deceased and quite possibly retain some of the essence of the deceased (the person's odor, interests, ways of dressing, etc.). So people may be reluctant to dispose of things, because they are treasured reminders, but they also may come to feel held back by those things from going on with life. Jo-Ellen talked about dealing with treasured reminders of her son, who died at age 4 of leukemia.

Jo-Ellen: I remember . . . closing his bedroom door, 'cause I just couldn't deal with it. . . . As time went on, probably about a month, I realized I needed to deal with it. And I remember going to his room to open the door, and I couldn't do it. . . . The next day...I went in and I laid across his bed, and I broke. I just cried. I just cried. I was like, "Wait, wait." And I cried till I felt like I was gonna throw up. It was a feeling of loneliness. It was a void that I couldn't fill. . . . I had been busy, but I couldn't fill it. . . . The first . . . morning I had got up, and I . . . looked out the front window. And I watched people going to work, and I remember standing there thinking, "(snort of disgust) Life hasn't stopped. It feels like it has stopped, but it hasn't. Look at these people. They don't even know. They don't know what I'm feeling. And I can't let life stop. . . ." When I did go into his room . . . I would . . . lay across his bed and cry. . . .

Beverly: Did you feel like you were closer to him when you were there?

Jo-Ellen: No, I felt like I probably wanted to be, but I couldn't. He wasn't there. . . . I had a girl friend that lost her daughter. . . . She would say . . . , "You could still smell their fragrance, their body in the room." Especially laying across the bed and on the pillow. But he wasn't there. . . . You're here; you smell him; it's almost like you feel him, but you know he's not here. Face that reality, and my crying was facing that reality. "I don't care how many of his clothes I have here. I don't care that I can look at the fire engine and remember his laughter. I don't care that I can pick up a piece of his clothes and remember him wearing it. He is not here. You've got to get rid of this stuff. Your holding onto it is not gonna bring him back . . ." That was hard, because part of you says, "Wait, but if I hold onto all this, I can hold onto him." But the part of me that deals with reality says, "Wait a minute. Come on. Stop. What are you prolonging this thing? You (snort of contempt), this is not reality. You have to deal with reality." And so I packed up his clothes, and I was very intentional on who to give them to. It took me a while, because I wanted them to go to a mother that would appreciate them for her children.

☐ African American Cultural "Shoulds" about Early Grief

Quite a few interviewees talked about their sense of what is expected of grieving people in the African American community soon after the death. Although we believe those expectations are not unlike those that many Euro-Americans would report for their own communities, we believe that in the "shoulds" interviewees talked about there was still a distinctive African American flavor.

It's Okay, Maybe Even Necessary, to Cry

Typically narratives emphasized that it was perfectly okay to cry, or, as some people said, "Whoop and holler." Whooping and hollering have historically been part of African American expressions of pain going back into slavery times and before (Crawford, 2002, p. xii). And whooping and hollering and other strong emotional expressions soon after a death seems a widely recognized "should" of African American culture.

Charlotte: It's okay to feel bad that you lost a loved one. It's okay to roll around the floor, close the doors, scream and whoop and holler. But know that that person is okay, and know that you will be okay, because you will pull everything from your experience with them to sustain yourself. It's life. Death is life. . . . I would tell them that whatever you're going through, it's okay.

Even some people who said they didn't "whoop and holler" made clear that such action was common and even expected in their community.

Elsa: Most people were looking for me to just break down and cry and whoop and holler.

Beverly: And how did you grieve?

Elsa: Inside. Inside.

With "whooping and hollering" common and expected in some African American communities, it is not surprising that some narratives spoke of worry about not "breaking down." Not whooping and hollering could be a sign that something was wrong. However, as some narratives indicated, not breaking down could arise from a person's socialization to be relatively controlled or a dying process that made death, when it finally came, a release.

Cynthia: At first I thought that there was something wrong with me because I never really broke down, but this goes back to my grandmother, who had always prepared me for death. . . . She always said that it's inevitable and that we're all gonna die. . . . And if you go back to the Bible, . . . actually we're supposed to cry when a person comes into the world, because they're coming into a world of sin. And rejoice when they go out, because they're going out of a world of misery. And so whenever something like this happens I think of that. . . . Mother was in so much pain. . . . First I prayed that it would be His will to make her well. And then I prayed that if it be His will that He would just go ahead and take her out of her misery. . . . I didn't break down and cry. And people kept telling me that I needed to let go of my emotions, and basically I just wanted to be alone. . . . Even when I was alone I was not crying. . . . I was just reflecting.

Be Strong for Your Family

The cultural "should" to express grief seems primarily to apply to the days immediately after the death. A contradictory "should," to be strong in the sense of emotionally controlled and helpful to one's family, also seems important in the narratives of most of the people interviewed. Although the "should" to be strong may apply primarily to the days, months, and years following the initial funeral rituals, some interviewees talked about themselves or others being "strong" from the beginning.

Beverly: Did your brother cry a lot at the funeral . . . ?

Willa: No. I don't think he cried at all, at the funeral.

Statements like these lead us to believe that "being strong" can be a should even very early in grieving. However, most of what people had to say about being strong applied to times other than immediately after the death, so we reserve most of what we have to say about being strong for a later discussion (chapter 12).

☐ Conclusion

It seems that early in grief African Americans experience a great deal that what would be commonly reported by Euro-Americans. There may be an initial numbness, denial, or delay of grief. For some people there is a sense of losing their mind or a sense of loss of direction. A person may feel alone or lonely and may, early in grief, deal with the situation partly by keeping busy. Although keeping busy may be about distancing the pain, loneliness, and loss of direction, for many it is not difficult to keep busy because there are the legal, financial, property, and other practical issues to deal with as a result of the death.

Even though the numbness and so on could plausibly be featured in a chapter on initial grieving among Euro-Americans, the interviewees talked about "shoulds" in the African American community that seem to us to be different from shoulds that Euro-Americans might report. One should is that a grieving person should be emotional, even strongly emotional, early in the grieving process. A second should is that a grieving person should be strong for her or his family, which means to be controlled and helpful. These shoulds can be understood to come out of a culture that values openness of emotional express but also recognizes that, in a racist environment that keeps many families on the edge of coping, those families cannot afford to lose a grieving person's functioning.

8

Meaning Making

Meaning making is central to the grief process (Attig, 2001; Nadeau, 1998, 2001; Neimeyer, 2001; Stroebe & Schut, 2001). It may even be more important in the grief process of African Americans (Plumpp, 1972, p. 84), because racism threatens both the survival and the meaningfulness of life for African Americans. Inseparable from other aspects of grieving at every step of the way is the struggle to find meaning in the life of the person who died, the dying, the death, and what has happened since the death. The meaning making process is fueled by what is inside the grieving person—what the person has learned and the person's values, beliefs, and psychology. Meaning making is also fueled by what comes from the outside, from what people say, including sermons and eulogies, things read, including the Bible, and much more.

Rosalyn: It is quite interesting . . . how I just happen to come upon things that help me through my grief. . . . One day, I was in a lobby somewhere, and I saw some books on the table. And one of the books was, *Lonely, But Not Alone.* . . . I picked up that book . . . and it stated . . . "God says, 'I'll be better to you than your husband, your mother, your father. . . .'" That helped me along. And . . . a friend of mine . . . a pastor, when I called him and told him about my husband's death, I guess I was some-what bitter and . . . I might have been blaming myself. . . . He says, "I think you are in a very, very bad stage, and I would suggest you get the book *The Power of Positive Thinking.* I got that book. . . . It helped me along. And I picked up and I read scriptures on death.

☐ Meanings Given to How the Death Happened

The narratives of every person gave meaning to how the death happened. We discussed in chapter 2 how racism is an important part of some narratives about how a death came to be—for example, how denial of medical services or racism-caused poverty led to a death. With some deaths, people talked about other aspects of the larger environment being implicated in the cause of death; for example, the gangbanger culture in the case of a death by murder. But meanings about the cause of death are almost never just about the larger environment. They are also about the "near" environment, the family and the interviewee. Many people make meaning by seeing part of the cause in the family or in themselves. Maya, for example, talked about blaming her ex-husband for the stillborn death of her son.

Maya: I divorced my husband. . . . [He] was very abusive. . . . I found out that he was on crack cocaine. Then I really got to blame him, saying, "It was your fault. It was them impurities in your body that killed our baby." You see I was pointing the fingers and, you know, that might not have been the case. It could have been a combination of the fact that I was still taking the birth control pill not knowing that I was pregnant. It was what the doctor said.

When there is self-blame, there can be powerful feelings of guilt and regret.

Len: I remember callin' the hospice nurse and sayin', "[She's] really struggling to breathe. Is there somethin' we can do?" And she sent over some medication. . . . The medication was, I guess, designed to slow her breathing down and, you know, to ease. . . . Just put a drop on her tongue. . . . I started to doin' it and then said, "I can't do this." But not too long afterwards she died. And my guilt and shame is that, and I know it's nothing but how thoughts just kind of penetrate (chuckling) you some times. . . . "You killed her. It was the medication. Should have given her that medication." And I know it wasn't, but still, that was the thought. . . . That's the biggest thing. It sneaks up every once in a while.

☐ What Was Lost

Every narrative detailed what was lost because of the death, and in that detailing meaning is given to the person who died, the death, and the grief that has come afterward. For example, by saying the person who died was of enormous importance, one is providing meaning for that person while alive and for one's relationship with that person, and one is providing meaning as to why it is that the death is grieved so strongly.

Racism and the Magnitude of Loss

Many narratives reflect the importance of family members in a world where racism is a constant in African American life, where because of racism it is possible to fall into deep trouble, where because of racism families are relatively likely to be disrupted, and where because of racism African Americans are typically less well off economically. In such a world, a family member who supported one's self-esteem, who tried to keep one from deep trouble, who was there for one emotionally, or who provided for one economically in difficult circumstances would be sorely missed. That is not all that would be missed, but it is clear for some interviewees that what was lost reflects the difficult circumstances of many African American families in a racist society. Andrew talked about his mother, who had died 12 years prior to the interview.

Andrew: Whenever I have tough times . . . I called my mom, and she, "Get up, boy! . . . You go ask everybody for a dollar . . . and you'll have a thousand dollars before the day is over," and she always give me that. My mama didn't believe in failure. She said, "If you mess up, you turn around. . . ." I just learned so much from her. . . . "You're somebody. . . ." At a time when self-esteem wasn't talked about, that's all I learned. "You're somebody. You are somebody. You got to do it. If you don't do it, who's going to do it?" And she instilled that in me. . . . "You can make it. . . ." I could talk to my ma. . . . Whatever I was going through. . . . "You'll need to do that," but I could tell you, I messed up badly. She beat me, but she'd say, "You don't need to see that side of life," and she always worked hard to provide. . . . When my dad was living they'd send me these letters (still crying) with so much love, and knowing they were proud of me (still crying) 'cause I left the community and I went to school. And they'd send me these letters of love. Wasn't no money, 'cause they didn't have any money (crying), but we'd talk on the phone and they'd send me letters. . . . And (weeping) got this letter, and in it was this couple of hundred dollars from Mama, and I hadn't told her. I would never worry her. I kind of learned from her to be independent. I think that's what she like about me. . . . I wasn't going to tell her. She had to pull it out of me. "What's wrong with you, boy? You don't sound right." Then I'll break down, and tell her, and then she'd give me one of those pep talks. . . . I really needed this money. I didn't know how I was going to do that. But I prayed. Me and my mother prayed together. And so, bam (claps hands together). There came the letter, with the money in it. And I was able to move. I was able to make the transition. . . . My mom was so much to me. Was so much. She taught me so much about living.

Barbara: [Mama] was the glue that held everything together . . . because . . . Daddy had a temper. . . . She was just always there. . . . She had like maybe a third grade education. And I remember coming home from school some times, after I got in high school in particular, and I'd be trying to work out algebraic problems and stuff like that. Now she had no idea, she hadn't had algebra. But she'd say, "Why don't you just read it out loud?" . . . And she might ask me a question after I read it out loud that would help me to figure out what I needed to do, which was most amazing to me, truly amazing. And she didn't have a whole bunch of different kinds of skills, but she could make me the prettiest flour sack dresses in the world. You know, the little collar here, the puffed up sleeves here, and the bow. . . . They were cute dresses. And she would save money all through the year so that she could buy us something for Christmas.

Elsa: [My son] . . . was my friend. . . . We could talk about anything and every-thing, but he was not to lie. We didn't lie to each other. So if it came to the point where you had to tell me a lie, we don't discuss. . . . I never mentioned [my father sexually abusing me] to anybody in the family until after my father died. . . . I knew that . . . my son would've killed the man. He loved his mama (laughing), and he ain't gonna let nobody hurt his mama. No. No. So I never said anything. . . . Before he passed away he put two new hot water tanks in my house. He started working on the downstairs and installed [an] electrical ceiling fan and he started redoing the kitchen. . . . Since he's been gone the house is falling apart. We can't seem to get anything done. We don't have the monies to get it done . . . and when we hire these jacklegs, they take my money and no work gets done. . . . He took care of the cooking. . . . He'd fried chicken, he'd have mom some baked chicken on the side, and he did all the grocery shopping. . . . He had to know how to take care of hisself. And that's what he started doin' with his kids. . . . It was just me and him for many, many year. Just me and him. My sister [who died] got sick when he was 12, so it's just me and him. Yeah.

Beverly: And his dad?

Elsa: His dad died when he was 6. He was killed in a motorcycle accident. . . . [My son] was a protector for the women in the family.

One can also hear Euro-Americans talking about how important their deceased family members were while alive, but arguably the situations re-ferred to in the above three quotes are much more common among African Americans than among Euro-Americans. Each of the quotes refers to situations of desperate need and great scarcity of economic and other resources.

A few people went beyond the matters addressed in the above three quotes to talk about wealth (savings, real estate assets, and the like). African Ameri-cans average lower income levels than Euro-Americans and also much lower levels of wealth (savings, real estate, personal possessions) than Euro-Americans (U. S. Bureau of the Census, 2000, pp. 13–16; Collins, Leondar-Wright, & Sklar, 1999, p. 55). Economic loss can be part of what is grieved following a death in any group, but in comparison to Euro-Americans, African Americans who are in difficult economic circumstances may on the average grieve economic losses more intensely following a death. Andrew, for example, said that economic loss was part of what many people grieved, that if a loved one who was an economic provider did not leave substantial wealth behind to sustain one, there was more to grieve.

Andrew: Not only do you hurt, but then if it's a husband or a wife . . . "I don't have nothing. . . . Now I've got to face this world, sho' enough, with." Now if I left you with two hundred . . . thousand dollars, then you can pay off the house, and you can have a little nest egg to pinch off of as you go to work. "Hey, I'm grieving, but I can make it." For us it's a whole loss of income. So whatever you was bringing in, if we don't have a good insurance policy. And we find a lot of African Americans on that side.

Because African American families are relatively often disrupted by premature death (see citations in chapter 2) and by economic and other factors, relatively often a grandmother or somebody else other than a parent has a crucial parental role in a person's growing up (Landrine & Klonoff, 1996; Minkler, Roe, & Robertson-Beckley, 1994; Ruiz & Carlton-LaNey, 1999; Sandven & Resnick, 1990). That means relatively often the death of a grandparent, stepparent, foster parent, or adult other than a mother or father will be grieved with the kind of intensity that might be seen relatively often in Euro-Americans grieving a parent's death. Here is an example of that. Kenneth, who lost his grandfather, a man central in bringing him up, missed the rapport he had with his grandfather and the ways his grandfather and he were special to each other.

Kenneth: He'd give me a look to let me know when someone was blowing smoke. "And don't take it too seriously. . . ." It was a rapport. It was a rapport. It was a communication system that was built in from being brought up by this man. . . . I treasure those things, and the memory of Grandfather.

Here is another example in which a grandmother was grieved for the parental support she provided.

Toni: I adored my grandmother. She was just life to me. . . .

Beverly: How did your grandmother's death affect your daily life?

Toni: I had nobody to call. I talked to my grandmother every day. And I had nobody to correct me or to teach me. . . . I was a newlywed, and I had no one to teach me to be a woman, and she would have taught me things. . . . I had nobody to teach me, so I kinda had to stumble around.

Perhaps anyone who loses somebody important can feel a loss of identity. But it might be relatively common for African Americans that it is the death of a parental figure other than a mother or father that shakes identity. Moreover, losing a person whose interactions were central to identity increases the difficulty of meaning making during grief, because without a strong sense of self one lacks footing to come to narratives, to define what has happened, or to make sense of what is going on in one. Here is an example of that, with Franklin reflecting on the death of his stepfather.

Franklin: Immobility is not unheard of for folks who are really grieving, because of the high loss, that person is my identity too. That I have lost me as well as them. That I am only someone in respect to them. That if there is any measurement of me, it is by them. So given that, once they're dead, I disappear (chuckles). Almost. I may go through the motions, but, I don't know. Do you really exist?

With parental figures other than actual parents so often important in African American families, the death of a parent may be grieved partly in terms of what the parent would have provided one's child.

Clyde: [My son] didn't get a chance to get some of her stuff that [my mother] passed on to me first hand. . . . So I think he was kind of cheated. I do the best I can, but it would've been totally different coming from her. . . .

Beverly: You're talking about wisdom?

Clyde: Wisdom, all kinds of sayings . . . traditions, boy, you'd be surprised. 'Cause the idea of . . . mirror, kids need that mirror. . . . That's what make us who we are. And we can only be who we see. I mean we have to see, whoever we see when we're around, that's who we're gonna be like. . . . He just didn't get that mirror. . . . He should've been able to get some of that. He should've had his butt spanked by her. . . . That's a tradition in itself. I got my ass whopping. (laughs)

Because African American economic situations are often relatively insecure, the death of a person whose economic support was vital will involve meaning making that emphasizes, among other things, the magnitude of economic loss. In the quotation below, Jane talked about the death of her husband, who was her economic provider. A piece of what she said, which we think reflects African American culture as it has developed in a racist economic world, is the importance of the house. In a racist world where it is very difficult for African Americans to accumulate wealth and where the people who help to maintain one economically may die prematurely or be no longer able to provide for other reasons, a woman with a house has security. Jane talked about losing the material support and the sweetness her husband provided, but she also talked about her husband giving her a house. Another aspect of the quote that we think would be more likely to be heard from African American interviewees is what is said about welfare. The difficult economic situation of African Americans makes it more likely that an African American interviewee would talk about how someone who provided material support helped one to cope with the inadequate economic support of welfare or other government support systems.

Jane: He did so much for me. He bought my home. He wanted to make sure that I had a home to live in before anything happened to him. . . . He was a nice, caring person. . . . He would do anything in the world for you. . . . He knew a lot of people. . . . He was 25 years older than I am, but that didn't make a difference. . . . He was just a sweet person. Everybody . . . liked him. And they always talked about what a nice person he is. . . . He would try to help you all he could. And he helped me a whole lot in my lifetime, 'cause after I got divorced from my first husband, I went on welfare. And it was hard for me to try to live on welfare. At the end of the month we'd run out of food, and he would always, "Come on. You need food, just call me. If you need anything, need to go anyplace, just call me. I'll come." And he did, so there were lots of months . . . he would buy food and bring it in. And he didn't look for nothing. He just did that. . . . My grandma said . . . "Girl, that's a good man. You better try grab that man. . . ." We had two kids together. . . . He would get up in the night and change the baby. . . . He was a good father to all four of my kids. Yeah, they all called him, "Dad." They all loved him. . . . His death, ah, that's hard. It's a start over in my life. It's me being by myself. . . . I had him there to help me. Now I don't have that. And that's hard for me. . . . I'm learnin' how to do things that I have never did before in my life. I'm learnin' how to take care of a house, and I'm learnin' how to take care of business. . . . He did all of that.

☐ Meeting the Standards of the Deceased

Sometimes an important part of the meaning making in grief is to come to see oneself as meeting the standards of the deceased. Then one can think, "I have lost the person but I have some of that person in me or at least I am trying to still live in a way that respects that person's standards." Sometimes the meaning making involves a realization that one cannot meet those standards, but in that realization is an acknowledgment and respect for the standards the deceased represented. Although we think that what interviewees said about these matters are on the surface similar to what one might hear from whites, we think there are subtle but important differences. Among the differences are that relatively often the person whose standards are referred to as being very important is a parental figure but not a parent. And relatively often there is a sense that this one person's standards were crucial in one's life. We think that it is not so often for African Americans as for Euro-Americans that there are two or more people jointly providing standards.

Franklin: Maybe I will come out of the shadow of whether or not I am good enough in [my stepfather's] eyes or not good enough . . . because he meant so very much to me.

And when it is a parent whose standards are discussed, we think it is more often, than for Euro-Americans, that the parent whose standards are mentioned is a mother. Proportionately more African Americans would have grown up in a household with a single mother or a mother who was central to standard setting.

Barbara: I knew that she would want me to be the best that I could be, to be on my best behavior. To be a good person. All of those things. So that was that, that fight going on, trying to be what I knew she wanted me to be.

☐ Religious Meanings

Kalish and Reynolds (1981, p. 210) reported that African Americans were considerably more likely than white Americans to say that religion (including mystical experiences) influenced their attitudes toward death the most. That may mean that religious themes, ideas, and imagery are relatively likely to have a central role in African American grieving.

Historically, the church has been central to social life and to coping with difficulties in the African American community (Early & Akers, 1993; Holloway, 2002). Traditions in African American religion of religious imagery, song, and action have had an important role in enduring and distancing racist oppression (Boyd-Franklin & Lockwood, 1999).

Another aspect of religious faith that is salient in African American grieving is the idea of death as a return home to God and a freeing from the trials of life (Barrett, 1995, 1998, 2003; Holloway, 2002; Meagher & Bell, 1993; Moore & Bryant, 2003; Smith, 2002; Tully, 1999). So people are seen as passing on to home in heaven, to the afterlife, to a place where one day family members may be reunited (Abrums, 2000; Holloway, 2002; hooks, 1993b; Smith, 2002). That way of thinking may be relatively salient in African American narratives about a death, because life on earth can be seen by African Americans as more a life of trials than it is for whites (Brice, 1999, p. 49). In addition, the oppressed can be seen in Christian terms as on stronger theological grounds to return to God's bosom than are the oppressors.

Although religion and spirituality can be, for anyone, a powerful language for talking about personal pain (Boyd-Franklin, Aleman, Jean-Gilles, & Lewis, 1995; Boyd-Franklin & Lockwood, 1999) and a powerful source of healing and of dealing with grief, they can also block people from their feelings and lead to religiospiritual concepts derailing processes that could lead to self-awareness and deep healing. Perhaps related to this, Prouty (1983), using MMPI-type personality measures, reported a higher level of denial in a sample of grieving African Americans than in a matched sample of grieving whites.

In any group in the United States, religious meanings may be important in making sense of a death and what has happened since the death. But for proportionately more African Americans, religion may have a central role. The African American church, in all its diversity, has been central to helping many African Americans cope with a harsh world. The people interviewed seemed like African Americans described in other research (e.g., Smith, 2002) in finding religious meanings in the death. God brought the deceased home. Death is about God's will. God wanted the deceased to suffer no more. God saw that the grieving person or the deceased was ready to let go. The death was not meaningless but represented what God wanted. The deceased has not disappeared into nothingingness but is with God. The grieving person has not been ignored by God. God looks after the deceased and the survivors.

Reliance on religion and on God can create a substantial challenge when a death occurs to someone important to one. How can God take away this person on whom I rely so much, who I love so much, who loves me so much? Thus, religious beliefs may be challenged by a death. When that happens, it seems important for meaning-making narrative to address how the death fits into God's plans. Barbara was a teenager at the time of her mother's death, which occurred several decades prior to the interview. Barbara had relied heavily on her mother and shortly after her mother's death was sent to live with relatives 1000 miles away.

Barbara: Finally I got it worked out in my head. And the way I worked it out was (breathes out loudly) that God had this garden up there. And that He really didn't need any thorny things. And he needed this one special flower. And she was it. So that's how I worked it out. But otherwise I was having a hard time.

Religious meaning shapes feelings, though it is also true that grieving people can have doubts that the religious meaning available to them allows them to deal fully and consciously with their feelings of loss.

Calvin: I had enough of a foundation biblically to understand that life is just an interim period. . . . I find comfort in the fact that [Mom] lived a good life. She lived a real good life. She lived happy. She wasn't abused or anything like that. And I've just accepted that fact with the hope of the resurrection and eternal life and the ultimate reunion. Some times when I think about it . . . I cry. And I don't think that's strange. . . . I just left [the funeral] saying, "Mom would want you to live on and be the man, the Christian man that she raised you to be," and embrace the promise that the absence of the body is to be present with the Lord. And so hopefully then, "By me shall ye never die." And Christ is the resurrection, and I just embraced those promises, and [kept] moving. I don't know. Maybe subconsciously maybe I wasn't dealing with it.

A key idea from the African American church has been that in a world of oppression, poverty, brutality, and premature death, there is a better world waiting for one. Thus, it is not surprising that an important part of some narratives is how the person who died is better off for having died. Although a statement like the following could be heard from a white person, in the context of the African American church and the history of oppression of African Americans, this statement resonates with what many African Americans would have heard in church every week.

Gwen: A barrage of things went through my mind as: if [my son] would live, what kind of life would he have with this debilitating thing going on? And so I decided that it was much better for him, and that's how I've been able to accept the whole thing, that he doesn't have to suffer that stuff anymore. . . . I understood that this isn't about me. I mean, it is, but it isn't. It's about him, being free from whatever pains. From the way he had the seizures, I don't know if he was in pain, but to me it just seemed like he should have been. And he didn't have to suffer that any- more. And that's where my mind has been through the years, that he will not suffer anymore. He'll never have that problem anymore. So he's in a better place than being here with me. And I understand that it's my wanting him to be with me. . . . For him it was better. For me it was a hard time. And sometimes still [30 years later] a hard time.

From another perspective, with the church and religion being important in the lives of African Americans it is not surprising that some narratives about the deceased and the grieving person's relationship with the deceased would speak extensively about the African American church. For example, a woman talked about the special rapport she lost when her father died and about her connection, originally through him, with the church.

Verna: My dad used to be called "the singing...preacher." Before he was or- dained he was a gospel singer. And all of my childhood memories was of him in church and me with him. And he did my nurturing, mostly. And so I was closest to him. . . . I was looked upon as a gift from God. I was treated as a gift from God, and pretty spoiled (chuckles). . . . So it grieves me often that I can't talk to him. . . . I find myself wishing that he was around. . . . He was my caregiver. He was so proud to have this child that he took me from my mother and he would take me to church and he would show me off. And everywhere he'd go, I'd go. I'd be at rehearsals. I remember him always giving me to some little old lady to hold, while he would go to the pulpit.

In another example that reflects the importance of the African American church, Gwen talked about the talents of her son who died and his aspirations to be a preacher.

Gwen: He was a pleasant little boy, a very intelligent little boy (chuckles). He was a funny little boy. . . . He used to jump on the table and preach. . . . He decided . . . he was gonna be a preacher, and so . . . he wouldn't go to church without a suit on. . . . He would get on this table, and he would talk, and somebody'd come around smoking a cigarette he says, "Thou shalt not smoke. . . ." He began to sing the song: "Wonderful savior is Jesus my Lord. A wonderful savior to me. He hideth my soul in the depths of His love, and covered me in (humming music), there with His hands, and covered me. . . ." And then some of the chorus, "He hideth my soul in the depths of His soul."

Scripture

Consistent with the idea of religion being important to meaning making in African American grief, 16 of the 26 people who were interviewed talked about scripture. Some found in Biblical texts support, encouragement, and teaching that helped them to have faith in God and to cope with their loss. Some saw the Bible as the place to turn to for help for anyone who was grieving.

Some had ways of making use of the Bible in dealing with their loss; for example, reading and rereading Psalms or letting God direct their gaze into the Bible.

Gwen: I think you can get through anything, like the scripture says, "through Christ, who strengtheneth me, I can do all things through Christ." And I do believe that. . . . Psalms is a wonderful book. I have found in the down times, through the tears, that Psalms is the book. . . . I say, "Okay, Lord. I've opened this book. And You place my eyes on what I need to see. I don't even need to tell You how I feel right now. Lord, You know what I'm feeling, so I'm opening this book." Psalms. And whatever pages it is, when I open my eyes and stick it on it, it's what I need. . . . talk to Him, and I believe Him, and I trust Him, and He hasn't failed me yet. . . . I've always [let] Him to do that for me, and I think I probably started it with [my son's] death. . . . You can endure anything . . . if you know who He is, and know that He is a compassionate and loving God. . . . That is the only way I have survived a lot of the things that I've had to go through, but especially my child's death, and knowing that in the pain that it caused me it was still God's mercy.

Just as Gwen turned primarily to Psalms, some others also turned to a specific book of the Bible or a specific passage that dealt with death or affliction. Len, for example, found great help in the Book of Job.

Len: God ministered to me through the Book of Job. . . . God really ministered to me in terms of just understanding life and why evil could happen to good. . . . In Job it talks about the wife comes out, and I think that's the one who talks about why don't you just curse God and die. And for a while I misunderstood what that curse means. And that curse scene I believe in the Book of Job is not, "God blank-blank-blank-blank." But the cursing was denying God His true character, saying that God was not just, or God was unmerciful. . . . Job wasn't about doubting, 'cause Job doubted. It wasn't about being angry; Job got angry. . . . The cursing that Job would not do despite his pain, despite his disappointment, despite his loss, was to deny God's character. God is still God, and He's good, and He's merciful; He's just. Even though I don't understand. . . . That really ministered to me, 'cause I don't have to have an understanding of everything. . . . There was something that God planted in my heart to carry me through, 'cause it's not all of a sudden I had that thought. It came out of anguish and study. . . . It's almost like the thought was given to me, and then I went through the journey or the process of anguishing and the grief process and everything else. It's almost like, I'm gonna plant the seed in you. . . . The other thing that God showed me in the book of Job . . . is . . . God speaks to Job through the thunderstorm. (*Beverly:* Umhm. Saying "Where were you?") Yeah . . . here you have Job laying on the ground . . . probably with boils on his arms or all over. . . . The last thing in the world I want to see is a thunderstorm with hard rain rolling up over the horizon. . . . [But] Job embraced the storm, and heard God speak to him out of the storm, and so that really ministered to me in terms of Job's ability to see God's goodness and justice and mercy in very difficult times, even though he didn't understand it. . . . Job heard God, even though he see pain in his whole life on the horizon. And so for me God really helped me to realize the lessons that I could learn and life growth that I can get from [my wife's] death. As painful as it was, it was like God planted seeds . . . before I had to use them. So when it came time, I could use them to survive . . . I've seen Job be implanted in my heart before I really understood it. And as I started to go back to those places of hard times, I started my anger towards God. I could see the thunder cloud. And I can remember, Job did not curse God, and the relief to me was understanding that . . . Job would not deny God's character. . . . Without that assurance and affirmation that . . . God is in character, there's no trust. Without trust, there's no faith. Without faith, there's no hope. And without hope, there's sure death.

☐ Memory and Meaning

A key to the meaning making process is finding ways to focus on memories of the deceased. With those, one can feel less that one has lost all. And the memories become the ingredients for defining the person who has died, the death, and the ways one is grieving. Also, memories, in a sense, make the death less of a death. The person is gone, but the memories live on.

Barbara: If we're taught to know that they're still there with us as long as we want them there, because of the memories . . . the grieving won't be as long or as hard. I think the grieving part of it is really the loss of the physical body, and not really reconciling that piece. I didn't grieve with my sister['s death]. I was sad and I hurt. I was sorry that I wasn't going to have her physical body, but still anytime I want to I can hear that laugh of hers (laughs); I can see her laughing. I can also see her sternness. . . . I can see all of that. And so she is really alive and well with me.

Beverly: What advice would you have for another African American going through the loss of a mother?

Willa: Remember all the good things, because they may be gone in body but the memories are there forever. Remember the funny things. . . . Somebody told me I would laugh through my tears, thinkin' about . . . stuff that she did. We did such funny things, like, oh, for example, if somebody . . . walked around with beady hair, (chuckles) she would do this, and I would know what she meant (laughing). She'd go (both laugh). She was such a funny person, so I just remember all those.

Elsa: We do have those memories, you know, chasin' the kids through the house, pinching you on your butt (chuckling), standin' up in the middle of my bed, jumpin' up and down so I can chase you through the house (chuckling). . . . That's my son. . . .

Beverly: What would you tell someone else who lost a son?

Elsa: Keep the memories. . . . I know it's a loss. And it's a process you have to go through. . . . You can't dwell on the circumstance. You have to take the memories and let 'em go, 'cause they bring you peace. . . . The good memories.

A part of the grief process connected to memory, as some people talked about it, was relating to important reminders of the person who died. A house, for example, could be such an important aid to memory that a central part of the grief process might be the choice to keep it. Similarly, the clothing of the deceased might be held on to because of its place in memory. But also, holding on to things can be a part of staying at a specific place in the grief process. One may not be able to dispose of them until farther down the grieving pathway.

Rosalyn: At one point I was gonna sell the house. . . . And I got so sentimental about it (laughs), I rushed and took the house off the market. And I'm still living in it. I don't know if that's good or not. I think about it now. Should I just move into something else, and let me put that behind me. But . . . this is . . . something we shared together, and I don't want to let go. . . . I've prayed about it. "Lord, why can't I just let him go?" You know, I have released him to the Lord, but . . . I still have his clothes hanging in the closet, just like he still lives there. I don't know if that's good or not. . . . The thought of just packing the things up. That's the end, when I do that.

From another perspective, many African Americans who lived through the latter half of the 20th century had experiences that whites did not have. They saw grinding poverty in African American communities and the desperate need of many people in those communities. At the same time, they saw the hope of the civil rights era. Not infrequently they found themselves with a role in trying to make changes in the African American community or in the larger society as it affected the African American community. So narratives about deceased African Americans, even if superficially like what one might hear about whites who had died, would have a unique African American content. For example, it might be about work with impoverished African Americans and about participating in organizations in and for the African American community. Thus, in the memories that were the building blocks of meaning making were the history of Jim Crow, the civil rights movement, and all else that was unique to African American life. Loretta, for example, talking about the death of her 70-year-old mother seven years prior to the interview, described her mother's activities in a northern city.

Loretta: She was very much a trail blazer. She was politically active. . . . She worked on all sorts of causes. . . . She brought the foster grandparent program to [our hometown]. She served on probably 20 boards. Very well respected and loved. She gave to strangers. She would give anything. She'd see a kid walking down the street, in fact my cousin married a guy and he says his memories as a kid, he was walking down the street with no shoes, and she stopped him and asked him where was his shoes, and he has on some really raggedy clothes. His parents had passed and he was being raised by his grandparents. And my mother put him in the car and took him to the store, bought him shoes, and he said, about five pair of pants, five shirts, underwear, and socks. She bought him more clothes than he had ever had in his life, and she bought him a suit, and told him that he had to go to church and wear that suit. And that's his memory of my mother. That was the story he said at her funeral. We did not know that he would marry my cousin . . . years later. But that's who my mother was. . . . If you had a need and she could fulfill it, she would. . . . She brought programs to the city that had never been thought of, and she did things for women who couldn't afford clothing. She started a sewing circle, and had the factories, because sewing was a big thing there, we had a lot of clothing companies there, she had them donate the scraps . . . and she taught women how to sew.

☐ **Conclusion**

Meaning making is a central part of the grieving process for many people. As in studies of people who were largely or entirely Euro-Americans (e.g., Nadeau, 1998), the African American interviewees developed meanings for how the death happened, who the deceased person was, their relationship with the deceased, and the grief process. They talked about how much they lost and how important and valuable the deceased was in their life. Many relied heavily on religious meanings and scripture. Some talked about finding meaning for their loss, their life, and the place the deceased had held in their life in part by trying to meet what they saw as the standards of the deceased. And it was important in the grieving process to relate to memories of the deceased and, for some, to hang onto things (a house, for example, or clothing of the deceased) that were reminders of the deceased and repositories of memories.

Although African American meaning making as reflected in the interviews seems to us to have strong resemblances to Euro-American meaning making, there were what seemed to us to be significant differences. For losses that seemed to in part result from racism, meaning making connected to racism. Many elements of meaning-making narratives related to aspects of the African American world that are not quite like anything in the Euro-American world, everything from gangbangers to the African American church.

In talking about what was lost, it seems clear that because racism deprives many African Americans of a great deal, the people in their lives who are supportive and helpful are, relatively speaking, very important. Not to diminish the magnitude of Euro-American losses and grieving, but it seems as though quite a few of the African American interviewees had relied with relatively great, even desperate, intensity on the person for whom they were grieving. If they lived in a society where African American families were not so often disrupted, economic resources not so scarce for African American families, and the pain and frustration created by racism absent, their meaning making in grief might be more like that of Euro-Americans.

Although religion is certainly important in the meaning making of many Euro-Americans, African American religion, in all its diversity, has elements of meaning making connected to the history of slavery, racism, and oppression that bring religious meaning making in grief to somewhat different places. For example, prominent elements include death as a homecoming and as freeing from the trials of life.

9
CHAPTER

Grief Over the Long Run

☐ Going On with Life

Some people talked about "going on," the idea that as one gets past the first intense pain of grief one has to move forward with life. That does not mean one stops grieving or forgets the person who died, but it does mean that the grief process is, as people talked about it, something that eventually allows room for other thoughts and activities than grieving. And also it may seem that going on with life is what the deceased would have wanted, so going on can be seen as honoring the wishes of the deceased.

Cynthia: It's okay to grieve, but you still can't bring that person back. So then life just goes on. . . . After you've become accustomed to the fact that that person's . . . not there, then you realize that you have to go on.

Angela: It's hard to go through, but you have to go on. And you have to remember that that person wouldn't want you to stop your life, or stop living. They would want you to go on.

☐ Grief Goes On and On

For major losses, the people interviewed for this book, as has been asserted about people in general (Klass, Silverman, & Nickman, 1996), experience grief as not having an end. In the long run grief is not constantly present, but it comes up again and again. Even long after one thinks one has gone through to some kind of completion of the grieving, it can return.

Verna: You . . . never know when the grieving process will come back to haunt you. It isn't a one-time thing and go through it.

Gwen: You're gonna carry it around, but you do get to a place where you can tolerate . . . and . . . handle this thing. . . . It doesn't stop the grieving any, because I know I still grieve for my son]. But it's not like it was 30-some years ago, but then at the same time some days are good. Some days I'm gonna be a nut.

Clyde: Sometimes grief goes on for years and years and years. Sometimes you never get over someone's death. I think I've never gotten over my mom's death [12 years ago]. I think I never will. . . . You go days without even thinking, and then something happens, something you see, and you know that, "Gee, that was Mo-," you know, something about my mom there. . . . It hits you that, "Yep, that was something my mom would say."

Ron: [It] is a journey, and everybody experiences it and expresses it differently. . . . It takes time. There's part of it that you'll never get over. You will go through confusion, frustration, anger, sadness, fear, and all of these are to be experienced. And it's okay, and it's necessary.

☐ When Do You Feel the Loss the Most?

After the first months or years of grieving, occasions for the recurrence of grief become rather predictable. People can say when they will feel the loss the most, because certain events that come up repeatedly will bring up grief feelings. What interviewees said about when they feel the loss the most seems to us to be like what Euro-Americans might say (e.g., Rosenblatt, 1983). Holidays and the birthday of the deceased were often when people felt the loss intensely.

Beverly: When do you experience your mom's loss the most?

Andrew: Holidays, Christmas, Thanksgiving. My mom was a great cook. . . . Mom invited everybody, so all the family met in Mama's house. . . . I miss that.

Beverly: When do you feel the loss of your grandfather the most?

Kenneth: I guess on . . . his birthday.

Beverly: When is it the hardest for you?

Jane: I would say probably Christmas time.

Maya: I think his birthday is the hardest for me.

Beverly: You said . . . that you missed the phone calls. Are there any other times when you miss your mother the most?

Cynthia: During the holidays. Christmas used to be very, very difficult for me. . . . My mother and I were the chefs for the Christmas meal. . . . And we would have eggnog spiced with rum (laughing), and turn up the music, be really loud with all of her Bobby Blue Blan, and (singing) "Oh, oh," Zing-Zee, what is it? Hill and all that and just have music blasting through, and we would just be laughing and her sipping on her cocktails, and cooking.

Sometimes a person feels the loss the most at times when, if the deceased were alive, the two would be emotionally close.

Andrew: I just miss, I'd go over and (starting to cry), I'd go over and we'd have coffee. She'd got coffee. My mom fixed me breakfast all through high school. See, my mom believed in breakfast. . . . It was nothing for me before I go to work to go by my mom's at 6:00 and sit up and talk with her a couple of hours, and she's going to go and open her day care. . . . And I'm going to go on and go to my work. And it was just that sharing time, so sometime early in the morning when I get up, just every now and then, it might come over [me]. 'Cause it'd be just me and her. Papa would be asleep, and if my brother was there . . . he's asleep. But me and her would. . . .

Sometimes one misses the deceased the most when confronted by the tasks the deceased used to do.

Beverly: When do you feel the loss [of your son] the most?

Elsa: When I look at the work that needs to be done around my house (laughs). That's the biggest thing. Things get broken, don't get fixed right away.

Verna: At times of crisis I think, "I wish you were here, because we need you." I don't know how to take care of Mother in this situation, and one of [Father's] message[s] . . . since we were little kids, "Always take care of your mother. She brought you into the world. . . . " Wishing that he was here to do that or help us with it. She is a spry little old lady. . . . She's working . . . but now we're starting to see that she is getting tired, and . . . we do need to take care of her. And so the other day I was . . . saying, "Oh, I wish you were here, and I miss you, and I'm not so sure I'm doing good with Mom," and so I kind of start crying then. So it comes in waves, and I do believe there's events that trigger it.

Sometimes somebody who looks like the person who died sets off strong feelings of loss.

Verna: My patient died this week. He looked like Dad. . . . I'd go home and cry, you know, that he looked so much like Dad [who died about four years ago].

Beverly: When do you miss [your mother] the most?

Loretta: (pause) When I look at my daughter. [She] looks like my mother, acts like my mother, smiles like my mother. Her mannerisms are my mother. Her interests are the same as my mother's. Even her taste in food is my mother. . . . One of [my daughter's] favorite foods is black eyed peas. I can't do that (laughs). The girl will cook black eyed peas and cornbread for herself. I didn't go that way. She goes out in the yard and picks poke salad. I don't go that way. Sewing. She sews; she makes pan pillows and she does a lot of needlework. My mother was into that, so I wouldn't do it. And now here comes my daughter. She has taken to wearing some of the stuff that my mom had. They have the same . . . taste in shoes. . . . I guess that's when I miss both of my parents, because [my daughter] has never known a grandparent.

Sometimes the loss is felt most intensely when one goes to a place associated with the life or death of the deceased.

Jo-Ellen: I had never went back to the hospital [my son] died in. And a girl friend of mine had a daughter that was very, very, very, very disabled. And she was gonna have surgery. And I went to the hospital with her, to see her child, and it was on the same ward. And I remember walking through the hall, and it was overwhelming, and I went into a bathroom and sat on the floor in the bathroom. Just cried. Trying to pull it together to support her.

Sometimes the loss is felt most intensely when one wishes one could talk to the deceased about a difficult or vexing issue.

Andrew: When I'm making real decisions, I always bounced it off my mom. . . . My mom was the only person that I could tell her whatever it was, and she said, "Well, you better think about how you're going to deal with it." And so I miss her at those times.

Barbara: Times when questions come up about what we're doing or how the children are doing, decisions we're making. Sometimes I feel like it would be good to talk to [my mother], because her judgment was pretty good about things, and it was so fair. And sometimes I needed somebody (chuckling) who was fair to help me with a good decision. So those are those times I miss her most.

Verna: The only thing that pulls me back toward my dad is when there's lack of affection in my life, or I don't perceive a relationship with a man. . . . I say out loud, "Dad, is this how it's going to be? I'm going to die alone? A widow. I don't see no black man, no white man. There is no man in my life. At least if you were here. . . ." So I grieve once in a while that I can't talk to him about where am I gonna find a man.

The death of somebody important means that at times one will be confronted with the difficult or vexing things one would typically have discussed with the person who died. So there is a kind of double burden from a major loss, losing the person and losing the conversation and advice that the person would have provided that would have helped one to deal with the loss. The need for the conversation and advice might recur for a long time, depending on what sorts of difficulties the death created. Barbara's mother died more than 30 years prior to the interview. As a teen whose mother had just died, Barbara was sent to live with relatives far away. For years she had times of loneliness, frustration, fear, and confusion, and at those times she sorely missed her mother.

Barbara: I (crying) always, I always wished I could talk to her . . . about things. I was lonely [at the place they sent me]. And that's when I missed her most, being up there, and just away from everything I knew.

Even a deceased loved one who had been unable to speak near the end of life might still be missed as a listener.

Loretta: Just the realization that I was an orphan, just an orphan. And even though [mother] had been in a nursing home . . . when things were bothering me I did have the ability to go vent to my mother, even though she couldn't respond.

Sometimes when something new and important happens—an achievement, becoming a parent, the birth of a grandchild—a person misses the deceased, especially a parent or parental figure.

Willa: I found myself, especially this past summer, real teary eyed a lot of the time, because I became a mother. And I wanted to share that with my mother. And she wasn't here.

Beverly: When have you felt the loss of your mom most sharply?

Barbara: I guess when the children were born. I would like for them to have had the opportunity to spend time with her. She had a special way with the children. And I know all of the other grandchildren who were born beforehand, they would get a chance to come down and spend a week or so on the farm. And cousins and nieces and nephews all got to come down. So I missed that. . . . Even though . . . my oldest brother was (chuckling) down there, it still wasn't the same as having Mama down. So if Mama had been here, then of course the children would have gone and probably spent the whole summer. So it was then, those times.

Also, one can miss the deceased when one has quiet time by oneself for reflection.

Len: Sometimes when you're just settin' at the lake, you know, sometimes you just, in the shower, sometimes you're watchin' a TV show, so it comes.

☐ Not Letting Go

If ending grief means letting go of the deceased, many people may continue to grieve (Brice, 1989, 1991a, 1991b). They will not want to let go of the deceased. Rosalyn, whose husband had died 11 years prior to the interview, talked about the matter as a dilemma which required her to choose between healing and not letting go.

Rosalyn: It's still not healed. . . . I want the healing to take place. . . . It's been hard for me to let go. One night I was home, I was so miserable. I even called . . . the psych number, to ask her some questions. And she did say, you [really loved] that person . . . and that's one of the reasons it's hard for you to let go. . . . It has been hard for me to let go. And I know I haven't let go. . . . He will always be a part of me.

☐ Conclusion

The African Americans whose narratives are the basis of this book talked about grieving over the long run in ways that seemed to us similar to what Euro-Americans would say. A grieving person will go on with life; there is little choice in the matter. But grief is felt recurrently over many years, quite possibly over an entire lifetime. After the first months of grieving, it will often bubble up at predictable times; for example, holidays, the birthday of the deceased, times when one is faced with a big decision, when one sees someone who looks like the deceased, at times when one would have been emotionally close to the deceased, when the work or wisdom of the deceased would be most useful, when something new and important happens in one's life. There is, for some people, a tension between healing and letting go, and they may feel in some ways that they must let go, but nobody interviewed for this book let go completely in the sense of shutting out thoughts and memories of the deceased. All still felt the loss and their connection with the deceased.

10

The Family Grief Process

In many ways, the family grieving the interviewees described seemed to us to be like family grieving described in research that focuses largely or entirely on Euro-Americans (e.g., Detmer & Lamberti, 1991; Gilbert, 1996; Nadeau, 1998, 2001; Rosenblatt, 2000a; Rosenblatt & Elde, 1990; Rosenblatt & Karis, 1993; Shapiro, 1994). For example, many interviewees said that some family members knew quite a bit about other family member's grieving. These family members witnessed the grieving of others in the family, a witnessing that could be understood as affirmation and support of the grieving. At another level, when others in the family are aware of a person's grieving, they are on alert to help if the person seems to be going into deep depression or some other extremely painful or dangerous place. Evelyn, who had lost an adult son to cancer two years prior to the interview, talked about the struggles of a surviving son.

Beverly: So your other son felt the loss too.

Evelyn: Oh yes, oh yes, he was really, really, really lost.

Beverly: Did he have a hard time with it?

Evelyn: Yeah, he did, he really had a hard time with it because he said, " . . . . . . You don't know just what kind of imagination I'm going through. . . . I just can't get him out of my mind." But . . . we all prayed about it, and we got better now.

What the interviewees had to say about the family grief process built on what they observed in other family members and what they experienced in interaction with them. For many interviewees, the narratives of grief were in important ways about how family members grieved together and worked at getting along.

☐ Family Talk about the Loss and about Feelings

Some people, like Patricia, felt that they benefited from conversation with other family members about the person who had died and about grieving.

Patricia: [My oldest brother and I] like to tell each other what reminds us of our mom in us. It is such a fun thing to do, but he's more like her because he's quiet and private. He doesn't draw attention to himself. So he's a lot like her. My second oldest brother is totally opposite. . . . I kind of need that, and that's why I always ask. . . . I still talk about my mama. . . . My oldest sister, we talk about it a little bit, 'cause we talk about how sometimes you drive along and you think about her. And we both remember the smile of my mom's look. . . . It was almost that smile of, "I really hate to bother you."

Part of what Patricia received from other family members was the reassurance of knowing that others felt the way she did.

Patricia: There was one time I was . . . cleaning out stuff in my mom's house. . . . And there was just all the things that she loved. . . . And something just overcame me, and I just could not stop crying for like I don't know how long. And it wasn't until my oldest nephew came in. . . . It was like, (sounding tearful) "I think about Mommy all the time. . . ." He said, "There's not a day that doesn't go by that I don't think about her," so he was able to calm me down.

Talk with family members can be a sharing of feelings which may help everyone to feel less alone in their grief.

Evelyn: Who have I talked with the most? My son and my niece. . . . We used to talk about him quite a bit, 'cause my son he was just as upset. He just said, "I just can't believe it. I can't believe it about him. . . ." I said, "Yeah, it's hard; it's hard," and we used to sit around and talk about it. And my niece, they practically grew up together, she said, "I just can't get over it. He used to come by after . . . work . . . and call me out. . . . 'Come on. Let's go fishing.' . . . Now he's gone, and I don't have nobody to come by and get me out to go fishing."

Some family conversation about a shared loss led to conflict, but the conversation could still be a good thing in that it enabled people to know where each of them was, and to establish the emotional space for their differences to be acceptable. Norma and Ron, a married couple, talked about the death of Norma's parents, who had been central to Norma and Ron's individual, couple, and family life.

Norma: The family grieves both individually and collectively. . . . In that process those of us who are adults, we also have to share with some of our kids sometimes what we're going through, and also find out what they're going through.

Beverly: How did the two of you grieve as a couple?

Ron: We would talk with each other.

Norma: We talked a lot. . . .

Ron: Give you an example. I would say something about what I was feeling. She'd say, "You don't know nothin'. You didn't lose your mom and dad." I'd say, "Wait a minute. They are my mom and dad. You can't dismiss my feelings. Like they don't count." So we would have to talk like that. . . . We just kept talking.

Perhaps similar to the situation of Ron and Norma, other families also had challenging conversations; for example, because of discrepant views of the person who died, the death, the funeral, or how to behave soon after the loss. The death, more than 30 years prior to the interview, of Gwen's 4-year-old son still would set off difficult conversations for Gwen with two of her surviving daughters.

Gwen: We've had to kind of retalk some things out, because [the two younger girls] remember things differently than the way they really happened. And [my oldest daughter] and I both have decided that that is probably all stuck right in there. They can't process everything that happened during that time, and I think that is age related. . . . Their visions and remembrance of a whole lot of things is distorted, and then when we talk about it, they bring it up when we talk about it. It's almost amazing how distorted it is.

When one grieves in front of family members, one claims the freedom to have feelings and to have them out in the open. Len, who was able to grieve the death of his first wife in the presence of his second wife, felt that it was very helpful that his second wife allowed and even encouraged that grieving.

Beverly: With whom have you talked the most about the death?

Len: Probably [my new wife]. Umhm. We really have a open communication. . . . We have a open relationship, real good communication. And very empathetic with each other. And I think partly because she's there for me. And she knows that there's a time of reflection and thought and grief, and she gives me permission to do that. I think even when we were in the dating stage, and we knew it was . . . serious, more serious than just being a friend of the family, we talked about . . . memories, and the right to have memories, and how not to be intimidated by memories or jealous of memories.

In some families, people seem to have protected one another at times by avoiding talk about the person who died, the death, or their grief. Evelyn talked about the ways that her family seemed to try to protect her from thinking and feeling about the cancer death of an adult son two years prior to the interview.

Evelyn: [My family] didn't talk much about it. . . . Now my son if I bring up something I would say, "Oh, I sure miss him," he would mention something, but they didn't want me, I guess by me having this heart surgery they didn't want to (*Beverly:* upset you). . . .

Beverly: How did that make you feel that they wouldn't talk about it in front of you?

Evelyn: I figured they just didn't want to upset me. . . . They are very careful about not upsetting me. My son will always say, "Now don't do this, don't get yourself upset. . . ."(laughs) I think that there was times when I would want to talk about it, and then I figured they didn't want to . . . because they might start crying or getting upset. . . . Then I wouldn't say nothing about it. I would just let it slide because I didn't want them to get upset because I would get upset.

Family Events to Celebrate the Deceased

The members of some families grieved together by celebrating the deceased at certain times, for example, on the anniversary of the person's birth, and some of these celebrations involved cemetery visits.

Jane: We celebrate my husband['s] birthday. . . . We [go] out to the cemetery. We usually go out to eat, me and the kids do. And then the day he died we celebrate. [I ask] the kids to take me out to a restaurant . . . to eat and just, we celebrate. My husband . . . was really close to his kids. We was like a close-knit family. And we celebrate his death, and his birthday, just like he was still here. . . . Father's Day we go to the cemetery. We go to the cemetery a lot.

Another form of shared celebration involved joining other family members in looking at family photos.

Ron: One of the . . . things I think that really helped . . . was when y'all got together and went through them pictures, right here (*Norma:* Oh, yeah). . . . [Our older daughter] was here and then both of your sisters . . . and [our younger daughter]. And everybody's talking about, "Remember this," and "Here, you take these pictures."

☐ Anger as Part of the Family Grief Process

There were many stories about anger among family members after a death. The anger had many sources, including conflict over how to do the funeral, conflict over fairness of workload in end-of-life care for the person who died, paying for the funeral, a family member stealing from the estate, insults and slights, and battles concerning whose idea about the deceased should prevail.

Loretta: I can't tell you how [my brother] responded to my mother's death. I was so angry with him. . . . I was doing everything, calling folks. . . . He was the first person I called. And I'm like, "Can you go tell our aunts?" They, he lived three blocks away from. "Could you tell people there . . . ?" And I gave him assignments for him to handle while I handled everything else here. Did he do it? He made it to the corner. To my . . . mother's youngest sister's first husband's house. Told him. And they smoked some reefer. They got high. And that's as far as he made it, and that's the only person he told. . . . No one had called me . . . so I called his wife to see where he was at. She didn't know. So then I told her. She said, "He didn't tell me." I'm like, "He was at home, 'cause I just called him here." She said, "Yeah, he . . . talked to you, and he got up and walked out." I called my aunt. Said, "What're you doin'?" She said, "Oh, I'm getting ready to go to work." I said, "Okay. He ain't told her either." So then I called my cousin (laughs), told my cousin. He said, "I'll handle it." And he went around, because I didn't want to tell my mother's sisters on the phone. I wanted someone to tell them in person, and take care of them. So . . . my cousin . . . had to go do that. And when he finished doing that, he went and looked for [my brother]. By this time [my brother] had left that house and had made it all the way to the real dope house. And he was high. . . . I still have a lot of resentment and hostility towards the way he handled my mother and her death, because he was Mama's boy. . . . His light, gas, water bill came to [her] . . . to pay. His taxes came here for my mother to pay. . . . [When] his house was up for sale for not paying his taxes, the notice came to my house. And at that point his taxes were five years behind, 'cause it had been five years since I had paid them, so I paid 'em. And yelled and screamed and cussed and fussed, and said, "You're on your own. You're older than me. You handle this." They didn't get paid again until his daughter paid 'em, and right now he's living in the projects. I am grrr with my brother.

Sometimes anger directed at a family member following a death seems to be not about what that person did but about the death or about what other people did.

Norma: I didn't feel angry. I . . . felt abandoned. . . .

Ron: The angers usually jump out at me. . . . She was angry. And displacing it at me.

Norma: Well, I would be angry about some of the stuff I had to do that [my sisters] would not do. . . . All the workload was on me, as usual. I was angry about that. Because they seemed like they were incapacitated to make a decision. . . . I was angry . . . the more we find out about the money.

Some anger was about withdrawal of life supports just before the death.

Norma: Our kids were very mad. They thought we had just killed [Papa]. It was very hard on them. It's taken them a long time to get over. . . .

Ron: We took him off life supports. . . .

Norma: Even my brother has second guessed it. . . . To this day my brother says, "Sometime I do wonder if." I said, "You did not see him every day like I did. . . . I'm telling you, he did not want to be any lesser than at what level he was already at."

In one family there was anger centered on one person blaming others in the family for the death.

Charlotte: [My aunt] . . . said to me one day that we drove my mother to her death. . . . This was when I was still a child. . . . I didn't go over there for years after that. . . . I couldn't believe she said that to me.

In another case, a child's biological father blamed the mother for their son's death.

Jo-Ellen: His father was in San Francisco at the time of his death, and I couldn't find him. . . . He was in prison when [the boy] was real, real sick. Then he got out, and he had wrote me a couple of times. And then when he died, some . . . old friends, street friends, they called pool halls and everything in San Francisco. They left messages everywhere. And he finally got the message, but he got it a day after the funeral. So he called to blame me for his death. "It's your fault. What did you do? My son should not be dead." I didn't pay no attention to him. "You're crazy. I didn't kill him."

Some anger was about how family members let the interviewee down. For Norma there was anger that one sibling lacked maturity and the other was looting their deceased mother's estate.

Beverly: How did you grieve your mom's death?

Norma: Drank too much.

Ron: And that's where the anger was coming from. (*Norma:* And tried to make sense) See, that's why she was angry.

Norma: And tried to make sense of, which I still never have, my sisters, both of their behaviors. . . . One acted like she was 2 years old, and then the other one we found out was robbing [Mother] blind. . . . I felt like they had just dumped all of it on my back, and in order for the good name of [Mother], I was gonna make sure nothing was not handled properly or right, and then all those who loved her they were not privy to a lot of this going on. And felt bad a lot for us as the siblings because we had just lost our dad, and then . . . her.

Toni's anger was about the family pattern of blocking talk about feelings and about an attempt by her mother to use her as a substitute for the mother's mother [Toni's grandmother], who had died.

Toni: Part of our family system is repression. . . . We just repress grief. . . . I don't know the psychological terms for it, but [my mother] just substituted 'cause my grandmother also babied her a lot, and so now . . . my mother will call me and, "Mommy just needs to sit on her other mommy's knee, and I just want to get on your lap. . . ." Oh, some of the sickest shit I ever heard (laughing).

Loretta felt anger at her brother for his ignoring their mother's 10 years of terminal illness and at his inability to carry a share of the load of dealing with the funeral for their mother and all that surrounded it. She also felt considerable anger at her mother for having favored her brother and for leaving the care of a multiply disabled foster child to Loretta.

Loretta: My brother, he was the emotional one, and I think that was not so much the emotion of losing a mother, but the guilt [due] to the fact that he had not seen her in 10 years. He had not done anything for her the last 10 years of her illness. He . . . wasn't there to support me. I would say, "She had two kids, not one." He said, "Whatever you do is fine with me." He never saw her in a nursing home. Why he didn't see her for 10 years! . . . When will I stop having resentment and start the grieving . . . or . . . the emotional healing? Not ready for that. And part of that goes to forgiveness. And I don't know how to do that. I flunked forgiveness. . . . I don't know how to forgive my mother for sticking me with [her blind, retarded foster child]. I don't know how to forgive her for [my brother] being her favorite, and me ending up being the one taking care of her. Even in her will, he got more than I did. And how do I get over that? I'm not that mature. In regards of that I'm very petty.

☐ Loss of an Important Family Link

If the person who died was the main link among family members, and this was most often so if a mother died, family members might lose their connection with one another. This is only speculation, but it is possible that among African Americans the loss of a kinkeeper (Leach & Braithwaite, 1996;

Rosenthal, 1985), a person whose communication connects some family members with others, might be more common and more challenging than among Euro-Americans. For example, proportionately more African American families have a single parent, so the loss of that parent means the loss of the parental link among the parent's children and with other relatives. And the shorter life expectancy of African Americans means that more people are young adults when a kinkeeper dies and may have fewer social and economic resources to maintain the connections that the kinkeeper maintained. At any rate, some people talked about the challenges of losing a person who linked family members. Another family member might try to be that link. And that person may succeed and want to continue, may fail, or, after trying out the role, may decide the burden of the role is too heavy.

Andrew: I pulled my family together for years. . . . I did all the Thanksgiving dinners; I did all the Christmas; I did all the summer barbecues. If I didn't do it, my brothers and sisters and cousins would not come together. They would not. Well, I stopped doing it . . . maybe 10 years ago. . . . . You get family members that come and they bring friends and they just abuse you.

With a kinkeeper gone, surviving family members may become more distant. And they may prefer superficial warmth from a distance to the conflict that would occur if they were close.

Franklin: With the death of my father then obviously you get a chance to really see it. . . . BANG! it's right there in your face. Because all of us are together. . . . We try to stay away from each other, rather than to engage in . . . conflict. . . . Everybody can be nice and kind, but from a distance. It's easy (laughs). . . . But when you're close and personal, and when all of you are together, then it does come out. And the pain of it does come out.

There was also distance in some cases because after the death of a kinkeeper another key member of the family wandered away from the immediate family to find such things as support, joy, numbing, that could not be found in the immediate family. For example, in one case when a mother died, the widower/father withdrew from the surviving children.

Charlotte: After my mother died . . . Daddy would be away from the house. . . . He had girl friends. Well, he had friends. I don't know what they were to him. . . . I remember the first one. . . . She was a hairdresser. . . . I can't remember when he started dating, but I remember him not . . . coming home at night.

Loretta had anticipated that the death of the family kinkeeper, her mother, would be disastrous for family relationships and spoke about the matter at her mother's funeral. But speaking about it did not make a difference; family members drew apart.

Loretta: Everybody was running around . . . crying. . . . The loss was profound, and when I had to get up and do my piece . . . my charge to the family was this was the last time my mother would ever bring all of us together again. Because she was the peacemaker. No matter who had fallen out with whom over what, she was the peacemaker, and at the time of her death, we were so fractionalized. . . . The whole family was literally crumbling, and that is what affected me then was the fact that this is the last time she can bring us together, and it's up to us to stay together. In the infighting, in the bickering, this is the last time. . . . Hell, and we ain't been together since. (laughs)

But the loss of a kinkeeper and the experience of increased interpersonal distance is not necessarily a lifetime thing. In some families, people stayed apart for years after the death of the kinkeeper, then realized how much family contact they were losing, and arranged to become better connected.

Cynthia: The family has gotten to the point to where we were sort of at a loss after she died. And one of my sisters would try to pull things together, but now we've gotten to the point to where we more agreeably come together. . . . They were . . . sort of like pulling away from the family, and it just seemed like to me the older they got the more they saw how important family was for the holiday, and so everybody looks forward to coming together now.

Also, sometimes the death of the kinkeeper drew family members closer, because they could relate more easily to one another instead of always relating through the kinkeeper.

Beverly: How did your mom's death . . . affect your relationship with other family members?

Cynthia: It made us closer, made me get closer to them. Not that I was distant, but I mostly talked with her, and then after she died then we started communicating more . . . even by telephone, and they started coming up to visit.

☐ We've Grown Closer to Each Other

The death seemed to draw people in some other families closer to each other, perhaps to support one another and to be sure others were okay.

Calvin: We rallied around one another to get through. But our relationships have never been divided. . . .

Beverly: What about your relationship with your dad? With your losing a mom and he losing his wife?

Calvin: That probably got closer, 'cause I think I made a point to communicate with him a lot more regularly.

Jane: Me and my kids got closer when [my husband] died. They was always over here. Like the night he died, we all slept in the room. We cleaned the bed up . . . real good. And we all slept in the room the night he died. In the same bed he died in. . . . We just changed the sheets and cleaned the bed all real good. And they love coming over now, right today, going in that room . . . sleeping there, being in there with me. . . . My son . . . moved in, because he wanted to be here . . . the man of the house, 'cause it was just me and my daughter who was left here. And he felt that he should be here at night with us, to take care of us, and do the yard work, and all the necessary stuff that a woman can't do. . . . So he's been here ever since. . . . He lives downstairs. . . . If anything, my kids have got closer to me, because they all concerned about me. They don't want to lose their ma. They love their ma. . . . We're a real close family. We argue every once in a while, but that's a family.

In some families, concern about someone grieving intensely drew other family members to the grieving person's side. Sometimes the closeness after a death came because somebody who was grieving needed to be around other family members to try to cope with difficult feelings.

Evelyn: I found myself some time I think getting a little depressed. When I felt that way (chuckling) I would get up and go over to my brother's or over to my niece's. I'd get myself around somebody. I wouldn't set here by myself because I didn't like that feeling (laughs). . . . I set here by myself I would get into that type of what where I wouldn't want to go nowhere; I wouldn't want to see nobody; I wouldn't want talk to anybody, and I said I can't let myself be like that. I've got to keep moving. I got to get around people. . . . It seem like I kinda drawn more closer because I had lost something dear to me and I wanted to get close to my family. Yeah. The closer we got, the stronger I felt.

In some families, one person is a caregiver for others. A death may move the caregiver to a higher level of responsibility.

Beverly: How did losing your mom affect your relationship with other family members?

Willa: It put more responsibility on me. I am the caregiver, the nurturer, the archivist. I have all the family pictures; all that stuff came to me. I was the one who had to basically pack up the house, get it ready for sale, all that.

☐ Moving Far from Some Family Members after a Death

As was mentioned in earlier chapters, some families were split up after the death of a parent or parent figure, with some younger children moving or being moved far from others. So the death led to long-term, perhaps permanent separations. Barbara, who as a teenager was sent to live with an adult brother's family shortly after her mother died, talked about the ways that such separation could mean that one was deprived of key people with whom to talk or safe situations in which to talk.

Barbara: The reason I got here was because . . . my brother . . . lived here. . . . He promised Daddy I'd get my education . . . and Daddy, he just revered education. So Daddy signed over my guardianship. . . . I came here. . . . I finished up a year and a half of high school. Left everybody, everything I knew. . . . Somehow or another I felt that if I didn't make this work that it would hurt [my dead mother]. So I tried to make it work. So my relationships here were finding out what people were like. And then making the adjustment. Not really feeling very close to anybody, not even my brother, because he married this woman and I thought they lived in a mansion. I thought she had come from something very rich. . . . She made me feel not welcome. So even though he said that they had talked about it, I think he talked about it. She said, "okay," but she didn't really want to. . . . There was nobody that I really could talk to about the death of my mom, where I could talk it out. And talk about all of my feelings. Saying that I was angry enough to box with God was not something I could say right then, because folks would look at you like you're blaspheming. . . . So it took a while for me to be able to say out loud how angry I was. . . . Had I stayed . . . , then sure, I probably would have talked to our pastor. I would've talked about how angry I was, and there were probably others I could have talked to about it. But leaving to come right up here, there weren't. Who am I going to trust to talk to about something like that?

We speculate that these kinds of long distance moves are more common in African American families, because the shorter life expectancy and the relatively high frequency of single parents means that more minor children are left without a parent or parent figure or at least one who is able to care for them following the death.

☐ The Property of the Deceased

The property of the deceased, the clothing and other personal possession, the real estate, the household goods, the insurance policies, and other assets are all potentially family matters.

Economic Disadvantage

We have already talked, at several places in this book, about the economic disadvantage that racism causes African Americans and also about the entanglement of estate issues in the grief process. Here we want to add to what we have said by pointing out that economic disadvantage seems to show up when it comes to inheritance and insurance proceeds following a death. Some narratives spoke of how much less there was to an estate after a family death than there might have been. A substantial estate could help someone who had been struggling economically to "stand on his feet," but often there was not much to an estate.

Charlotte: My brother . . . spent his entire inheritance. . . . He's gone through that, whereas I used mine to buy a house. . . . There wasn't a lot, 'cause that's one thing that black people don't do well, is to plan for their children. . . . Of course we all love our kids. And we want to do things for them. My mother was still carrying health insurance and life insurance on *us.* I'm like, "If she wanted to help, she'd 've taken more life insurance on herself. . . . " I don't think she had $20,000 life insurance. . . . So basically all that we got was whatever money she had. The little bit of money that was left after we paid for the funeral expenses and the new burial plots and the sale of the house. And the house, because it was in the location that it was in, which was the best for black folks back when we were growing up, but now, you know, the house went for next to nothing. 'Cause I mean even now, you can buy a house in a lovely location in (that town) for $75,000. . . . Ours . . . wasn't in a particularly nice location.

Looting the Estate

In some families, following a death, it was discovered that one or more family members had been looting the estate. So the financial value of the estate was much less than it might have been, and there were strong family animosities as a result. This kind of thing might happen in any ethnic group (Titus, Rosenblatt, & Anderson, 1979), and we do not know that it is more likely to occur in African American families than in Euro-American families. We can speculate that at least in part, because of the economic disadvantages of African Americans and because of drug issues in some communities, there are certainly African American families in which someone is so desperate or needy as to loot the estate of an elderly family member.

Norma: We would find out my sister was . . . spending quite a bit of money out of [our parents'] checking account. And so things that were supposed to be real weren't really as they were. And she swore our mom knew that, and we were not so sure. . . . I was angry about that, about her and the money. . . . The way I found out was that one of the checks she wrote . . . the funeral home, bounced. And then that's when . . . she had started owning up. . . . We were like, "There's no way in the world." We knew exactly what Dad's retirement and his social security and [Mom's] retirement and all the, there was no way there should've been any type of cash flow problems. And so what is the deal with this check? And of all places, too. The funeral home! Fortunately they know our family. . . . But there should have been enough. . . . I was angry about that. There was no question. You were too . . .

Ron: We later found out she was on crack. So she fucked up big. They had a condo that they let her stay.

Norma: 'Cause she didn't have anywhere to live.

Ron: She didn't have anywhere to live, wound up messing that up.

Norma: Lost it totally. We had no money out of it. We couldn't sell it. It was in arrears. It was foreclosed.

Following a death, personal possessions might disappear in what seemed to be a looting by neighbors or family members. But with people having relatively little in economic resources, it would not be surprising that looting might occur. The following story is about a family and community of southern sharecroppers several decades ago, but stories like these can also come nowadays from urban settings.

Barbara: A cousin had told me . . . "If there's anything of your mom's that you want, you should take it now." And I said, "No, everything will be fine." She said, "No, really. You better take it now." I didn't listen to her, 'cause I'm thinking like Mama now. "Everything will be fine. Daddy's still here. I don't want to take stuff out when Daddy's still here." Well . . . that stuff was taken. Daddy'd be out in the field, folk come to visit, the house was left open (laughs). They'd come in, 'cause she had a trunk that she kept things in. My little baby ring that my older sister had given me, that was gone. Never found that. There was a little bitty lamp, just a miniature lamp that you had to put kerosene in, that was gone. And she had a whole bunch of sheets and towels for company. . . . Daddy didn't know. He wasn't going up checking on stuff after people left. Just one of us will come home and we'll say, "Daddy, where are so and so and so?" "Why? Isn't in there?" "No, Daddy. It's gone." So he figured out what was going, and the thing that hurt most though was there were a lot of pictures taken. And they think they know the cousin that took 'em (laughing). 'Cause that cousin has a room that she won't let any of my family members in.

In some families, one person took all the personal possessions of the deceased in a way that another family member might experience as looting. The "looting" can be a sore point with some people for many reasons, including that they then do not have meaningful mementoes from the estate.

Clyde: Leading up to the burial . . . what was really different for me was how people treat things that people have . . . while they're alive, clothes, jewelry. . . . It was a real grab kind of a thing. . . . This was before the funeral. . . . My sister loaded up the car with all kinds of bedspreads and . . . things, and took the jewelry, because, "My mom said I should have it. . . . " That really bothered me. I think that bothered me more than anything, and, you know, I only have one picture of my mom, and there's lots of other pictures.

Beverly: Who has the others?

Clyde: My sister has those too. So it was funny. It was like this is where the buck stops, in the sense that my mom's gone now. Whatever I want about my mom or from my mom, I gotta go to this person and ask. . . . I'm crazy about that, but I don't want to go, I didn't want to deal with that. But that piece bothered me more than anything else. That really bothered me.

Some families blocked looting by organizing immediately after the death to pack up and store things that might be of value.

Willa: It must have been the night after her funeral, because the house was going to be empty for a while. And I did not want people coming in just helping themselves to things. So called [my brother] (laughs). He had said he would help any way he could. I said, "We need to move some of her things to a storage facility, because the house is going to be empty. So all of the decent pieces of furniture were moved. And all of the stuff that was . . . sentimental but . . . not really valuable, we left. But we packed up her dining room, because it was solid cherry. Same thing with her bedroom . . . the TVs, the VCRs, microwaves, things that people could lay their hands on and sell real quickly. . . . My brother and I divided them up. He took the dining room, except for the buffet, 'cause I wanted the buffet. . . . He also took a marble top table that was in the living room . . . and . . . glassware and dishes.

When One Person Gets the Bulk of the Estate

Sometimes the family decides that one person is the neediest or most deserving, and so that person gets most of the estate of the deceased.

Andrew: We gave everything to my sister. . . . My sister was down there [where Mama had been living and where she died]. . . . So we said, "Everything is yours." And that's how we dealt with it. Everything in the house. . . . I took a couple of keepsake things. . . . That was it.

When one person takes all the personal possessions of the deceased, that person would be the one who would dispense them to others, if any were to be dispensed.

Calvin: The only kind of misunderstanding was, my sister had to let everybody know that everything in that house that belonged to her mom was hers.

Beverly: And what did you say?

Calvin: Amen. Amen to that. I know my mother and she was one of those with the big hats and the fur stole . . . and so some relatives uh, "[Your mom] said I could have this." "This" "Everything back there. . . ." My dad [said], "Everything back there is hers. Every purse, every shoe, everything is hers. She's the only daughter. . . . If she wants to give you something, then that's okay. But right now is not the time to be talking [about] it, 'cause we kind of grieving."

Keeping Mementoes

People may hold onto some of the clothing or other personal possessions of the deceased, often because they want to maintain connection with the deceased.

Patricia: She's mostly here (*Beverly:* In your heart?), umhm. That's where, and then she's in things that I do and things that I have. . . . I kind of wore. A lot of her clothes are, just had to have certain things about her.

In some families, anyone might be able to claim a few personal possessions of the deceased, but there would also be a sense that some of it is more appropriately given to one specific person. However, if the financial value of the things going to that person is great, the person might be expected to pay others in the family a certain amount for those things.

Calvin: Daddy had his will. . . . Nobody fought over anything. They told me to come get certain things out of the house. . . . My oldest brother, he's the only real handyman, so Dad probably had $10,000 worth of tools. We did say, "Well, what's the value of these tools? Give me $2000 for them. We can do that." He's the handyman. "You take the tools." That's the way it was with us. And all those circular saws, and all those other things, I wouldn't know how to use. . . . Six foot ruler. That's all I took. Took a saw (chuckling), T-square. And nobody said, "Oh." We just did all that. Praise God.

The House

In chapter 8 we referred to the importance to some African Americans of owning a house. When people are in difficult economic circumstances, a house can be a lifesaver. One family hung on to the house of the deceased, reserving it as a permanent refuge for the extended family, particularly for those who might "really, really need" it.

Patricia: The way she raised us and the way we are . . . we needed to take care of her house. We still own it. A couple of nephews live there, and it's there in the event somebody one day might really, really need there.

Keeping Things of Value in the Family

In some African American families, as in some Euro-American families, it is important that things of value stay in the family. It is not just cash values, but the meanings inherent in specific objects. So, for example, a widow who did not want to keep the bed she and her husband had shared passed it to a grandchild.

Jane: I gave it to my granddaughter. . . . I guess I wanted to just start all over again, start new, and 'cause I knew if I gave the bedroom set to my grandbaby it would still be in our family. It's still a nice bedroom.

Loss of Financial Assets

Sometimes family financial assets were lost because the family did not do enough talking, planning, or insuring to hang onto them. Is that more characteristic of African American families than other families? One man suggested it was.

Beverly: How did her death affect your daily living after she was gone?

Len: Immediately afterwards (laughs), drastically. . . . [She] was the bread-[winner]. . . . We didn't financially bring a lot of things to closure, even the power of attorney. That was never passed over. . . . The house that I live in currently, we had purchased together. . . . So that was no big deal, but we had another house that was in [her] name, and I remember calling the bank to try to make some type of arrangement for it, and he told me they couldn't give me any information . . . because it wasn't in my name. And so basically I just let it foreclose. . . . They said I'd have to go through probate to get it, and I said, "I'm not gonna pay another $6000 for a lawyer to take it through probate, and then I'm still gotta pay (laughs) a mortgage on two houses . . . (laughs), so you guys can have it. . . . She [didn't have] life insurance. . . . I think the tendency probably is [in] black families [for] . . . death [to be] something that is real sacred. . . . When it happens, or going to happen, all of our energy and focus is on . . . that. . . . We don't think practically. It's almost like taboo, you know, "Who are you to be talking about business (laughing)? . . ." So that was a piece that we never really dealt with. And I never really pushed, because I thought it would bring stress to [my wife], and the last thing I wanted to do was have her stressed about anything. . . . She was such a fighter. She was gonna fight to the end. "And I [don't] want you tellin' me . . . that I'm gonna die. . . . I don't want to bring closure yet. . . . I'm still alive." It's really her words: "I'm still alive. I'm still alive."

☐ Conclusion

In many ways, the family grief dynamics as described by the people who were interviewed seem to us quite a bit like what Euro-Americans report. Family members were often aware of some of the grief of other family members. Family conversations connected to the death and the grieving were important to many people. There might be family disagreements about what was true concerning such matters as the deceased, the dying, the death, the funeral. There might be considerable anger connected to the end-of-life care, the funeral, the grieving, and related matters.

One difference, we speculate, between African American and Euro-American family grieving is that it may be more common in African American families that the death of a kinkeeper (e.g., a mother who links her children together) may lead to long-term disruption of the relationships that were maintained by the kinkeeper.

Another difference, consistent with what was said in earlier chapters, is that because of a shorter life expectancy and the relatively high proportion of single parent families, relatively often in African American families a death leads to minor and young adult children being separated from siblings and other family members as they are sent to geographically distant family members who can care for them.

The economic oppression of racism shows up, we think, in the economic life of grieving African American families. First of all, there is a lower likelihood that there will be a substantial estate, so a family death does not often mean that family members gain substantial wealth. Second, and if it is more common among African Americans than Euro-Americans it may be because of the economic oppression of racism, we heard a number of reports of what seemed like looting of the estate, either prior to the death or soon afterwards. An adult child, for example, might drain the economic resources of an elderly parent, perhaps to pay the rent, perhaps to support a drug habit. Soon after the death, the economically valuable possessions of the deceased might be removed, either by an aggressive family member who felt entitled to them or by family members or neighbors whose identity and motives remain unclear.

A house can be an important asset in any ethnic group, but it might be a particularly important asset to an African American family. It might be a place of security, have important family meanings, and be seen as a long-term resource to family members in need. Perhaps for African Americans more than Euro-Americans it is important that certain possessions, the house but also various kinds of portable possessions, remain in the family.

Finally, it is possible, as several interviewees speculated, that African Americans more than Euro-Americans have difficulty retaining financial assets after a death.

God

For many of the people who were interviewed, religion, scripture, and the African American church were important in meaning making about a death. This fits with what Smith (2002) found in a study of African American women grieving for a mother's death, "Religious beliefs provid[e] important ways of thinking about and coping with their elderly mothers' deaths" (Smith, 2002, p. 316).

Although the interview did not probe people's understanding of the gendering of God, many but not all interviewees used the masculine pronoun *He,* in talking about God. Our impression is that some used "He" even though they belonged to congregations in which the clergyperson took the position that God is not gendered, is ambigendered, or is female. In quoting people talking about God, we honor their choice of gender terms.

☐ Trusting God

For some people, a key to dealing with the death was to trust that God had good reasons for taking the person who died.

Gwen: It is a bad thing, and you're gonna have to get through this somehow, but you're gonna have the reassurance that this was not God's retaliation on you for whatever you might have done. This was God's mercy. And the minute I understood that, it didn't shake me no more, because I understood that God was taking [my son]. He had suffered enough. . . . Grandfather was a preacher, and he said, "Our children are not ours.

They're lent to us by God." And so (laughs) all of those things flooded back into my mind when [the doctor said my son died of natural causes]. When [my son] came, he was only loaned to me for 4 years and 9 months. . . . That's all the Lord had intended. . . . The Lord [also] decided I had too much on my plate. I had two seriously ill babies. And when he was home from the hospital, she was in the hospital. And it was one thing after another. . . . It was from birth with him and from birth with her. I was just running ragged in two directions here. I couldn't get over one thing before I was into another thing. . . . I think . . . [my son's] death was one way the Lord just was relieving some of that pressure.

Many people said that they trusted that God would take care of the person who died (which is also what Smith, 2002, reported) and that God would take care of them as they dealt with the loss. Rosalyn talked about the hours after she learned, 11 years prior to the interview, that her husband had been killed in an auto accident. She was home with her son:

Rosalyn: I says to my son, "God's going to take care of us." He said, "Yes, Mom." (she's crying). . . . It's seemed like God was with me at every step. He made that most difficult task seem just easy. . . . He was in God's hands.

Calvin talked about the death of his mother putting it to him that, after years of working as a pastor telling others to trust in God, now he was going to find out how much help it was to trust in God.

Calvin: The loss of my mom was the first opportunity to really experience . . . what a relationship with God can mean. I've been going to the graveyard with folk, ashes to ashes, dust to dust [for many years]. But when it's your mom that's laying out there, that's the whole big ball game. I've been telling folk for years, "Hold up your head and trust in God. . . ." That was an experience where I had to apply those same principles that I had been giving to someone else, and found them to be (claps hands once) valid.

Beverly: Was it difficult for you to apply those principles to your own life and your loss?

Calvin: Not with the help of the Holy Ghost. Not with the help of the Holy Ghost.

Trusting in God can mean that a person does not feel alone, that even though the death means they have lost a spouse, a parent, or some other close relative, they will not be alone because God will be with them.

Rosalyn: One lady said, "You don't have nobody to come home to. . . ." I says, "Oh, yes I do. I have the Lord." Matter of fact, when I came from burying my husband, I said, "Lord, I know there's going to be empty house." When I put the key in my door I say, "Lord, you come on here with me. And I know you're going to come on in," and He did.

To some people, trusting God means that they do not question God but accept what has happened, though in their not questioning there may be an awareness of the questions they could ask. Patricia talked about her mother's death seven and a half years prior to the interview.

Patricia: He knows best. . . . I think God doesn't have like a specific thing, "Well, you all don't need him anymore." Or "You're gonna need to make it." Or "I needed her here." Or, "I didn't want her to suffer anymore." "She was tired." You hear all kinds of reasons. Before I want to put up a question like that to God, I start . . . to think, "Do you [need] an explanation for everything?" I mean, everything that happens in life we could almost ask why or why not. But I think while I'm asking that why, I might want to ask Him, "Why did You still decide to leave me healthy? . . ." There's just a certain, I started to use the word *comfort* or *resolve* about just accepting that God knows best. . . . I just trust that it was the best, that it was His will. . . . I'm able to live on without understanding fully why God chose for my mom to be with Him now instead of here. Yeah, I could spend some time and all that, but what more am I going to gain? . . . The way I understand it is that that's God's will as He chose to do, and so be it. . . . I felt a void in my life when she left, because I missed her and I still would love to have her here now; I want her here. But God still provides me what I need. I'm blessed in so many ways. . . . He is using me in ways that my mother would have been so pleased and proud of, and that I thank Him for. I have my health. I have so many things. . . . I just thank God so much (crying) that He gave her to me, that I . . . was able to gain what I was by her being my mother, and my friend, and sister, and my everything. . . . There are things that I still want to discuss and explore, but . . . it's not like, "I want that so much that I can't live any further without having it." It's okay. Yeah, I need to find out what is it that I would really still want to know from God. And I've asked Him a couple of questions. . . . I've looked at those questions I asked earlier and I think half of them were answered.

Len's first wife died six years prior to the interview.

Len: It was God's mercy to take [my wife], and to allow her to live, versus looking at it as a . . . deficit . . . a negative . . . thing. You know, "God, why are those people who are tryin' to live for You die, and people who don't care a blank of what they do to other people or themselves or anything else, you know, why do they seem to prosper?" And that really helped me to . . . check myself in my attitudes to the Holy One. "Who are you to judge and to condemn . . . ? God is a loving God, a compassionate God, and a merciful God. And here is an example of God's mercy."

Trusting in God doesn't necessarily mean that a person will not question God about the death. A person can have faith in God and trust God while still questioning. Rosalyn talked about interactions she had right after the visitation.

Rosalyn: Everybody was saying, "Will you stop saying, 'Why?'" But I say, "The Lord is understanding me, why I am asking 'Why?'" And I asked for His forgiveness too. "If I should not ask You 'Why,' forgive me."

Gwen talked about questioning God in the hour immediately after her son died.

Gwen: In the first hour . . . I was questioning God, telling God off (chuckles). . . . I'm not a cursey person, so there was none of that, but I was very angry, and "How could You let this . . . happen? You let us come here to do this?" And I know that's why [the doctor] had to come back and tell me [that my son died of natural causes that would have killed him anywhere], because that was the Lord answering my "Why? . . ." [Then] it was just so plain, and I could accept it. It was because I needed to be there. I could not have been at home.

☐ God Gives Solace and Strength

Previous research has shown that grieving African American women often cope through prayer (Ellison & Taylor, 1996). Presumably the same is true for African American men. In fact, some people who were interviewed for this research talked about receiving solace and strength through their relationship with God, and that relationship often included prayer.

Beverly: Who took care of you?

Cynthia: Nobody. Just the good Lord.

Beverly: Do you ever regret that (*Cynthia:* No) or wish that someone was there for you?

Cynthia: I feel that there was somebody there. The Lord was there, so I had solace.

Evelyn: God had given me strength through this illness that [my son] had. I had found strength to go on through it. . . . I just kept praying and kept going, studying my Bible and asking God to give me strength for the day and so I found strength in that, more strength than I thought I would have. . . . I kept praying about it, and that's where I found my strength . . . daily prayer. 'Cause otherwise I don't know (chuckle), but it was a tough time, but God gave me strength to go through it, and I'll say that without prayer we're lost. We can't make it unless we focus on God.

Some people added that it was important for others who are grieving to trust that if they turn to God they will receive God's solace.

Beverly: What would you say to others who have lost their mother, who have gone through what you have gone through?

Charlotte: I would say your heart is broken, child. You're on your knees. You think you're not gonna make it some days, and it's okay. Go ahead, go to the mercy seat, let Him put His arms around you. . . . So this is what God's plan was. And I accept it. I accept it, because where He wanted me to have light, He gave me light. Where He wanted me to have gifts, where I needed a gift, He gave me a gift. Where I needed my strengths, He gave me the strengths, based on what His plans were. Because this was some ugly stuff. It was life, but it was ugly.

☐ God Teaches

Some people talked about God teaching them things through the death and its aftermath.

Vickie: I truly believe that [mother's] passing on, I really do think there was a lesson in that. . . . To be more thoughtful and to be more spiritual is one of them.

The teaching might take many forms. For some people, scripture was key (see chapter 8 for more on scripture). After her son died of leukemia, Jo-Ellen had been upset with God for taking her son and confused about why the death happened. But in the Bible she found a release from being stuck in those feelings and thoughts.

Jo-Ellen: I knew that I had been a good mother, and I had opposed all of the legalistic things that had been fed to me, because I just couldn't imagine that God could be that way. "If I as a mother loved my child this much, and he's God, then, my God, what are you? A crazy?" And I remember telling Him that if this is really You that would do this, then You're sick. And I can't live for You. I can't be in a relationship with you, 'cause something's wrong here. "And I remember going through the Bible, and I found a scripture, and I can't even tell you exactly where it is now, but basically it summed up that the blood of another person, they're accountable for their own stuff. And that's all I needed to see. It's like, "Whoa. It's all over then." And then I remember reading about David, when his son died, and how he fasted. He went through all those changes, but then after it was over, he got dressed. You know (chuckles), life did go on.

☐ The Death Brought Me Closer to God

Some people said that the death brought them closer to God, partly because they prayed and read the Bible more.

Jane: The good Lord blessed us. We was 27 years together, two kids. . . . [My husband's] death . . . brought me close to God, because God had brought me a long ways from even before I met my husband. God been in my life all my life, 'cause my grand daddy was a deacon in the church. So I've been in the church all my life just about. But when my husband died, my relationship with God got closer, because . . . I prayed to God more than I had been doing. I read the Bible more than I had been. . . . I thank God what I have, and what He done did for me. I thank God for the 27 years he gave me with my husband. I don't have nothing to regret. . . . God has been good to me, and [my husband] was a good husband, and a good father.

Beverly: How did your relationship to religion and spirituality change after your son's death?

Elsa: Closer. . . . I felt that I needed answers and the only person that could answer me was God. And He told me He would answer me. . . .

Beverly: What were some of the questions you had of God?

Elsa: Who? For sure. Because we don't know for sure [who killed my son]. I didn't ask why, but I asked who, and . . . I still don't know if it's because Satan wants me, and this was my sacrifice. So I don't know. . . . This was my sacrifice, but I know of a better place, and I also know that God makes all the decisions.

Some felt they became closer to God because after the loss of someone they had always turned to for help they had to turn to God.

Loretta: Aside from being a orphan now, it's like the reality that I had no parents that I could rely on. Before, no matter what happened in my life, my parents were there to bale me out. No matter what I needed. . . . No matter what I wanted, my parents were there to provide. . . . When I buried my mother, my husband made the comment, "You're on your own now. You don't have anybody else to depend on." And that realization said, "Okay, you *are* on your own." And I sat down and it's like, "Who can I depend on?" And then your religious upbringing comes back to you. The only one you can depend on is God. And I had to develop a closer walk with God. It was out of necessity. I didn't go willingly. . . . I really began that walk during [Mother's] illness, because I had no one that I could talk to. When I was at the end of my rope and just wanted to scream, I had no one there. . . . I had to talk to God. That little Stevie Wonder song, *Just Go Have a Talk with God.* That was it.

☐ Communication from and to God

Some people believed that God communicated with them concerning the death. The typical communication was one that said that the person who died was in heaven and was okay.

Rosalyn: I had a dream about my husband. . . . but I couldn't see a face. The face was all blacked out or covered up. And he said, "Look up over the hill." And when I looked up over the hill, there were homes, beautiful, gorgeous homes. . . . It looked like a paradise. And in the dream he said, "That's where I am." I woke up with a sense of comfort from that dream. . . . Each time I dream about him, they're comforting dreams. One time I dreamt that we were walking along the park, and we were just holding hands. The dreams never continue, because I wake up. And I have that feeling of comfort. And then one time I had a dream about my husband, and he uh, "Look up over the hill. There's a light." That's God telling me something, I believe.

Jo-Ellen talked of an extended interaction with God about what she should do with her life following the death of her son. The following is atypical of interview narratives in this study in the detail, the vividness, and the extent to which it seems that her life and death were in the balance during this crucial event, but it is typical of narratives about communication with God in that God is good and helpful.

Jo-Ellen: A week after [he] died . . . I remember tellin' God, "I can't do this. . . . What do I have to live for? . . . I remember . . . getting on my knees and praying . . . , "God, please take me home. Because I don't know that. . . . can live for You the way that they're tellin' me I need to live. . . . But now I know I'm at peace, and so Your best bet (chuckling) is to take me now (laughs), 'cause I don't know what my future holds. . . . I don't know that I can deal with the loss of [my son]. I don't know where it will take me. I can't deal with this pain. I can't deal with this void." And I remember crying . . . and I closed my eyes, and all of a sudden it was like I was looking down at myself. . . . Here was this image, and it was white, this white robe with this . . . blinding glow. I couldn't see the clarity of the face, but the person was holding [my son]. And they said, "You wanted to be with him." And they handed me, and . . . I'm sitting and . . . crying and . . . laughing, all at the same time. . . . I'm feeling him, and I'm holding him, and it's like it was a minute of holding him, but it was like it was hours. And then . . . this same image coming back, and they said, "You have a choice. You can stay here and be with your son, or you can go back and do the work that I've called you to do. . . ." And He pointed this way, and there was this lo-o-ong table. "This table will be full of those that I have used you to reach. . . ." At the very end was my son, but all the other was empty. . . . Again He handed me my son. . . . Now I'm really crying, 'cause I'm torn. I'm thinking of my mother; I'm thinking of my best girl friend. . . . I'm holding my child, and I'm like, "[I'm] here, but they're there. What am I gonna do? . . ." Next I hand my child to this image . . . this image I call "The Lord." And then all of a sudden I'm seeing my body again. But I'm not able to get into it. . . . I was laying, and it was like (breathing out), and tears were coming, but I couldn't breathe, I just couldn't breathe. . . . I was like (breathing out), "Wait, wait. In the name of Jesus," and it was like someone hit me with a sledge hammer, literally hit me hard in my chest, and I was wide awake. And that was 32 years ago. And I was not a minister. I was nothing. And I was still smoking weed (chuckles). I wasn't lookin' to be a minister. No, I wasn't. All I was thinkin', "Oh, I've got to tell my girl friend about Jesus, and my mama (laughs). . . ." Now here, years later, I've . . . had opportunity on top of opportunity to share Christ with individuals from the streets.

Jo-Ellen was one of a few people who felt that God communicated with them to prepare them emotionally and spiritually for the death and to enable them to cope.

Jo-Ellen: I went back to the hospital to see [my son]. . . . I had wrote a letter to God that day, thanking Him that my child was alive. . . . Two weeks before that a woman had . . . told my minister to tell me that unless my life got in order that God was going to take my child. And I was struggling at that point with fornication. Looking for affection, but going further. But one evening I had fornicated and after I got done I felt extremely guilty, just like crazy guilty. Because here was this fear in the back of my mind, "Is God going to kill my child because of me messing up?" And I remember going into the bathroom and . . . crying and looking in the mirror, and all of a sudden it was like I saw my child in a coffin. And I just panicked. I remember falling to my knees in the bathroom. "Oh, my God! Please don't, please, I'm trying so hard. I don't mean to do this. I just needed to be held. I don't want to do the other." And I was just begging like crazy. And then it was a week later that he went into a relapse and became very ill. So I had wrote this note to God thanking Him so much for being there, for keeping my child alive. . . . I remember trying to stay awake. . . . I was afraid that if I fell asleep he would die. . . . And . . . I felt like the spirit of the Lord spoke to me and told me to go lay down. And at first I thought, "Oh, that couldn't be God. . . . I've gotta be awake. . . ." And I felt like I heard it again. . . . So I went and laid down on the bed that was across from [my son]. . . . I must have fell asleep as soon as my head hit the pillow. And then all of a sudden it's like I heard all kinds of people in the room. And I opened my eyes, and there were doctors all around his bed, and his breathing was slow. And I jumped up and I felt like, again, God said, "Lay down. I'm gonna take you home." But it was real peaceful. I was totally at peace, and that's not who I am. And especially my fear of losing my child. . . . But I had this calmness, and I laid back down and I listened, and the room was just (whispering) quiet. (back to normal loudness) And all I could hear was his breathing, and it was like his breathing was just (speaking more quietly with each word) slower and slower. It just stopped. . . . (back to normal loudness) They weren't able to revive him. . . . I was tempted to go over to his bed and pick him up and hold him. And I thought, "No. He's not there. That's only gonna to do more damage than good to hold his dead body. . . ." And I walked out of the room. . . . I didn't want to see him dead dead. So I didn't even look.

Len provided another example of a communication from God received before a death.

Len: I woke up that morning [before my wife died], and I really had a sense of peace. And almost hearing a audible voice . . . but it was just in my mind . . . , "Be still." And just that whole day it was just that consistent thought or message to be still.

Sometimes it was only in retrospect that people felt that God had tried to communicate with them prior to the death, to prepare them for the death. Evelyn, for example, came to understand dreams she had before her son died as messages from God.

Evelyn: Before this thing happened, I had a dream . . . about my son, but I didn't know what it was, and it looked like I was standing arguing with somebody about him, and it looked like I was saying, "No, he is not going with you." But I thought it was just . . . somebody I didn't want him to associate with, and I was just standing there arguing, and so finally I woke up. I said, "I wonder what that was about?" And then . . . it was about a month before we got the news that he was sick, but you know what? I would start praying. I would pray three times a day after that, 'cause I said, "There's something on my mind. He's on my mind." I don't know what it was, and I was praying about it. And then when I found out I said, "This is what it was." When I found out the tragedy, that was what it was. It was a . . . vision.

Rosalyn and Willa were among several people who found great comfort in communicating with God.

Rosalyn: I talk to God a lot. . . . He will not go and repeat (laughs). It stays with the Lord. . . . Some people will say, "You are . . . strange. . . ." They have told me that. I talk to God like I'm sitting talking to you. I do. I talk to God the things that I don't . . . want to talk with my sisters about it. I didn't want them to be upset, because we have all had our share of problems and pain.

Willa: I think if anything [my mother's death] strengthened my faith. Because I had to hang onto something, someone. And a lot of people my age never have a spouse or somebody . . . to physically hang onto. I didn't have that. But I had my faith. I had God. And I talked to Him a lot, believe me. . . . I got on real good terms with [Him]. So, I think it strengthened it. Because I knew her spirituality was so strong. And I knew that she was fine. Like I told everybody else, she's fine. We're the ones who are suffering. She's fine. I don't worry about her at all.

☐ Challenging God

For people whose faith is deep and who believe in God's wisdom and fairness, an untimely death, the death of a good person, or the death of a person who was doing good works, could shake their belief in God. As has been true in research in which the people interviewed were Euro-Americans (e.g., Gilbert, 1992), some African American interviewees reacted to a death that seemed somehow unjust with anger and by challenging God. Jo-Ellen is quoted earlier in this chapter in that regard, and Barbara is quoted in chapter 6 as being so angry with God she wanted to box him. Franklin talked about his challenging God after his sister's death in a motor vehicle accident.

Franklin: I challenged God, and I mean I challenged God. I threatened God in every which way that I could think of, and I flew across a bridge that was a killer bridge, trying to challenge God. If You're so mad, why didn't You take me instead of [my sister].

Challenges to God often ended in an understanding of how it might be appropriate that God had taken the person who died. But before reaching that point people might find it difficult to go to church or to pray.

Beverly: You talked about boxing with God. (*Barbara:* uh huh) How long did you have that desire?

Barbara: . . . It took that six years for me to reconcile. It was after I figured out, "Okay, okay, You needed her in Your garden. I still don't like it, but anyway I forgive You."

Beverly: How did it affect your spirituality? Or your religiosity?

Barbara: It changed it in that I couldn't go back to church. . . .

Beverly: So during that six-year period you weren't able to go to church?

Barbara: Not really.

On the other hand, some people seemed to question those who challenge God. For them, faith in God meant one did not challenge.

Patricia: I'm not one to really question God. I don't think I'm close enough to be intelligent [enough] to question God. All these brilliant people who do, I don't know where they get it, people who argue with God. So I didn't go through all that phase of being angry with God. . . . I was really thankful that He gave [mother] to me the time that He had.

☐ Conclusion

Many people talked about the place of God in their grieving. Sounding to us like many Euro-Americans for whom God is important, they talked about trusting that God's benevolent hand was involved in the death and that God would take care of them and of the deceased. Some talked about God giving them solace and strength following the death and teaching them through the death and its aftermath. Some felt that God communicated with them concerning the death and that the death had brought them closer to God. Some who felt that a death was unjust or untimely challenged God, but in the end came to accept the death and God's hand in it.

Being Strong in Grief

Grieving people of any ethnicity may talk about needing to be strong in dealing with a loss and may be encouraged by others to be strong. But our belief is that African Americans talk about being strong in dealing with deaths more than Euro-Americans do. In fact, quite a few of the African Americans who were interviewed talked about being strong in grief.

☐ What Is Involved in Being Strong in Grief

An important part of what people seemed to mean about being strong in grief was that either in general or after the funeral and burial they grieved only in private. Consistent with this, Boyd-Franklin and Lockwood (1999) have said that for many African Americans, grieving is very private and personal. Why grieve privately? A person might not want others to know that she or he is hurting and also might not want to affect others, to set off their pain and grieving.

Rosalyn: How do we grieve? (pause) Within. I think we grieve it within.

Beverly: Why do we grieve within?

Rosalyn: We don't want it to affect someone else, or we don't want to let someone else know how we're hurting.

One's own strength (grieving only in private) could help others in the family to be strong in the same way, and their strength could help one to be strong in that way. So privacy of grieving is not only an individual thing, it can be a mutually reinforced family pattern.

Jane: [My children] never saw me cry. . . . I didn't want to break down in front of them. I wanted them to think that I was strong so they could be strong too. I'm just a very private person. I like to cry . . . by myself (chuckles). I don't like to be around a lot of people and cry. When [my husband] died, I did a lot of crying in my room, and in the bathroom. . . . I think I cried more when he died than I have cried in years. . . . They didn't cry in front of me, because they didn't want to break down in front of me because they knew I'd probably start crying. If they saw me crying, they'd be crying.

In order to be strong (private, controlled) in grieving, a person might have to avoid reminders, events, or people that could set off grieving, particularly public grieving. Patricia thought it ironic that her oldest brother had been the strongest of the siblings emotionally and yet had never been able to read a letter their mother had written to her children. In her view, strength goes with being able to face what might be emotionally jarring. And yet strength, such as that of Patricia's brother, also might require a person to distance things that would challenge emotional control.

Patricia: Before Mother even became ill, she wrote us a letter, and I still carry the letter around. My oldest brother hasn't read it yet. . . . One of the things that she said in her letter was how much she admired the way the [family] loved each other. . . .

Beverly: Why hasn't [your brother] read it?

Patricia: He's probably afraid of what that letter might do to him. He used the phrase one time that I found so affectionate, when we were reflecting on what Mom was like, "That was my girl. . . ." When somebody says, "That's my girl," you can't mess with her; there's nothing I won't do for her; she is the ultimate. And so I just feel like the love my brother has for my mom is so great that it's not as great for the rest of us. And he, even though he was the oldest and has always been the strongest of all of us emotionally and the most level-headed and all of that, it's ironic that he's the least able to do that.

Based on the interviews, it seems that emotional distancing is a strategy often used when people work at being strong. They distance what challenges their emotional equanimity, perhaps even if it means walking out of the wake or funeral of a loved one.

Cynthia: I remember seeing my youngest brother get up and walk out of the wake, and was gone for a period of time, and then he came back, and I knew then that he was dealing with his emotions, and he just did not want people to see him crying. . . . My sisters wept openly, but the boys were really trying to control themselves.

Distancing of feelings and being strong are related in another way. Some people are strong in grief in the sense of taking care of others who are also grieving, and by focusing so much on others they may be able to stay away from their own pain.

Beverly: Did you feel that anyone let you down during that period?

Cynthia: No. I never thought about it (laughs). I guess maybe my taking care of everybody else . . . I was too preoccupied with that . . . to be thinking of things for myself, and it kept me busy and kept my mind occupied. . . . I guess I'm a born caregiver. So it's just like as long as I have something to put emotions and everything into then I'll be fine.

☐ Strength in Grief Is Valued

Although, as we say later in this chapter, some African Americans have mixed feelings about strength in grief, many interviewees valued strength. Willa, for example, talked about her mother's strength following the death of her father. It was strength not only about keeping grief feelings secret and suppressed but also about being both father and mother to her children and supporting them.

Willa: She was a very strong woman. She raised my brother and me alone, after my dad died, when I was 9 and my brother was 6. So I learned to become very strong, I think, and independent as a result. I had to kind of grow up a little bit fast. . . . I don't think she ever realized it, but I was always kind of worried about her, and kind of, "How's Mom doing today?" I would catch her crying when she didn't think I saw her. . . . I think it . . . sped up my maturity a little bit. But she was a great mama. She was very supportive for all of the things my brother and I did. And I remember she would be the only mother who would be sitting in a car waiting for us at the high school to come back from band trips. Everywhere else it was dads waiting.

☐ Strength in Grief as African American

We think there are unique aspects of African American history and experience that have pushed African Americans toward being "strong" in grief. African Americans have faced enormous adversity for hundreds of years. They have often lacked financial, legal, medical, and many other resources for dealing with their difficulties. They may have had the support of others in their community, of family, and of faith, but with few other resources they had to rely often on their own strength. In fact, some African Americans may say that their only source of support is their own strength (McDonald, 1987), and because they have had to rely so much on their own resources of strength many African American widows may agree with statements like, "Black women are stronger than white women" (McDonald, 1987, pp. 153–154).

In addition, African Americans have at times had to hide their grief because revealing it could give white oppressors information about how to hurt and control them and could also give those oppressors sadistic satisfaction (hooks, 1993b). Since white cruelty and suppression continued past the end of slavery into contemporary times, African Americans may continue to feel that controlling emotions in certain situations keeps them safer than they otherwise would be. From another angle, hooks (1993b) sees the strength as a defense against allowing oneself to fall apart at the recognition of personal pain and difficulties. So African Americans may have learned to face the special stresses of their lives with what they considered strength, which includes distancing feelings and keeping feelings private (Brice, 1999, pp. 51, 105, 121; Shenk, 2000). Thus for African Americans, grieving may be constrained and shaped by efforts to distance feelings, keep them private, or act in other ways they consider to be "strong" (Abrums, 2000; Brice, 1999, pp. 51, 105, 121; Hines, 1986, 1991). But despite the scholarship behind this analysis of the historical context of strength in African American grief, only a few of the people who were interviewed mentioned something resembling that context. One of the few people who linked strength to African American history was Kenneth, who saw strength in grief as a carryover from slavery times, when the slave owner did not allow those who were newly grieving any time off.

Kenneth: When you're a slave and something is taken from you, massa not gonna give you three days off sick leave.

Beverly: So what you're saying is, we don't have the luxury or the opportunity

Kenneth: We didn't. We didn't. We did not as slaves. We did not have the luxury or opportunity to take any time off to mourn for the loss of our loved ones, simply because we weren't considered human. We were cattle. So that's a part of that process of making adjustments to how we grieve.

☐ Being Strong and Having Nobody to Whom to Turn

In all domains of life, and perhaps across ethnicities, being strong might be engendered and even demanded by situations where one has nobody to whom to turn for help and support. A single mother may have to be strong in parenting if she has no other adult to help her parent. Similarly, a grieving person might feel forced to limit and control strong grief feelings because she or he lacks someone to provide support, nurturance, or help with tasks that must be done. "Being strong" in grief is then at least partly about feeling alone. Loretta talked about feeling alone in dealing with her mother's dementia and her mother's death seven years prior to the interview.

Loretta: With my mother, money couldn't fix it. . . . I couldn't give anything to make it right. I couldn't give her back memories. I couldn't give her back her life. I couldn't even give her back herself. And looking into her eyes, and her eyes seemed to have gotten larger, and there was nothing behind them. There was no substance. There was no feeling. There was no passion. There was nothing. There was just sorrow and confusion. . . . I couldn't do anything. I could not control that situation. . . . And I have a refusal to go see my aunts, because they have the same freakin' gray eyes, and I don't want to see that. And maybe if I did go, I would begin your grievin' process. Maybe I would then be removed from the situation enough to allow myself to cry.

Beverly: Do you want to cry?

Loretta: You know (breathing out in exasperation), sometimes I think I do, and I have this thought that if I could just get all of this stuff out of me, that I would be the better for it. Until I started crying.

Beverly: And then what happened?

Loretta: The hopelessness, the despair, and the needing of someone to comfort me.

Beverly: And there was no one there.

Loretta: And there was no one there.

☐ **Becoming Strong**

Many people who were interviewed talked about family and community forces that pushed them to become strong. They did not get to their "strength" in a social vacuum but learned it from and were pushed toward it by family members and others in their community.

For Charlotte, a childhood lesson in being strong came following her mother's death, when her father told her: "Your mother wouldn't want you to cry."

Several people talked about parents setting the standard for grieving in private by themselves grieving in private. Andrew, for example, talked about his mother's grieving not a death but the losses associated with her son, the respondent's brother, being a drug addict.

Andrew: She wanted to raise a boy that could have some strength in him. . . . She was a strong, courageous woman, but she cried. . . . But she ain't gonna cry outside of that door. She ain't gonna cry with no,

"Your brother hurt me." She just cried. She cried at me. And I sit there and cry, "Well, Ma's it's gonna be all right. He gonna be all right. . . . She knew she could cry to me. But she's going to be strong when she gets through crying. . . . My mama was one of them people that, "This is family. So what your brother's a drug addict? . . ."

Beverly: Do you think you learned from your mom not to talk with other people about your grief and your pain?

Andrew: Yeah. Yeah.

Toni talked about seeing her mother respond without visible grieving to the death of her mother's mother (the interviewee's grandmother).

Toni: I remember watching my father walk out to the car and tell my mother, and my mother sat up (*Beverly:* straight), sat up straight. You know, never a tear. And in all fairness I know now she was doing her duty. She wasn't just being callous. She was performing her duty, to stay erect and to take care of her business. . . .

Beverly: How did your mother grieve?

Toni: She never did. What she told me was that she had made amends with her mother in the spirit, prior to her dying. But I don't think she ever grieved.

Kenneth talked about the pressure on all men in his extended family not to cry.

Beverly: What do you think about men in your family not showing each other the tears?

Kenneth: I think it has a lot to do with um, it's a display . . . of remorse. And for many of the men in my family, weakness was not something that was easily tolerated.

Beverly: Okay, so if you cried then you were weak?

Kenneth: That could have been interpreted as a sign of weakness. . . . They just didn't [cry]; you didn't see it. I'm not saying that they didn't. They might go somewhere and be by themselves.

Beverly: All right. That's interesting, because oftentimes we tell our boys, "Don't cry" or "You gotta be a man," or something like that. . . .

Kenneth: I was never told to talk that way. It was just a code . . . from growing up, and being a competitor, playing sports. Okay? It was never taught. It wasn't something that was said. It was a matter of being in competition and watching somebody on the football field or playing basketball. When they got hurt, if they cried, you (laughs). . . . And if they found out that you were going to cry, they would do things to you, because they wanted to play your spot on the team. . . . So . . . it wasn't a taught thing that I learned from my family.

☐ Mixed Feelings about Being Strong

Many people admired strength in others. They could see it as something to appreciate and emulate, something to pray for and to incorporate into their own ways of dealing with pain and difficulty. And yet feelings about strength were often mixed. For example, Rosalyn saw strength in the sense of holding emotion in as only good if one could handle it, but not to the point where it could harm one emotionally or physically.

Beverly: Do you think it's helpful that we grieve by holding it in?

Rosalyn: . . . It all depends on how much of it you can handle, within. If it's to the point where it's going to affect you emotionally and physically, then "no." Let it out. Go somewhere, to grief counseling.

Clyde talked about how harmful it is for men to work hard at being strong, because then they are not in touch with who they are or what is going on inside of them, and in a sense that makes them less human.

Clyde: I just don't, no offense to those males that don't show any emotion, but I don't think they in touch with who they are. . . . A lot of men have this idea about who men are, and they don't want to show any frail, being fragile. That's more of a woman, feminine kind of a thing. . . . It took me a while to get in touch with my masculine as well as my feminine piece. . . . I think it's something that we kind of make latent. I think it's there, if men deal with it. But emotional, I think it also makes you human. And we've been taught to be someone what's bigger and stronger and tougher and mightier . . . and so to let somebody else see that we can be just fragile as anything . . . unun, no. . . . Sometimes I think we don't know how to grieve. . . . Some of us have to be taught how to grieve. . . . I think we always, all of us have some preconceived notions about how men should be, if our dad or whoever the male was in our lives, how they grieved, that's the way you gonna grieve more than likely. So if they held back and didn't cry, it's probably what you're gonna do. But now they never ask the question, "Why am I doing this? And I'm feeling really sad now to be cryin'. I really ought to have some tears, 'cause there're some tears up in those ducts, believe me." And it's okay. See, I guess that's the thing. It's okay to cry. It's okay to feel bad, feel sad, feel that feeling for that person that ain't here no more. . . . Somebody, maybe a wife, somebody gotta tell 'em, "Okay, it's cool. You can cry, brother, baby. You can bawl and cry now." And most men don't want other men to see them in that kind of a (*Beverly:* vulnerable) vulnerable position.

Charlotte is quoted earlier in this chapter as saying that when she was a child and her mother died her father told her that her mother wouldn't want her to cry. Now as an adult she can talk about how being strong in the sense of being emotionally controlled is lonely and ultimately can lead to feeling that one is "going crazy."

Charlotte: All I know is to be under control. That's lonely stuff. All you know is to be under control, but yet you know you're going crazy.

Willa also talked about how lonely it was to be strong.

Beverly: How does it feel having to be the strong black woman?

Willa: Sometimes really lonely. I've never been married, and I would like to be . . . because I need emotional support, and just somebody to say, "It's going to be okay. It'll be all right. We'll work it out." (Sighs)

People can also worry that when loved ones work at being strong in grief they can risk serious health problems.

Willa: [My brother] always bottles things up, and so that worries me about him. Because I can see him having a heart attack one of these days.

Jo-Ellen thought that the strength others saw in her following her child's death was actually her distancing ("freezing") her feelings of grief. Instead of engaging in a grieving process, her efforts at control "froze" her until years later there was a thaw and the grief came rushing back.

Jo-Ellen: As they got ready to close the casket. . . . I broke. Then I began to feel it. Then it's like, "Oh, my God. Wait! Wait!" And with my father I did that same thing, "Wait!" With my child I did the same thing, "Wait!" And I realize now, years later, back then the way I dealt with grief was, "Let me get control. Let me freeze what needs to freeze, and I'll feel what I can control." And so they did stop the funeral. I went and put the one rose in his casket. But what it did, it allowed me to pull myself together again. And we went to the cemetery, and we did it, and I was just mechanical. And people said, "She's so strong. I don't know how she's so strong." Six months later, I got married. And my husband wouldn't allow me to have any pictures of my child at all. Zero. So in a matter of six months I really made a decision way too soon (*Beverly:* to put closure), to put closure, and a decision to marry. Because a year hadn't even went by. I really was still froze. And so then, not being able to deal with it, I didn't start dealing with my son's death until . . . now.

☐ It Is Hard to Let Go of Being Strong in Grief

Even if the African Americans who were interviewed have mixed feelings or negative feelings about being strong, they can find it hard to let go of that strength. Being strong emotionally can seem the safest place to be. If a person has worked for a long time at being strong, it fits who they are in many ways. So then, when they try to stop being strong, it may be difficult. And, as Loretta said in a statement quoted immediately below, there can be that fear that letting go can open one up to horrifying things that one cannot handle.

Loretta: I can't be in a position where I need. And I even called someone, and said, "I just need you to hold me," but even in front of them I couldn't allow myself to cry, because I had to be strong. I had to put on a whole different persona. So, yeah, I would probably be able to sleep at night if I let it out. Okay? But yeah, I had this history, and all of these people that constantly said, "Be strong. Be strong. . . ." Do I want to be weak? Yeah, it would be really, really nice just to be weak for a day. And I came close. I really came close. And didn't like where I was. And considered if I completed the process would it be over or would it open the floodgate for other things?

Some people talked about taking steps to let go emotionally. That does not mean they stopped being strong, but they found a path that enabled them at times to feel their feelings and take care of themselves better than they would have if they had concentrated only on being strong. Sometimes it only takes permission from someone else to allow oneself to be less strong for a while.

Beverly: When do you let yourself not be strong?

Elsa: I don't. I don't. Oh, I cry, yeah. And I went to a retreat. . . . The church had a women's retreat that called me and said that the church had paid my way. And there was a minister there, a prophetess, and she said, "The Lord said you can grieve. And He knows when it's time for you to cry." And I started crying, and I couldn't quit crying, and that was the best cry I had. But I still, I don't, I blocked out the tragedy of what happened, but the memories of it, I keep those memories.

☐ Conclusion

Strength was an important value in the narratives of many of the people who were interviewed. It is perfectly understandable why a people who have experienced centuries of oppression and who still face many difficulties and disadvantages would value strength. Strength is often vital to well-being, one's own and that of others who rely on one. So we applaud the strength of African Americans in the face of adversities of all sorts. However, in this chapter we focus on a specific kind of strength, strength in grief, what one does with feelings of loss. Although we could make a case for strength in grief being about facing and expressing painful feelings or talking openly with others about feelings, the people we interviewed generally saw strength in grief as about keeping feelings private and perhaps even thoroughly bottled up. That kind of strength is understandable because it is connected to so much, including the scarcity of many kinds of resources as a result of societal oppression, the centuries during which revealing pain to oppressors invited the oppressors to inflict more pain, and not wanting to set off bouts of pain

in others. And yet, strength in grief was also seen by many who were interviewed as a cause of difficulty. Keeping feelings private and to oneself may
take a terrible emotional and physical toll on oneself and others around one.
It may mean that for years one suppresses one's grieving. Since that kind of
strength is often taught and modeled by parents and others who are close to
one and is often valued in the community, it is not easy to let go of. But
several people had stories of how much they benefited when they were able
to let go. So it seems to us that a case can be made that strength in grief can
create considerable difficulty for an African American.

13
CHAPTER

Continuing Contact with the Deceased

It is often said that many African Americans believe strongly in the continuation of a person's spirit beyond death (e.g., Barrett, 1998, 2003; Pleck, 2000). So it should come as little surprise that 19 of the 26 interviewees talked about having or anticipating continuing contact with the person who died. As with African American women studied by Smith (2002), and as in research where most or all the people who were studied probably were white (e.g., Bennett, 1999; Conant, 1996; Klass, 1988, pp. 18–19, 1993, 1996, 1997, 1999; Klass & Walter, 2001; Sormanti & August, 1997), the deceased person was not gone from interviewees' lives. They might know they will meet with the person in heaven. They might experience a sense that the person is watching them from somewhere. They might hear the person talking to them, or see some signal that the person is present.

Sometimes the contact was that they continued to imagine or say aloud things they would say to the person were the person alive and present. For example, Vickie talked about the conversations she had with her mother who had died 15 months before the interview.

Vickie: I do go back and visit her. I have little chats with her now. "How are you doing? Just want you to know. . . ."

Barbara talked about her ongoing contact with visual representations of her deceased mother, and also the times she remembered her mother, talked with her mother, or even talked about people connected to her mother.

Barbara: I have a picture that was drawn . . . from a photograph . . . of her right there. . . . At some point I . . . realized that all the things we say to other people, that the person is not gone. As long as you remember them . . . that person is not gone, 'cause their spirit will dwell with you. . . . Every time I talk about her best friend . . . I'm talking about her too. . . . I feel I can talk to [Mom], but not to get an answer.

☐ Cemetery Connections

For some people, a cemetery visit provides a sense of communing with, remembering, and caring about the deceased.

Verna: Me and Mother go to the gravesite. My sister believes Dad is not there, so she won't go to the gravesite. She says, "Mother, Dad's gone. And that's just a body there, and you waste your time." But because his body's there, because she wants to talk, or clean up, or put flowers there, I'll go with her.

Some people think of a cemetery as a place where loved ones can be together in death.

Willa: When we bought the plot over in the white cemetery (chuckles) for my mom and dad, we bought an extra plot, 'cause my brother hadn't decided whether he's going to be cremated or buried. I know I'm going to be cremated, so I said, "Well, she can just share this plot." So what we'll do (chuckles) is have a marker made. . . . I'll have a marker put in where . . . you can set an urn into the marker. "And that'll be me, and you'll be down here."

With the loved ones buried there, some families take cemetery photos to record the connection they have with the burial site.

Jane: We go out to the cemetery and put flowers on his grave, take pictures. We got a lot of pictures of the cemetery. We got (laughing) a whole book full.

In one family, the cemetery connection with loved ones who had died was so powerful that they brought a new family member to the cemetery to, in a sense, introduce her to family members who were buried there.

Ron: When we picked up our new daughter-in-law from the airport, it was a beautiful day, we stopped [at the cemetery].

Sometimes a visit to the cemetery enables a person who had been avoiding grieving a death to enter into the grief process.

Jo-Ellen: Seven years ago when I left my . . . husband . . . I began to go back over where I was when I married him . . . 'cause it was a mentally abusive relationship. So I had lost myself. So I had to go all the way back to find myself. . . . I decided I was gonna go to the cemetery [where my son from a prior relationship was buried]. And [my husband hadn't] let me go. . . . I wanted to deal with the death of my child. . . . I was on [the road] to the cemetery. And I saw the exit I was to come off on. It was as if I was in the limousine all over again. . . . I had. . . . [a rose] that I was taking to the cemetery. . . . I knew that I didn't remember where he was buried. But I remember the day of the funeral I had looked up and saw a street sign and a tree. And I had remembered that spot. . . . As I got ready to get off [that] street, this panic hit me . . . uncontrollable panic. I began to cry, till I couldn't even see. . . . I was petrified. . . . I couldn't even breathe. But I was determined that I had to do it. And it wasn't that I was crying because of something I feared. I was feeling. I was coming unthawed. . . . And I was talking to God. "God, I don't know what to feel, but I choose to feel. . . . Let me start trying to figure this out. . . ." Just . . . feel what I needed to feel. Not try to label it . . . but feel it. And so . . . I drove to the area. . . . I saw . . . the street and I saw the tree. I thought, "Oh, this is it." And when I stepped out, I could not find it. . . . I felt like I went crazy for a minute, 'cause I felt so much guilt that I didn't have a grave head for him. I felt ashamed. . . . I just stood there and . . . cried. . . . I felt like I couldn't turn the page to the next chapter, and I had to. . . . It felt like the funeral all over. . . . But . . . I couldn't find his grave. . . . I thought, "You know where the tree is. Just sit by the tree. God knows. . . . You know [my son] ain't here anyway. This really isn't about [him]. This is about you." And so I . . . sat under the tree . . . and I chose a little area that I called his grave. And I left the rose, and I prayed, and I even talked. . . . I apologized, without feeling guilty. After I calmed down, after I got past the panic, I didn't feel guilt. I just felt like, "I'm here." I felt complete. . . . I sat under that tree, and I thanked God for carrying me through. . . . I remember saying to [my child], "I know you're not here, but I'm here. A lot is happening in Mom's life. I'm glad you're with the Lord. I don't think you could have endured the things that did happen to me. I don't think it would have been healthy for you to have been here. . . . I've never forgot you." And I remember putting down the flower and crying. . . . I kinda picked up where I left off. . . . And so to be able to cry and feel the sadness of not having him, and yet the joy of being able to be there. And to return to a place that I could be thawed out, and not fear that tears were going to destroy me. But that tears were now a point of joy and . . . freedom. . . . And I . . . came back again in about a week . . . and . . . tried to find the grave, and that's when I felt . . . anger at myself and said, "Someday I'm going to raise enough money to put a headstone there. . . ." But even if I never do, it's not a issue. . . . I would like to know exactly the spot, but I've made my own little spot, and made my own little cross . . . and sat there.

For some, cemetery visits are a way to remember, connect with, and honor a loved one who died.

Willa: [Mother] was the reason that I would go back to my hometown. I haven't been in a while. . . . I'm going to go back . . . on Memorial Day weekend, so that I can go myself to put flowers . . . on [her] grave.

☐ Reunion in Heaven

Some people talked about their plans to reunite in heaven with the person who died (which is what Smith, 2002, found in her study of African American women grieving for the death of an elderly mother). This is similar to what is found in studies of people most or all of whom are white—for example, in studies of grieving parents (Klass, 1999; Rosenblatt, 2000a). The loved one was gone from earth but was still a reality for the survivors to think about, pray about, pray to, and plan to meet again in heaven. And it stands to reason that if, for many African Americans, death is a homecoming, that the deceased would be in heaven for them when they got there (Sullivan, 1995).

Andrew: One day I'm going to be free, and me and Mama believed that. I believe it. I don't know nothing about no life after death, but I believe we're going to meet up. . . . I just know we all going to be up there. My day going to come. It ain't no ifs, ands, or buts. . . .

Beverly: Do you think your mom is some place else . . . ?

Andrew: Yeah. . . . In heaven. . . . Mom was a good person.

Willa: I'll be with my mom, my dad, and I'll catch them up on everything. . . . And they'll tell me, "Oh, we know all about it, because we've been watching."

Elsa: Spiritually, I believe, I will see him again. My mom, my sister, we will all be together again.

Reunion in heaven with a spouse who died might seem more challenging for widows or widowers who have remarried. Perhaps that is why Len talked the way he did about someday meeting his deceased first wife in heaven.

Beverly: After somebody important in their life dies, many people at times experience the presence of the person, maybe they see and hear the person, or maybe they just have a sense of the person being nearby. Have you had experiences like that after [your first wife] died?

Len: (pause) No. Not in the sense of really feeling that like there's a manifestation of her spirit present. I think in the sense of her thoughts or what she stood for in life, being reminded and having clear visions of who she was, her presence in the sense of her character and her commitment and her energy, I would say, "yes." But in the sense of having kind of a spiritual presence in the room, no. And part of that is my belief system. . . . I would hope that, "You don't have to linger around here anymore. . . . Go ahead and enjoy your new life and celebrate the universe, and someday I'll be out there kinda checking things out too."

As some interviewees talk about it, "reunion in heaven" may be abstract, something like disembodied spiritual essences coming together, rather than like two humans who love and have a lot to say to each other getting together. But for others, reunion in heaven seems to be quite a human thing in that they talk about doing concrete things together in heaven. For example, Calvin talked about introducing the interviewer to his mother when they were all together in heaven.

Calvin: Praise God. Praise the Lord. When we get to heaven I'll introduce you to her.

Although most people looked forward to reunion in heaven with their deceased relative, Loretta definitely did not.

Loretta: My mom . . . I think that when I die she's going to give me a royal cussin' out. . . . I have this real fear of dying and having to face her.

Beverly: And why are you afraid?

Loretta: . . . Probably those two weeks [at the end of her life] that I didn't go see her, that psychological guilt behind that. Yeah, and the fact that I haven't put a stone on her grave. . . . I know she pissed. If there's any way to be pissed off in the next life, she's there. (whining, nagging, critical voice) "You ain't put a stone on my grave."

A deceased family member can live in a person's heart, in the name one gives a child, and in the sense that she or he is looking down protectively from heaven.

Willa: She's in my heart always. I mean, the way she raised me. The kind of person that I am, I think, had a lot to do with her. . . . [My daughter] has her name as her middle name. . . . I just feel like she's looking down and watching over us. . . . I really do think people have guardian angels, and I think most of the time they were relatives who have gone on before. . . . That's why I think people who are insincere and didn't like the person in life, don't be making on over them in death, 'cause they're up there somewhere watching everything that's going on.

☐ Sense of Presence

Kalish and Reynolds (1973; 1981, p. 215) reported that their black informants were considerably more likely than white informants, and also more likely than Japanese-American and Mexican-American informants, to say that they had at some time experienced or felt the presence of someone after that person had died. This may be a corollary of the belief that a family member who has died has passed to the afterlife and exists there (Abrums, 2000).

Help and Protection

Consistent with the work of Kalish and Reynolds, among our 26 interviewees, some talked about a sense of presence. Such experiences are reported often enough in studies where most or all of the people studied are Euro-Americans (e.g., Frantz, Trolley, & Johil, 1996), so we would not necessarily assume that what the interviewees said was different from what Euro-Americans would say. But Toni talked about her experiences being African and mystical. She also talked about the deceased coming to be a helpful presence at a time of great need. And that may be a more common experience for African Americans, that sense of presence comes when the person, if alive, would be present to help.

Toni: The African piece is I understood that my grandmother was gone, but she wasn't too far away (chuckle) . . . when I was getting ready to have [my baby] and . . . I went into labor. . . . My water had not broken, and I had a midwife, and she didn't want to break my water until I was already dilated because she said, "The longer you can keep this water intact, you won't have as much pain." And there was a piece of the labor that just got real hard, and . . . I knew my grandmother was in that room. . . . I could hear her. I could smell her, and I felt she did something to [the baby]. Now [the baby] wasn't breach, but she like moved her down because I literally felt her push on my abdomen, on my uterus. And I said, "Oh, Granny," and she smiled. . . . My grandmother has been with me, she has been a companion along the way for me. So I have missed her in her physical form. I've seen her. I've seen my grandmother. So she has corrected me. She has come in my dreams and beat me, you know, verbally, "I know you not trying to do that (laughs)." And I know that it is not a psychosis. I know this is real. I know my grandmother's presence is real as you sitting there.

Beverly: How often does she come to you? How often do you see her in dreams?

Toni: (breathes out audibly) I don't know. It's not like a set pattern, and it's not even when I think I desperately need her. It kinda comes when she thinks she should come, but she's always busy. She's always working. . . . I know my grandmother goes with me. . . . When she visits me she is as real as you are.

Angela talked about her deceased father sometimes warning her of dangers.

Beverly: Do you ever experience your dad being present in your life?

Angela: At times, yeah. . . . Sometimes I can walk in to my house or I can get into my car and I feel him. And sometimes I can be with a crowd of people and . . . I can feel. . . .

Beverly: Does your dad talk with you when he appears to you?

Angela: I think, yeah, and . . . it seems like he warns me sometimes about some things.

Franklin talked about the time his sister, who had died sometime before, saved his life and also about the times she communicated with him that something was wrong back home.

Beverly: [With] people [who] died we sometimes say that they appeared to us. Has [your stepfather] appeared to you since his death?

Franklin: No. No. And (crying, pause) when my sister was killed, she did. . . . I know that my sister saved my life one time, after she was dead. Speeding along in a car, out carousing . . . in a car that I used to race every night, and I fell asleep doing about 100, maybe 110. And her voice came, "Fool! What's wrong with you, boy? You better wake up!" In only her voice and her way, her mannerisms. I woke up, and I was heading right for a bridge, and I swerved and missed it. Pulled over to the side, had a conversation with her. She never spoke back after that, but I had my conversation with her. . . . After my sister was killed, if something was wrong [back home] that affected somebody strongly, I would smell roses. And I'd call. And there'd be something wrong (chuckles). Because the night before she was killed she and I walked together. And she had me walk with her in this little town, going to visit people. And every one of them she talked with, "If I don't see you no more, I just want a dozen red roses at my funeral." And after the third one I told her, "If you don't cut that out, me and you gonna have to go to war right out here." "Ah, boy, don't be silly." She got killed the next day.

Andrew talked about the way his deceased mother continued to encourage him to go on when things had knocked him down.

Beverly: Do you feel that your mom ever communicates with you?

Andrew: All the time. Her and God. . . . My mama wasn't a quitter, so at points in my life that I want to give up, I can hear Mama saying, "Get up, boy. Get up. Okay, all right. That's over. Now get up. What you gonna do?" I can hear her plain say, "What you gonna do?" . . . I can hear Mama saying, "Boy, is you crazy?" I just can hear her and feel her. . . . Or "You didn't make up your bed. . . . I can hear, and especially like I said when I go through tough times, and when I feel lonely. Her and God. I can hear their saying, "You're all right. Get up. . . . You're all right. . . ." I think Mama knew she was getting older and, ". . . I ain't did nothing with my [life], but you got to do . . . something with your life. You gotta be true to your ministry. You gotta do it. You can't be none of them old fake preachers." And I can . . . hear her.

Rosalyn talked about not wanting to move from the house she had shared with her husband who had died, because she felt his protective presence there.

Rosalyn: I still live in the same house. And everybody asks me, most people that are widows, they say they have to move. They can no longer stay in the house. "Well, how do you feel?" And I say, "I feel like I have a whole house full of people. I'm surrounded." I don't feel afraid. And I just feel like his presence is still there.

Verna felt the presence of her deceased father at times when she was in need of great assistance.

Beverly: When do you experience your dad's presence the most?

Verna: Holidays, when families are around. . . . Certain church services. And when I'm in the pulpit. And the first time I did a funeral . . . I froze and couldn't talk. And he was sitting in the pulpit behind me, and he got up, and he came and he whispered in the back of my ear, "You can do this. The Lord is with you. You can do this." And so I always hear that in the pulpit, the Lord is with me; I can do this.

She talked about the most recent time she had seen him, and what she saw was a ghostly version of him, not the man she would have seen if he were still alive. And she also said that her mother saw him at the same time, at a time when her mother needed assistance and support.

Verna: I saw him (pause) last Monday. . . . It was him, but it was like a ghost. It was like a shadow. . . . We had just finished AIDS school, and Mother [walked] out. (pause) And he went directly behind . . . and I jumped like, "Boy! What's going on?" And so when I got in the car I says, "Mom, I have to tell you. I thought I saw Dad," and she said, "Yeah, he was there." And I says, "Well, why?" And she says, "'Cause I was scared." "'Cause you were scared of what?" She said, "I was scared of them mices in the bath when I was tryin' to go to the bathroom." (both laughing) No, I'm serious. She says, "I'm telling you. He was there." "Okay, well I saw him. But I don't want to scare you. And I don't want to bring up something that's going to upset you. . . . I know he was there."

Norma talked about her deceased mother being a protective presence. At first she felt abandoned when her mother died. But later she realized that her mother was still in contact with her, watching over her and guiding her.

Norma: It was like, "You don't have your Mama no more," no more. Just to call up and rant and rave to her. Or discuss career options or whatever, 'cause I could talk with her about anything, at any time about anyone, about my own feeling, whatever, and so I really felt like she just was gone. Then I realized that she really wasn't, and I have a lot of psychic experiences sometime with my people who are close to me. And I realized then that she was really still very much with me and watching over me and watching over my family, and guiding me still.

☐ Just a Presence

Not everyone had a sense of the deceased as a helpful presence. Some had more a sense of the deceased as a presence, in continuing contact with them but not necessarily warning them, helping them in time of danger, or supporting them. The situations of mere presence seem more like times of either being a companion or witnessing a significant family event. For example, Jane talked about her experience of her deceased husband.

Jane: I was sittin' in the livin' room one day and sound like I heard somebody say, ". . . Come in. Come down. I want you to see something on TV. Come in." It just sounded like his voice was there, and he was calling me (laughs). I got up and went in (laughing). . . . When I'm here by myself, I be talking to him. I look at his picture and kiss his picture. Once I get ready to go to bed, I kiss him goodnight. . . . When he first died, I could feel him being there. . . . Specially when I was in bed, just felt like he was in the bed with me, but he never talked.

Ron and Norma talked about feeling her father in their house at Christmas Eve.

Ron: We would feel him in the house. We could hear him. We'd be . . . saying, "Pop's here tonight." Every Christmas Eve, he would have the whole clan get together. And that first Christmas, that bathroom door, there was nobody in there, and we forgot his aftershave lotion was sitting on that back of the door (*Norma:* From when he had stayed here), and it fell off and broke.

Norma: And everybody said, "Okay! Okay, Dad." (chuckles) Yeah.

Ron: 'Cause we could smell him. (*Norma:* Yep)

Beverly: Yeah, and you weren't afraid or anything. . . .

Norma: Oh, no, not our family, no (laughs), no.

Norma also talked about both of her deceased parents being present at a family wedding.

Norma: I was teasing the kids the other night [that] I explained the whole wedding to Daddy and Mama. And [one daughter] said, "Now Mama, really, how?" I said, "No, they . . . were right there, and we were laughing and talking, and I was telling 'em all about the wedding, and they told me they were there." And I said it, and [one son] told me the same thing. He said, "I could tell Grandpa was there."

Unwelcome Presence

Not everyone who had a sense of presence of a deceased family member welcomed it. Loretta, who was quoted in chapter 12 as being afraid of meeting her deceased mother in heaven, was apprehensive about her mother's presence.

Beverly: Do you feel your mother ever communicated or talked with you?

Loretta: . . . One or two times. . . . When she does, it scares the crap out of me. . . . The imagery scares me. I guess I never felt like I ever did enough, and so I still carry that baggage of being a disappointment to her.

In another example of the presence of the deceased being unwelcome, Jo-Ellen talked about sensing the presence of her deceased son and not wanting to have anything to do with it.

Jo-Ellen: I was laying in bed . . . asleep, and I had this overwhelming feeling of his presence in the room. . . . I could feel the presence getting closer. Then it was like the end of my bed and on my, "What the heck is going on?" And I remember laying then on my pillow and I opened my eyes. . . . "He has no business being here. He's not alive. He's not alive." And I remember thinking, "He's not alive. So he couldn't really be here. So I'm not accepting this." And I went on back to sleep. And . . . once . . . I was in the kitchen washing dishes, and all of a sudden I felt this overwhelming presence of [my son]. But it wasn't like he was in the room. It was like he was in the attic. And it's like this presence that was just like wanting to draw me up to the attic and almost like a thought, like, "If you go up there he's gonna be standing at the top of the stairs." And literally there was this pull. I remember the struggle, because it's like the presence was so strong, but I was like, "He's dead. . . . If I do go up there and see his spirit, what's that gonna do for me? How's it gonna benefit me? I'm gonna be in worse shape (chuckling), because I can't have it."

☐ Conclusion

Most people who were interviewed talked about continuing contact with the deceased. As in studies of Euro-Americans, they talked about reunion in heaven, a sense of the presence of the deceased, communications to and from the deceased, or going to the cemetery to be in contact with the deceased. Because death as a homecoming is so common in African American religious ideology and because the spirit is important and real for many African Americans, we conjecture that a belief in reunion in heaven is a more common reality for grieving African Americans. Also, there may be more concreteness to that reunion for proportionately more African Americans than Euro-Americans, a reunion in which people will talk and laugh together and relate as they did on earth. Another conjecture is that because in a racist society people are so important to African Americans, it may be that the deceased is a protective presence more often for African Americans than Euro-Americans. African Americans do not necessarily lose the help and watchfulness of someone who has died.

14

Talking about It, Crying about It with Others

After the initial condolences and hugs, the food brought over, the visitation, the funeral, the burial, and the final round of condolences, grieving people are much more on their own. Their supporters and the other mourners have, for the most part, gone back to their daily routines. But often, over the weeks, months, and even years following the death a grieving person might be in great pain. Then what? Are others there with and for the person? Does the person even want the help of others?

☐ I Don't Talk about It with Anybody Because It Hurts

A few people said that they had talked to nobody about the death. One reason they gave was that talking about the death and their feelings hurt too much. Echoing what was said about being strong (chapter 12), another reason people gave for not talking with others was that they did not like to cry.

Beverly: Who do you talk with . . . about . . . [your stepfather's] death?

Franklin: Nobody.

Beverly: No one? Why is that?

Franklin: I don't like crying. And I cry. . . . Crying is not a big deal. I just don't like doing it.

Beverly: With whom have you talked the most about your mother's death?

Loretta: You. (both laugh)

Beverly: . . . Why is that? Why haven't you talked with anyone else about your mother's death?

Loretta: Just don't. I just don't. . . . I do an awful good job of avoiding me. . . . I don't talk about me.

Beverly: And the reason for that?

Loretta: Damn! To talk (chuckles) about me would be to open up an area of emotion, and I don't do emotions, all right? I can't allow myself to be emotional. . . . When I get emotional, or when I have these insecure feelings or something, I want someone to make me feel like it's gonna be all right. Okay? Just somebody like to hold me or to comfort me or to say, "You're gonna make it through this. It'll be okay." And since I don't have that component in my life, rather than to be upset about being emotional and whatever I was emotional on, and ticked that I'm missing a viable component in my life, I just don't let myself go there and feel that.

☐   Talking about It with Others

As has been reported in the literature, which is based largely or entirely on white grief (e.g., Rosenblatt, 2000a), the grief process, as many of the interviewees talked about it, is at times social.

"Just Being Able to Talk about It Helps a Lot"

The grieving person talks to others and receives listening, advice, comfort, and sympathy. Talking often helps one to develop narrative about the dying, the death, the person who died, and the aftermath of the death. Sometimes it helps to put the loss in the perspective of losses others talk about. Some people find that it even helps to talk with someone who scarcely knows what to say. Just telling the story can help, and sometimes it is especially helpful to tell an upbeat part of the story.

Willa: Some days I just will be kinda blue. It happened . . . four, five months ago. One day I just was, ooh, in a blue funk. And [my friend] could sense this. She said, "What's wrong?" I said, "I miss my mother." And she almost didn't know what to say. . . . I talked to her, and she can't empathize when she's never been through it. She can sympathize. And just talking to her, and being able to talk about my mother helps a lot. Some of the funny things that she (chuckles) used to do, like that graveyard jam. . . . My mother had a million of them. I can just see them out in some farmer's field eating ice cream, in the south, in the '40s! Oh. So . . . it happens every now and then. But not too often.

Some people do not think of themselves as telling a story so much as telling memories.

Beverly: With whom have you talked the most about [your son's] death?

Jo-Ellen: Oh, anybody who would listen (both laugh). No. No, I don't necessarily talk about his death as much as I talk about him. I know he's dead,
but when I talk about my other children, and they're grown, I still talk
about when they were kids. Well, I'm the same with [my son who died].
I still talk about when he was a kid.

Some people, especially women, found quite a few people with whom to talk.

Norma: I think that just talking about it a lot with my friends helped me a lot.
A good friend of mine she lost her mother, and she was talking about
how long she grieved her mother. . . . Years had went by and she still
had not dealt with it fully, and . . . she was really angry with her dying,
and so talked a lot. . . . I think that helps a lot, and talking with [my
husband].

Jane: I had a lot of friends, close friends, that would call me all the time, talk
to me. . . . My doctor, he was so nice. He really helped me a whole lot
too. . . . I could sit in his office and cry and talk to him as long as I want.
He didn't pressure for time, although he had other patients. . . . I went
to him two weeks ago, and he said, "You know what? You look so good
compared to the first time I saw you when your husband passed. . . . You
really came a long ways. . . ."

Beverly: Who do you talk the most to about his death?

Jane: Oh, one of my girl friends, one of my real close girl friends. I just talk
to her, and that helped a lot.

Perhaps reflecting on her own experiences, Patricia thought African Americans needed to be pushed to seek support, because other African Americans
will assume one does not need or want it if one does not ask.

Patricia: Sometimes black people, we don't sit down and talk about stuff. We
just assume we are, unless you let me know you need something, you're
okay with it.

"You Don't Understand"

Some people talked about social encounters that did not help. Echoing what
is in research on Euro-Americans (e.g., Rosenblatt, 2000a), several people

said it does not help for someone to say to a grieving person, "I know how you feel."

Jane: I hated for people to say to me, "I know how you feel." "You don't know how I feel inside." Don't nobody know how I feel but myself, so don't say that.

Sometimes a support relationship is not easy and tranquil. The other may offer words of advice and consolation that set off anger and pain. But still the relationship might be experienced as supportive. In fact, being able to express the anger and pain might be part of what is helpful.

Maya: My friend . . . would always talk to me and always give me words of encouragement, and he would say, "You are loved; you have to stop . . . hiding behind your son. . . . You will always love him and one day you'll get to see him, but . . . accept that you are loved even beyond him, so you can stop that." And I'm like, "You don't understand!" And he was letting me just yell . . . , "You don't understand. You haven't lost a kid, ya-ya-ya-ya. That was my boy. That was mine, mine, mine! That was something that I could truly call mine."

"It Sure Helps to Help Somebody Else"

Some people said that they found it helpful to support others, that in helping others they found self-affirmation and a sense of doing something worthwhile.

Charlotte: Take it off of yourself. Do for somebody else, listen to somebody else's difficulties. It doesn't mean yours are not important. But it sure helps to help somebody else do something when you are not doing well, or feeling well.

Elsa: As long as I'm helpin' someone else, I think that helps me.

But others said that it was hard for them to help others who were grieving because they could not rely on their own experiences to know what was going on with someone else.

Maya: You don't know what to say because each person grieves their feelings differently.

☐   Therapy/Counseling/Support Groups

A number of studies have shown that African Americans in need typically make less use of mental health services (all but emergency mental health services) than do Euro-Americans (Cooper-Patrick et al., 1999; Ho, Snowden,

Jerrell, & Nguyen, 1991; Neighbors, 1985; Owen, Goode, & Haley, 2001). One reason for this disparity, hooks (1993b) suggested, is that racism denies African Americans all sorts of services. Also, there is reason to believe that a white therapist would not understand or would not know how to deal with certain issues connected to being African American (Jones, 1991). So it is not surprising that aftercare services for the bereaved are less likely to be available in black communities (Barrett, 2003). Perhaps also, many African Americans may be averse to seeking help because it is inconsistent with the notion of being strong. Nonetheless, some of the people who were interviewed had turned to a psychologist, psychiatrist, therapist, counselor, or support group for help.

Jane: I missed him so much I got really depressed. So I went to my doctor, and he (sighs) suggested I go and talk to a psychology. . . . I went and talked to her for a good two months. I had appointment with her. And that helped me a whole lot, to talk to her, and just talk things out.

Some people had brought family members to professional help after a death. Elsa, for example, brought her grandchildren, the children of her son who was murdered, to grief counseling.

Elsa: When it first happened, all the kids were wetting the bed. And we finally got 'em through that. They went through grief counseling, got a very positive outlook of that.

Although some who went for professional help had good support from friends and family, Vickie saw professional help as something one turns to when one does not find adequate support among family, friends, and others around one.

Vickie: You need to feel what you feel when you feel it. And if you don't have a really good support system, you need to find yourself one. You might have to pay for somebody, or if you find a free clinic that has a service. . . .

Vickie said that her family did not approve of finding professional help, so she kept her visits to a psychologist a secret.

Beverly: Did you go see someone?

Vickie: Umhm. That helped a lot. That helped a lot. My sisters would have me committed if they knew.

Beverly: Oh, you're not supposed to see a therapist.

Vickie: You're not su-, unun, because they don't believe in that.

For Vickie, and no doubt other African Americans, it is desirable that the professional who is seen for help is black, a person who can understand the world in which they function and can understand their cultural issues. Also, given that many African Americans mistrust the medical system (Barrett, 1998, 2003; Smedley, Stith, & Nelson, 2003, pp. 135–136, 174–175), a key way to minimize the mistrust is to see an African American professional.

Vickie: I wanted the stranger [I turned to for help] to kind of look like me. So I'm sure, I can only imagine what they say when I call the medical line and say, "I want to talk to a black person, so you look in your little file and you find out who's black." And they were like, "Uh, well, uh." I said, "Oh, I know you got records." I said, "You speak about how you're going to do it and then you get back with me. Okay?" So that was my preference, 'cause I really didn't want to go talk to a white person. I was not going to go talk to a white person.

From another angle, what Vickie said about not wanting to see a white therapist was put in a larger context by Kenneth, who talked about his family's pattern of not trusting white people.

Kenneth: I think that the institutionalized racism and the system of slavery pressed upon us a survival technique of sharpening all your skills all the time. And never trust white folk. Of any circumstances and conditions, never trust them. And so that's how it has affected my family, and they don't trust them. They do not trust them.

From that perspective, Vickie was fortunate to find a black therapist, and she also felt fortunate that the therapy dealt with issues beyond grief. The help Vickie said that she received from her therapist was not only about the specifics of the death and grief. It was also about broader issues of her relationship with her mother, the person whose death she was grieving.

Vickie: I saw him . . . probably four to six months, every other week or so, which was really a big help. . . . I explained it to him. I said, "I never really thought I would be upset when my mother died. I thought, 'Oh, this will end a lot of things. We can move on.'" You know, logical thought. I never thought I would be all jumbled up on the inside. That never crossed my mind once, until it happened, because I was so ticked with her. . . . She could never be consistent. And there was always just so much flux around the house. You never knew what she was gonna say when you went out or how she was going to act. . . . There were some good things that she had done. But I never quite balance them with the rest of her. . . . I can remember trying to figure out why she would act that way. . . . In those days . . . mental illness was not something that you talked about. And that was not something people even acknowledged existed, especially in black families. People might be a little different, a little peculiar, a little eccentric, but you really didn't talk about it like a disease. . . . My father said the file said she was paranoid schizophrenic. My sister says that is *not* true, and I'm thinking, "How do you know? You didn't read the file." And now I realize part of it is a whole sense of denial. We don't discuss it; therefore it does not exist.

A benefit of grief support groups is that one finds that one is not the only person in the world struggling with loss issues, so one's experiences are normalized, and one can learn from what others who are in a similar situation have to say.

Maya: I finally . . . found a grieving group where you can go, and I find I'm not the only person (chuckling) that has gone through this. . . . It doesn't hurt as bad as it used to, I guess because I've been able to talk about it and get more of an understanding of why I'm hurting and why that pain is there, and I don't think that pain will ever leave. I think I'm at a point where I'm kind of somewhat healing after all this time.

Beverly: And what's helping the healing?

Maya: To listen to other people's story and to know that my child wasn't taken because male people didn't love [me]. I had to find that out (laughs). Because that was a very big issue with me.

Beverly: Did anyone in the group tell you that?

Maya: Yeah, the counselor. She was like, "Oh, honey, no. That's not, no that's not so." And she even suggested that I go and talk with the people who I felt had hurt me and that has helped. . . . I finally got a chance to talk to my biological father and actually told him how I felt, and he said, "It wasn't even like that." When I got to hear his side of the story, I was like, "Oh, my God. I've been loved all this time and didn't even know." And I was like, "Oh, so my son wasn't taken. . . ."

Beverly: Did all of these people in your group lose a child?

Maya: They all lost a child. Everybody at different stages in different way and it was all hard for us on Mother's Day.

Elsa: We started the [grief support group in our church]. . . . Most times people are going through emotions and feelings and they don't know what they're dealing with, and they think they're going crazy. Or they think nobody wants to hear it. Or somebody else is gonna perceive them as being crazy. And the point is that people need to know that their feelings are okay, and that they're normal. And they're not alone. And the support groups offer them the opportunity to talk out their feelings with others that are going through the same feelings and emotions. And gives them a chance to let it go and let it out. . . . Years ago I couldn't tell you anything about grief. . . . But now I can do it. I can listen. I know I can listen. . . . And that's the purpose. I have prayed before [my son] got killed, for the black men to quit killing each other. . . . What makes you so angry that you can take a life? Because you're mad about nothin', or a rumor. Ninety percent of our young black men are killed over rumors. Lies be goin' between gangs. Police lyin' between the gangs. . . . But if we can stop it before it gets to the rage, we know that you've probably been through a divorce. We probably know that your daddy beat your mama every day. We know that you probably got your lights and gas cut off at one point. . . . Water got shut off. You don't know if you lost your home or not. But it's okay, because you ain't alone (chuckles). You're not alone.

Normalizing grief experiences and learning that what one feels makes sense and is not out of line also could come through grief therapy.

Norma: I went and [saw] that one grief counselor lady. She was good. . . . Even prior to my sister [dying], one of my very best friends died. She just all of a sudden dropped dead. So it was just gettin' kinda be a little bit of much. . . . So I went and talked to this woman . . . and she was very good. . . . I really felt like she was just kind of confirming what I was going through was pretty natural, and nothing that I was way out of line. I mean, way, way somewhere else . . . where you shouldn't be.

☐ Conclusion

A few people said that they kept their feelings to themselves, but many had talked to others about their grief. Some had found it helpful. Some, particularly women, had talked with quite a few others. Not all would-be supporters were helpful. Echoing what can be heard from Euro-Americans, it could be particularly annoying to have someone say, "I know how you feel." Also echoing some Euro-Americans, some African Americans said it helped them to help others.

Some people found it helpful to go to a therapist, counselor, or support group. As with some Euro-Americans, they might keep it secret from family, and one kind of help they valued was "normalizing" their feelings and experiences by being helped to see how they were like others who were grieving similar losses.

One difference from Euro-Americans was that some people wanted an African American therapist or valued being in a support group with other African Americans. There was, for some, a sense that the life experience of African Americans and the personal, family, and community issues of loss were much easier to deal with in a relationship with an African American professional or other grieving African Americans.

Our Grief and Theirs:
African Americans Compare
Their Grief with Euro-American Grief

Often it seems that a part of grieving is an examination of identity, one's own identity, the identity of the deceased, and the identity of important others who are grieving that person's death. Almost by definition, identity is in part about how one differs from some people and is similar to others. When one looks at grief from that perspective, it would not be surprising that for some African Americans the examination of identity would include comparison of African Americans with Euro-Americans. The comparison might include how the two groups deal with death, including funeral rituals, the emotionality of grief, and the grief process (e.g., Perry, 1993). At one level, such comparison means that racist oppression links African Americans to Euro-Americans. At another level, it could mean that a part of resisting racist oppression is to resist forces aimed at trivializing or obliterating how African American individuals, families, and communities deal with life and death.

The people who were interviewed were asked about their perceptions of white grief and how it compares with African American grief. Living in a society in which African Americans are often ignored, demeaned, mistreated, and misunderstood by whites, African Americans have found it helpful, and at times crucial to their welfare and survival, to observe whites (Davis, 2000; hooks, 1992). That does not mean whites know they are being observed (hooks, 1992), nor does it mean African Americans observe whites in order to imitate them. But it does mean that in many areas of life African Americans will have acquired enough information about whites to get a sense of how, if at all, whites differ from African Americans, and one such area is grief.

A few of the 26 people who were interviewed were reluctant to generalize about white grief, including one or two people who felt that they lived in such a segregated world that they did not know how whites grieve. Most were willing to draw a comparison. And most of them said there were differences between African American and white grief.

☐ Whites Show Feelings Less or Feel Less

Consistent with what others have written (e.g., Holloway, 2002, pp. 154–156; McIlwain, 2003, pp. 81–84; Perry, 1993), a large majority of the people who were interviewed said that they thought whites typically showed feelings less or were less open and honest with their feelings or even felt a loss less strongly than an African American would. The following is a statement like many that were made. It points out that in the less overtly segregated North it has been easier for the interviewee to see white grief. She sees diversity in both the African American and the white community, but she sees much more emotional control early in grief for whites than for African Americans (despite what she and many other interviewees are quoted as saying in chapter 12 about African American efforts to be strong in grief). And from her point of view, the greater emotional expression of African Americans is a good thing because it helps with the grieving process.

Beverly: Do you think there's something different about how African Americans grieve in comparison to how whites grieve?

Barbara: . . . Down South, when I was growing up, because it was segregated, there wasn't the same kind of chance to know. . . . I don't even remember anybody white passing when I was growing up that we would have had any idea . . . how they grieved. But . . . [up North] the thing that I noticed . . . was that people weren't supposed to show their emotion. And it was something unsaid, but known. . . . It didn't even appear that they gave folks time enough to grieve. So I've always felt that they did it differently. . . . Individually there have been some people that were extremely sad about . . . passings. But still they're . . . kind of in that thing of not showing anybody. . . .

Beverly: I know there's no typical African American way of grieving, but if you had to describe grieving in the African American community, what would you say?

Barbara: A lot of loud crying. Fainting, and drinking to medicate the pain. Some arguing. "She loved me more!" It is multifaceted, the grieving. But basically, you remember when Mahalia sang in *Imitation of Life*. . . . Before then and up to a more recent point, the grieving was sing that sad song and everybody in the church is crying. That was a good feeling. 'Cause she sure enough sang that song. And it was *Precious Lord*. Somebody sing "Precious Lord," and everybody falling out. . . . For a lot of people, it was like a cleansing crying. It took away . . . that pain and the hurt . . . so that when they got done they were basically okay.

Others also saw white grief as controlled or private or maybe not even very deep.

Kenneth: They seem to be very private about that.

Calvin: There's a level of emotion that a white person I'm not sure can reach.

Verna: We can be animated and very vocal and very expressionistic in the way we grieve. . . . I've seen people fall on the casket, and drag them and we pull them off, and they got to kiss them for the last time, and "No, my Pookie ain't gone," so I'm just like, "Boy, when I [go to] those white funerals, we're out in an hour."

Charlotte: I think they may be more private. This [white] woman . . . when her mother died, I didn't find out until later.

Willa: I think African Americans are more open with their grief. . . . People (crying sounds:) "oh-huh-huh-huh." And I think whites feel like they have to be controlled. . . . Tears are very healing. Let' em flow. . . . I think that we do tend to be more open in our grief.

Jane: Afro-American people grieve different than other people. . . . We celebrate, we celebrate. They don't. They don't cry. They don't let it all out. We do. Like we had my husband's funeral at the church, and the people was crying and everything. And most of the people who go to my church is white. They'd never seen a funeral like that. That was the first time they had ever seen a funeral that people cried and played the kind of music we played. And how we celebrate after it's over with. We have a big dinner. . . . We had all of this food, soul food. Everybody came back from the cemetery, and we celebrated. They don't. They don't cry. They don't let it out at they funeral. We do, and it makes us feel better.

Beverly: So after you cry it's over?

Jane: No, it's not over. Just, once you cry the hurt part, it's over for that time, but you know you're [gonna cry] again.

Clyde: I think we put on more of an exhibition. . . . We grieve verbally. We don't hold it in. . . . And I think we talk to people when they die. . . .

Beverly: Did that happen at your mother's funeral?

Clyde: I think some of that did. . . . I saw it more so with my second cousin and my aunt and some of the older members of the family, and how they reacted to the death and what they did during the funeral. . . . They yelled and screamed and then they talked to her like she was alive and right there, the spirit was there.

Marcia: I don't know if white folks grieve. . . . They do, but they don't show it. I think they internalize. . . . The European Americans that have attended funerals of African Americans almost seem to be, "Oh, gosh, I've never been to such an uplifting, moving, spirit-filled worship. . . ." There just seems to be such *distance,* and I don't know what that's about. . . . It's kind of sad. Their funerals are solemn. If you cry, "Don't cry about it. . . . I've never seen a usher come over to give a tissue. . . . If children cry, they're immediately taken out. Families don't necessarily sit together. I've never seen a reviewal or a processional. . . . It just seems cold, and I'm really saddened, 'cause I'm . . . thinking "How do they grieve?" I know they grieve; they must grieve privately.

The emotional control that many African American interviewees saw in grieving whites does not mean that the interviewees are unaware of their own efforts to "be strong" in grief (see chapter 12). Many interviewees were aware that they and other African Americans worked at being strong in ways that limited the expression of grief feelings, particularly in front of others (Smith, 2002). But they still saw whites as more controlled or feeling less.

We said in chapter 4 that we thought African Americans preferred open casket funerals. One woman thought that whites were less inclined to have open casket funerals because seeing a dead body would make it harder for them to control emotions.

Toni: We were Presbyterian; my grandmother belonged to that church. . . . It was an all-white church, and so at that time the trend in funerals, which is still true for Presbyterians, is that you buried the people first, so there's no open casket, 'cause white folk don't want to feel their grief. They don't want to see no dead bodies.

She also talked about white people being uncomfortable with the longer, more expressive funerals that are frequent in the African American community (see McIlwain, 2003, pp. 164–165 for corroborating comments about the duration of black and white funerals). For Toni, a key illustration of the difference between racial groups in funeral duration was what happened at a nationally televised funeral.

Toni: I can remember watching Daddy King's funeral on television, and who was the Vice President? . . . Whoever the white man was, 'course was on the dais, and Jesse Jackson was speaking. And whoever it was, was very uncomfortable 'cause it was taking all day for us to bury Daddy King (both laugh). And Jesse turned to him, and said, I'll never forget this because it just cracked me up but it was so true. He said, "Mr. Vice

President . . . I see you're uncomfortable, but we're gonna take our time. That's how we do it. This was our father, and he was everybody's father here, and so we are going to remember him till we get tired. So you just need to sit down and relax." Because the little white man was . . . like, "When are they getting over right now? Good Lord, what can they say?" We have traditionally given ourselves permission to take the time to grieve, even while we worked, so it was okay to cry. It was okay particularly in, not in our high church, but in the primitive churches. It was all right to weep and to wail.

Len was one of two people who talked about the difference between African Americans' emotionality at funerals and white emotionality, as reflecting patterns that were brought from Africa.

Len: I think there is a difference, even though it may be not really that . . . obvious. . . . But there is . . . a code of conduct. . . . There's a time . . . when you're supposed to mourn, and even I think one of the young guys said this to you . . . that they feel like they had to cry. . . . During a funeral there's times when it's almost like if you had a list of activities or an agenda . . . it'd be like, "Okay, more!" (laughs). "Mother cry." (chuckling) Or, "Father yell!" (chuckling) And I think that is wrapped up in our religious traditions. . . . And probably goes deeper than that. . . . I'm thinkin' it does have a African connection. I think there are some West African traditions that have been integrated into who we are as African Americans. . . . There's that whole thing about (chuckling), for the brothers who ain't here, libations and so forth. . . . I think in our grief process it gives you the *right* to speak about a person in a way that if they were alive you would never speak about them. . . . I hear young brothers who quote "lost a homey" talk about "I loved him." Now when that brother was alive you'd never say, "I love my homey. . . ." So our grieving process allows us, traditionally, to express and say words and do things that we're [not] allowed in any other scene to do. . . . I think that's one way that we grieve differently.

Building on his comment about pressure in the African American community to observe mourning decorum, he thought that not all the emotionality of such grief necessarily comes from deep, heartfelt places.

Len: In our community . . . there is a period of time that you're supposed to grieve, even though also traditionally, you always had your friends saying, "You need to get out there and . . . enjoy life. . . ." We say that, but I think . . . we want to see that grieving, because it affirms in our own sense that . . . look how much they loved this person. So as long as you hang your head low, and go around like you're broken and sad . . . people feel at ease about that. But as soon as you stop doing that, people feel uncomfortable with you, and I sensed some of that. As long as I was really a broken husband, then . . . it was kinda okay . . . but once I started moving on . . . with life . . . , "He's too busy; he's too happy . . . he's in denial; he's not really dealin' with it. . . ." Versus for me it was, "No, I grieved when [my wife] went through her thing. That was my biggest grief, watchin' her suffer." But once that ended, I took off the sackcloth.

Another person who said that African Americans sometimes respond to the demands of mourning decorum with grief that is not necessarily deeply felt, also said that African Americans grieve at a deeper emotional level than do whites.

Jo-Ellen: I think we're very emotional. We need to feel it. . . . We need to move from where we're at emotionally to a place of acceptance, and a place where we can actually be at peace with it. So we need to feel the anger. . . . I don't think that [whites] are on the same emotional level. . . . Now I think we African Americans sometimes think we're supposed to really put on a show. Lots of people almost jump in the coffin, and "Get out of there" (both laugh). Honestly, I've seen people just like, if they didn't just scream and holler, they felt like that they didn't grieve. . . . I've seen people upset at funerals and they didn't even know the person. . . . So I think we believe we have to be emotional.

☐ Emotional Difference in the Context of Racism

Some people saw the differences between the two groups in emotional expression at a death as connected to what African Americans have had to go through at the hands of whites. It is as though whites have steeled themselves to pain (the pain of others and their own pain about what they have done to others).

Patricia: There are some things that I feel that whites can't understand when it comes to some of the suffering that black people have experienced. . . . I think if they could understand more we wouldn't have as many problems trying to convince why affirmative action is a fair thing, or why blacks should be able to borrow loans. . . . I can't judge that people don't grieve the same, but I just think . . . whites and blacks express themselves differently. . . . When I was younger I used to almost wonder if white people had a different God than black people, 'cause it was like, how can they have the same God and treat, and it's not to say that blacks don't mistreat people, but to treat people differently because of their race. . . . I was thinking if they had the same God they would like us. And so . . . I used to think, "Do they relate to God differently?" 'Cause the way we express and sing, shout, do this and do that. Used to hear more black people acknowledging God in their regular daily conversations. . . . So . . . when it comes to grief . . . I used to almost . . . feel that . . . white people didn't feel as deeply about things. It almost felt like their feelings kind of like were on the surface. They can always just deal with 'em, and put them into like an academic form or intellectualize them . . . and then just kind of move on. . . . They seem to express their emotions differently, and it doesn't mean that it's right or wrong. But from my perspective I thought the more you express yourself, the deeper you feel. Or the more you are feeling. And so I used to wonder if things could bounce off them, like racism and slavery. . . . If you could just do stuff like that, maybe you couldn't feel as deeply or feel as much. . . . Comedians like to make jokes about (chuckles) how fast whites buried their people compared to blacks, and it's almost like, "okay" (snaps her fingers). They just take care of business. . . . I would imagine they hurt just as much as we hurt; they regret losing someone just as much as we do, because it's just like even when it comes to nursing homes. It just seems like whites can just quickly say, "We're going to have to place in a nursing home." But blacks go through the struggle of trying to keep them at home, bring the bed in there. . . . This doesn't mean everybody, but something seems different to me, and then I want to trace it further and say, "Are people able to be more compassionate . . . when they've gone through certain experiences that eventually . . . lead you closer to God? . . ." I don't think that's a Christian thing to even think that. . . . But I'm just saying . . . there are certain things that you experience that cause you to relate to people differently. . . . It's just like I think blacks relate probably more open to gays and people of other races or poor, because we know what it feels like to not have.

Elsa: They make the funerals quick and short. . . . If you don't talk about it, it's gonna be okay. And if you don't think about it. . . . Black families don't like to discuss it because it hurts. . . . We perceive (chuckles), this is sad, but we perceive [white people] not to really have that kind of feeling (laughs). . . . I think it goes back [to] the way they treated us they couldn't have had feelings. But in a way I think it hurts them more, and they hide it more. I think they hide it more than we do, because their suicidal rate's higher than . . . ours. We see what they want us to see, and they see in us what they want to see, broke down and hurt. And that broke down and hurt they don't show. Or it comes out in suicide.

Others who saw the emotionality difference as rooted in the history of white treatment of African Americans, emphasized how much more important family and other people are to African Americans. And it makes sense that greater emotionality after a death could be related to the crucial importance of relationships for African Americans. Much goes on to disrupt African American relationships, and the close relationships an African American has may represent, on the average, proportionately more of the capital an

African American individual or family has than what a Euro-American has (cf. Hines, 1986, 1991; Tully, 1999). In difficult situations and with few other resources, a person must rely very heavily on other people. And when one of those people dies, it hurts enormously. In a sense, the argument is that because African Americans have typically lived in much more difficult situations than whites, they may grieve their dead more intensely.

From another perspective, Hill (1997) argued that African Americans are relatively likely to be involved in caregiving for family members who are very sick (see also, Owen, Goode, & Haley, 2001), and they are also relatively likely to say that the caregiving is a good thing rather than onerous. Perhaps that kind of involvement in caregiving and that valuing of it is entangled in the grieving process following the death of a person one cared for. On the one hand, caregivers may feel less guilt and feel more as though they did what they could, and that may in some ways ease their initial grieving. On the other hand, the fact that they were involved in caregiving may make grief more intense, because the person who died was more entangled in their daily life and more a part of their identity.

Whatever the underlying factors, many people talked about African American emotional expression in grief being more open, intense, and authentic than white emotional expression.

Gwen: I think we're very honest with our feelings, and I don't think they are. You don't go to a funeral and see them whooping and hollering. . . . We . . . grieve differently. We're honest about how we feel. I don't think white people have ever been honest about their feelings. I don't think they know how to. I have a few friends that are white, and we've talked about a lot of things. And they can't comprehend our emotions, and I can't comprehend theirs. How do you not speak to your mother for 10 years? You've been angry with your mother and you don't speak; that's not a black thing. We gonna get mad, and we may never come back and say, "I'm sorry." But you are not gonna stop talking and seeing people because you are angry. Those things just kinda subside. . . . They subside with us, and they don't with them. . . . We are different. And thank God we're different. . . . Because you were brought from over there, and away from everything familiar to you, and forced to do what was unfamiliar to you, foreign as foreign could be to you, that makes us different. We appreciate family, because you had to then make a family. . . . You might have been the only person on that boat from your particular family, so you had to make a family. And we make families (laughs). "How many people is in your family really?" (both laugh) "Well, it's just me and my four kids, and my six grandkids." "I thought you said you had 20?" "Yeah, I do" (laughing). But biologically I have only six, and the rest of them are there and they belong (laughs). So, yeah, we are much different from them. . . . Religiously I watch them all the time, and I am so amazed.

They can just sit with no emotions. The man is preaching himself crazy. We are sitting there saying, "Amen!" (Here she sits staring with a blank look) That's them (both laugh). . . . I've watched us, and I've watched them, and, no, we don't do anything the same way. And I don't know why it's different today. I understood back when they were bringing the slaves here, there was that difference, but today because they say they're moving to a common bond. (Snorts) There is still a big difference in how blacks do things and how whites do things. . . . They stifle. And I think that's how we have learned, those of us that do that, we have learned to stifle because that's what they've taught us. But we only stifle to a point. (chuckles) We don't stifle totally. Sometimes when I've gone to some funerals that were white (pause), you can't always see hurt in their faces. And I'm thinking to myself, "Lord, (pause) that can't be me." I'm an emotional person, so you're gonna know what I feel. . . . So, yeah, I think that we're different when we . . . grieve.

Calvin: I think we're a little more dependent on one another in that the common struggles that we face, you know, wives comforting husbands who didn't get promotions, parents lamenting children who got a prison sentence, red lining. . . . So we're used to consoling one another and having a huddle every day or once a week and say, "Let's go back out there and fight. . . . If you have a bad day, I'll lick your wounds. If I have a bad day, you'll lick my wounds." It's like us against them. And I think that comes out in the grieving process, whereas I think with European Americans, that not having to worry about certain things that other races have to, I know I'm treading on some heavy ground here, but maybe in your home you haven't really experienced the degree of love that we have. I love my son. I pray for my son, because I know because he's black and articulate and if he gets a good job and can drive a nice car that he's going to be pulled over just because of that.

Maya talked about the racial difference partly being that African American grief includes anger and sorrow at what an African American who died had to go through because of white racism.

Maya: I guess I look at it in a way that if things had 've been fair, I wouldn't be so angry. . . . You know you have a lot of obstacles because of your skin color. I'd say it like that, and that a lot of times even though society has gotten a little better, you still have your prejudices in the workplace, in life, period. And I'm in a group and I am the only black, and my grief and the way that I do things is totally different (laughing) from theirs, but we only connect in the fact of the loss part. . . . White people don't, they have their fathers and mothers, whatever, but being a . . . young black girl and going through the things that I've grown up with and things that I know that happened in our families and that don't necessarily happen in theirs, and I don't know how to explain it. It's just, it's a big difference. It's a big difference.

Charlotte, who is quoted earlier in this chapter as saying that white people seem more private in their grieving, seemed also to say that it was possible for an African American to stuff grief feelings. She noted that as a child her dealing with racism took so much energy and focus that it got in the way of her grieving her mother's death.

Charlotte: This culture gives us so many other things to deal with that, hell, sometimes you can't even go through the grief process. My mother died, but I was battling the system. . . . I was in separate but equal . . . in terms of the very school I was in. This little complex they built to bus all these black kids to, as opposed to letting us go to the schools in our neighborhood. To me that was a . . . psychological burden. I can remember consciously knowing that I was not prepared to go on in the world, because I knew I had been ill-educated. . . . If you went to separate but equal, and if when you got your books they came from after white children got 'em, then, hell, you couldn't possible be prepared. If you in a lab and you don't have what you need in the lab, if you've got a math teacher and she's drunk, you know you're not prepared. And I remember feeling anxious about it. That was something the system put in place, the system put me, a child of tax-paying veterans, put me in that position. The system impacts the process. You don't even got a chance to grieve. It interferes with the natural process. You better (chuckles) get up from there and do what you need to do. I don't think you can wipe that out. I think that's a major component. And someone else might say, "Well, that's life." Wait a minute now. A white child ain't going through that that way. Don't tell me that's life.

On the other hand, Loretta said that under slavery and postslavery domination, African Americans were robbed of the identity that was the foundation for grieving. And they also, while enslaved, had to learn to suppress their emotional expression. Whites would not allow grieving to get in the way of work. Or whites would use African American expressions of grief as a source of knowledge of how to hurt African Americans more effectively. Loretta also thought that the demands of slave and postslave work shaped African American mourning customs in that African Americans were only allowed to grieve on the Sabbath.

Loretta: We have never really been allowed as African Americans to do that whole [grief] process. . . . In Africa we were able to mourn the loss and to grieve. But once we entered the ship and came across the ocean, we were stripped of that right. . . . When we came to . . . this country, we lost our identity, and when you don't have an identity you can't associate the grief process. . . . My great, great, great grandmother was sold . . . to a man in Mississippi, and she was allowed out of her six children to take three with her. . . . Was she allowed to grieve the loss of her husband and her other three children? No. . . . I went to the . . . place that my father was born and . . . recalled listening as a child to the white family talk about my grandmother delivering children in the field, and what a strong, sturdy worker she was, and feeling that anger. . . . One of those babies were my father. Okay? You learn to be strong. You don't grieve. You look at our tradition. We have funerals on weekends, because those are the days back in slavery that we were allowed to bury our dead. Because we couldn't take a day off from the fields to have a service during the week. And definitely you weren't allowed to cry and to mourn. And we still carry that. . . . We had to be [strong]. . . . I was my grandmother in that field. I am *her*. . . . If she could not take a day off to bear a child, who would also work in that same daggum sugarcane field, you talk about strong, then who am I to be so weak that I have to cry . . . ? That's the way we have been conditioned to be. . . . We weren't allowed to take the three days to cry, mourn, and sit up in the house and cry. . . . That's why . . . when we want to cry, we can't. . . . Massah can't see us cry, 'cause then massah will think we're weak. And it's just a whole mental mindset that has been handed down from generation to generation. . . . My great grandmother on my mother's side died at 134 years old. I was 16. She had the chain marks on her back where she was beaten. She didn't cry. You don't cry, because cryin' is a weakness, and when a white man sees that you are weak, you are now subject to that white man. So now we don't mourn. We don't cry. . . . I would never cry. And then you think about what is there to cry for, because someone passed on. They're away from this misery. This is the hell they ain't to be in no more. So why cry? Whatever the next phase is, it's got to be better than this phase. And hopefully in that phase there's a bit of equality, 'cause there sure wasn't any in this one.

Barbara said that racist limitation of African American grieving continues. She talked about white police and hospital officials being so alarmed at African American outpouring of grief that they try to suppress it.

Barbara: Remember when the young African man got shot off of West Broadway. His family, their grieving is very demonstrative, right then and there. And the police officers did not know how to handle it. "You better quiet down." Instead of knowing this person is grieving, and it's at the height, so you're telling somebody to quiet down, and they ended up arresting the person. (*Beverly:* Because they were grieving too loud.) Right. And they can do that. They can. If some young man gets shot and kins and family are down at the hospital, the hospital staff gets nervous. "Call the police." And so then here you are in pain, and you've got to figure out a way to clamp this down so that you won't go to jail. Or if you want to grieve, you can't, because you gotta try and pull everybody together so that nobody goes to jail because they're hurting. So that's that racism part. It's where folks don't know what to do, don't know how to treat it. They act like there's something wrong with you because you're hurt that somebody's gone.

☐ Racism May Be Making Some African Americans More Like Whites

A few people who were interviewed thought the differences between African Americans and whites were not as clear as in the past. Toni thought that the difference in emotionality was disappearing because more African Americans have come to accept the white notion that emotionality is not good.

Toni: Martin Luther King's funeral. . . . My parents made us sit and watch it, because this was a time for national community grief. We all grieved his death. . . . I remember Mahalia Jackson singing *Precious Lord,* and she had on a yellow and red striped suit, and she came out of the hospital to do it. . . . She was told not to leave the hospital 'cause she would risk a heart attack. And she said, "You don't understand; Martin is dead." And so grief for us was communal; it was not individual. It was a communal event, and so we had people leaving hospitals and whatever, and it wasn't just about Martin; it was about the community. . . . Grief was communal, and it was shared. Now we still had to work 'cause of our economy and who we were, but we worked it through, and it was okay. Not now. . . . We have taken on our oppressor's oppression of emotion. . . . We have bought the lie . . . that the intellect is the highest order, and feelings are the lower order. And so if you tap into your feelings that means you're lower. . . . So as we've tried to escape that definition that's oppressive to us, we lost our gift.

☐ Conclusion

With the exception of a few people who said they did not know any white people well enough to compare African American grief with white grief, almost everyone who was interviewed was willing to make the comparison and could make it with what seemed like confidence. Despite what many of the interviewees said about the importance to African Americans of being strong in grief, most said that it was whites, not African Americans, who show feelings less or who have less deep and intense feelings to show. Some readers might take what interviewees had to say (and the corroborating views of various scholarly observers) about differences between racial groups in grieving as stereotyping, sad evidence that stereotypes occur on both sides of the racial divide. But we think it would be respectful and useful not to dismiss the allegations of difference as stereotyping. Rather, we urge readers to explore the ways in which what interviewees and various scholars have said might be based on experience, and might have a validity that says something about racial group differences in overt grieving, and about the ways that past and current racial group relationships might be related to those differences.

As the people who were interviewed speculated about the difference, some said that white people are impatient with or puzzled by the emotionality of grieving African Americans, because whites prefer brief funerals and closed caskets. Although two people thought that the difference was partly about patterns that came with the Africans who were brought here as slaves, far more thought the difference was about white people needing to distance feelings in order to do what they did to others; for example, what they did via slavery, Jim Crow laws, and contemporary expressions of racism and discrimination.

Another explanation of what many interviewees saw as a difference between groups in grieving was that in a racist society those who are supportive and helpful are extraordinarily important to African Americans. To lose anyone who is there for one in a racist world is quite a blow. Whites, on the average, do not need as much as African Americans to rely on others that way, and so on the average they are not hit as hard by a loss of someone close to them.

Another explanation for the difference was that relatively often African Americans are involved in caring for their very ill family members, so they are closer to them when they die. And still another perspective was that African Americans grieve more intensely because they know how rough racism has made the life of the deceased.

On the other hand, some people talked about factors that undermined and blunted African American grieving, making it more like white grieving. Included in these factors were the demands of living in a racist society, the demands of white police and hospital officials who are uncomfortable with strong expressions of grief from African Americans, and the influence of white society on some African Americans.

16
CHAPTER

Understanding
African American Grief

☐ African American Grief Is and Is Not Like White Grief

Judging by what the people who were interviewed had to say, African American grief seems very much like Euro-American grief. And yet, as we point out throughout this book, there are what seem to us to be substantial differences and also differences that are subtle but still real and important. These differences suggest that if all one knew about grief was from experience with and research about Euro-Americans, one might be ill prepared to understand, empathize with, support, or help a grieving African American. To a large extent, the differences are linked to past and present racism and economic disadvantage and to distinctive aspects of African American culture(s). So to be supportive and helpful to a bereaved African American, it would be best to be attuned to and knowledgeable about racism in the United States and also to be broadly familiar with and knowledgeable about African American culture(s).

Although Barrett (1993, 1995, 1998) and others (Devore, 1990; Herskovits, 1958; Holloway, 2002) have made a strong case for the carryover of West African cultural institutions into contemporary African American grieving, almost no interviewee mentioned such carryover, and the two who did had little to say about it. One, Clyde, is quoted in the Introduction about the similarities he saw between West African and African American funerals, including forms of emotional expression, speaking in tongues, and funerals having the character of revivals. Another, Len, is quoted in chapter 15 about West African patterns being represented in contemporary African American funerals in the libations to the brothers not present and in certain forms of verbal intimacy at funerals. We do not doubt that there are carryovers of cultural patterns from West Africa into contemporary African American rituals when a death has occurred. But with interviewees saying so little about it, we have no basis in this report, based as it is on interview data, for addressing the carryover. On the other hand, the voices of the 26 people interviewed fill this book with aspects of African American culture. They refer to distinctively African American music, religious institutions, community life, values, culturally meaningful historical events and processes, foods, historically important and contemporary leaders, writings, and much else. Many quotes offer aspects of African American speech patterns—not only pronunciation, usage, and patterns of emphasis, but also metaphors, grammatical forms, and idioms. A person who was unfamiliar with African American culture could conceivably have a great deal of difficulty understanding important aspects of what a bereaved African American had to say.

☐ Cultural Grief and the Pileup of Losses

Some interviewees indicated that they and African Americans in general struggle with losses related to centuries of racism, discrimination, and oppression. This is a perspective that can be found in many writings about African American life (e.g., Brice, 1999, pp. 3–4; Burke, 1984; Cooper-Lewter, 1999; Holloway, 2002; W. R. Jones, 1998, pp. 21–22; Martin & Martin, 1995; Rosenblatt & Tubbs, 1998; St. Jean & Feagin, 2000). Perhaps the strongest allusions to cultural grief in the interview quotes include remarks by Kenneth quoted in the introductory chapter and in chapter 14, and remarks by Loretta quoted in chapter 15.

If one grants that there is such a thing as cultural grief it would then come as no surprise to one if some African Americans who are grieving a death are, at the same time, dealing with grief connected to racist oppression experienced by self, the deceased, the family, and all African Americans both recently and in the past; that is, dealing with cultural grief. It would also come as no surprise if an African American were grieving about losses in general, not about the death of any particular person.

☐ Grief Therapy/Support for African Americans

Because the grief of African Americans is often entangled with issues of racism and discrimination, therapy and support for grieving African Americans must be sensitive to these issues. A practitioner who is not well grounded in dealing with racism and discrimination in the lives of African Americans (and in the self of the practitioner) could be unhelpful or even hurtful to grieving African Americans.

Although many programs for training therapists and support group leaders seem to imply that they provide expertise in working with all who need therapy or group support, we believe that they often do not move beyond the rudimentary level in dealing with issues of race, class, racism, discrimination, and related matters. But even if these programs moved beyond the rudimentary level, some African Americans would say that it is impossible for a Euro-American to work sensitively and effectively with a grieving African American. At the very least, a Euro-American who hopes to work with African Americans needs to learn to escape the limits of what some people call "whiteness" (e.g., Nakayama & Martin, 1999). That would include escaping from obliviousness to white privilege and to racism, discrimination, and economic disadvantage in the lives of African Americans. It would include getting past stereotypes and mass media images of African Americans. It would include confronting one's own complicity in the racial system, and the ways one benefits from that system.

It is also important for a therapist who is not knowledgeable about African American culture(s) to become knowledgeable. One clinical training approach that can help white therapists to be more knowledgeable about African American culture(s) has been described by Jones and Block (1984). They talk about training clinical and counseling psychologists, particularly those who are white and lacking knowledge of African American culture, to work with African American clients using the TRIOS model. It is a model that sensitizes the therapist to understand, appreciate, and value important elements of the African American cultural milieu, time, rhythm, improvisation, oral communication, and spirituality.

A related matter is that a grieving African American in a support group may not be well served by being in a group with Euro-Americans. Will those who are Euro-American understand and sympathize with feelings and narratives related to issues of racism and discrimination? Will they even tolerate words that address racism and discrimination, or will they engage in something like defensive denial? It would take an especially sensitive and skillful support group leader to facilitate a group in which African Americans, who are trying to deal with heavy issues of grief, find themselves also having to deal with a discounting of the effects of racism and discrimination being directed at them from other support group members. This is, no doubt, part of what underlies the phenomenon described by Johnson-Moore and Phillips (1994), that African Americans are reluctant to participate in grief support groups out of fear of racism and discrimination by white participants and organizers.

Although grief support programs are less likely to be located in African American communities (Meagher & Bell, 1993), grief support groups that are provided by African American churches and other institutions serving the African American community might be especially helpful and draw substantial numbers of African American participants.

☐ African American Diversity

The research reported in this book was not organized to probe for systemic differences in grieving among African Americans differing in social class, religion, spirituality, cultural identification, or in other ways. There are certainly reasons to expect such differences. For example, Black and Rubinstein (1998–1999), suggested a pattern for grieving African Americans who are in deep poverty distancing questions about causes, perpetrators, and God as they relate to violent or drug-related deaths. Or, to take another example, Lee (1995) wrote about smiles and laughter among inner city African American children as a mask for explosive anger and unresolved grief. Or, to take another example, Barrett (1998) and Pleck (2000) wrote about how as African Americans move into the middle class, their funeral services may move toward what is common in white funeral services in terms of the expression of emotion, duration of ceremonies, formality, and the absence of a social gathering afterward. Within the limitations of our study, we have tried to speak to aspects of the diversity of the people who were interviewed and the much greater diversity of the 36 million other African Americans. It would be unfortunate for the outcome of this research to be a set of "facts" or generalizations that would be assumed to apply to all African Americans (see a similar point made by Gunaratnam, 1997, writing about blacks and other minority groups in Great Britain). Respectful, knowledgeable support of African Americans who are grieving will always require attention to the uniqueness of each individual, situation, and community. Still, it is hoped that this research will help to sharpen the focus on African American grief, while undermining the assumption that all that need be learned about African American grief can be acquired by studying grieving Euro-Americans.

☐ Revising How We Think about Grief

We do not think, from what we have learned from the 26 interviewees, that theories of grief dealing with Euro-Americans have to be abandoned in order to understand and help grieving African Americans. We think there were the same basic grief processes in African Americans that have been described in largely white populations. However, we think theories of grief need to take into account the sociological location of people and to make room for the effects of that location in grief. It is partly a matter of community and cultural ideas about how to grieve. But it is mostly that when groups differ in their location in the social class and racial caste systems, they differ in the conditions of loss, the meanings given to loss, the economic and social resources for dealing with loss, what it is they grieve, and much else. From this perspective, the experiences of many African Americans are so different from what is typical of Euro-Americans that we would never know about or understand African American grief if we simply generalized from white grief. For African Americans, a death may have different familial and economic consequences, may bring different feelings, and may lead to different narratives.

These differences would not be news to many African Americans, but for many Euro-Americans they may be. Just as in other areas of life, many Euro-Americans may ignore, misperceive, or deny the experiences of African Americans (e.g., hooks, 1992, McIntosh, 1988; Moon, 1999; Rosenblatt, Karis, & Powell, 1995; van Dijk, 1992; Zane, 1997). Euro-Americans may think discrimination has ended, that any African American can get ahead who wants to, that affirmative action has succeeded or is even an unfair advantage to African Americans. They may blame such problems as crime, drugs, poverty, and premature deaths in African American communities on the personal defects of African Americans or their culture. They may be oblivious to the experiences of African Americans, even to experiences such as racial profiling that have received an enormous amount of attention in the mass media. Ignorance, denial, and obliviousness would, of course, guarantee that a white person will not understand African American life or African American grief.

We think that grief researchers, grief counselors, and others who work with grieving people must expand their understanding of the people with whom they work. They must be willing to ask about experiences of racism and discrimination in the life of the grieving person and the life of the deceased. They must be open to the economic, familial, community, psychological, and spiritual impact of racism and discrimination, and how those impacts are entangled in grief. Focusing only on grief and not the societal context of loss and grief for African Americans and others will make for very limited understanding and help.

We also think that it is crucial that the United States be understood not as a homogenous society but as the location of many different cultures, with many different ways of understanding and dealing with dying, death, and grief. Rather than assume that everyone shares a common culture when it comes to loss, we think those who work with grieving people need to assume that they have to learn about a grieving person's cultural ways of dealing with dying, death, and grief.

At another level, what we have learned says that those who care about grieving people need to care about the ways that the United States is racist and discriminatory. Until African American life expectancy has moved up to the level of Euro-American life expectancy, until African Americans stop feeling that deaths in their community are caused by racism and discrimination, until the economic situation of African Americans and Euro-Americans is identical, and until African Americans no longer experience racism and discrimination, those who are compassionate about grief need to be compassionately interested in ending racism and discrimination. It is an act of support for all current and future grieving African Americans for Euro-Americans to work hard to end racism and discrimination.

APPENDIX

The People Who Were Interviewed and the Interview Guide

☐ People Who Were Interviewed

Andrew age 50, lost his mother
Angela age 30, lost her father
Barbara age 56, lost her mother
Calvin age 48, lost his mother
Charlotte age 50, lost her mother
Clyde age 47, lost his mother
Cynthia "older than 40," lost her mother
Elsa age 54, lost her adult son
Evelyn age 76, lost her adult son
Franklin age 58, lost his stepfather and sister
Gwen age 57, lost her 4-year-old son
Jane age 51, lost her husband
Jo-Ellen age 54, lost her 3-year old-son
Kenneth age 50, lost his grandfather
Len age 43, lost his first wife
Loretta age 47, lost her mother
Marcia age 51, lost her uncle
Maya age 32, lost her son (stillbirth)
Norma age 53, lost her mother, father, and sister
Patricia age 48, lost her mother
Ron age 54, lost his mother-in-law and father-in-law
Rosalyn age 61, lost her husband
Toni age 48, lost her grandmother
Verna age 51, lost her mother and father
Vickie age 40, lost her mother
Willa age 47, lost her mother

☐ The Interview Guide

Respondent(s)—name, gender, age, years of schooling, occupation, relationship to each other; is respondent from Twin Cities or somewhere else (and if from somewhere else, how long here?)

Other household members—name, gender, age, years of schooling, occupation, relationship to respondent(s)

Who else do you consider close family? [Note: Family is how the interviewee defines family.]—name, gender, age, relationship to respondent(s), how far away do they live

I. The Death

Who is the person whose death is the focus of the interview? (It can be any person you knew personally and whose death affected you strongly.) When was the death? How old was the person? How was the person connected to you?

Tell me the story of the death. Start wherever you want. (What was your last contact with X? Do you remember the last words X said? Where were you when X died? Was there a funeral? Is so, what was that like? Do you still have questions, concerns, or anything else that feels unresolved or incomplete about the death?)

II. Grieving

A. *The Person Who Died*

How would you describe X's life?

(What was X like as a person? What was your relationship with X? What was X's relationship with other family members? Do you think that looking back over her or his life X would have felt good about that life or mixed or not so good? Why? In what ways do you think X's life was affected by racism or discrimination? Do you think that racism or discrimination were connected to how or when X died?)

B. *Individual Grieving*

In what ways have you grieved the loss?

(How did the death affect your daily life? How did it affect your relationships with others? How did it affect you religiously? When have you felt the loss most sharply? Has your health been affected by your grieving?)

What does X's death mean to you?

(Does X's death have any particular religious meaning to you? Has it affected your relationship to God? Has it affected your participation in organized religion? Is there anything more you could say about how you make sense of X's death?)

After somebody important in their life dies many people at times experience the presence of the person—maybe they see and hear the person or maybe they just have a sense of the person being nearby. Have you had experiences like that since X died? Do you feel that X ever communicates with you? Do you feel that you can communicate with X? Has X showed up in your dreams?

When people grieve they sometimes think about other painful things that have happened in their life. Has that ever happened to you as you grieved for X? If so, could you tell me what other painful things came up for you?

In what ways is X in your life nowadays?

Do you think of X as being somewhere now? If so, where? (Do you think X is in heaven?)

Is there anything else you want to say about how religion or religiosity affected your grieving or the grieving of anyone else in your family?

With whom have you talked the most about the death? Have you gone to particular people, like counselors, clergy, doctors, or friends for help in dealing with the death? Did you read anything that helped you to deal with the death? Did you talk to other people who had to deal with similar deaths? There are support groups for bereaved people. Have you been involved in a support group? If so, can you tell me about that? If not, why not?

Was there anybody whom you felt really let you down; for example, unwilling to listen to you, not being supportive enough, saying hurtful things? (If so, has that changed your relationship with that person/those persons?)

Is there any music that has been particularly important to you as you have dealt with X's death?

C. Grief and Family

Do you think other family members understood and experienced the loss in the same way you have?

(If not, what were the differences? How did those differences affect your relationship with each other? Even people who understand a death in the same way almost always grieve differently and follow a different time course in grieving. Have you observed that in your family? Has it created any problems in your family to grieve differently or over a different time course? If so, tell me about those problems? Have you talked with any family members about the differences in grieving? If so, what things came up as you talked?)

How did the loss affect your relationships with other family members? (Do you think your relationships with other family members were affected by your grieving? Were there disagreements or hard feelings about inheritance or about what happened to possessions of the deceased? Were relationships in your family affected by economic problems related to the death and its aftermath? Were relationships in your family affected by you or somebody else in the family becoming immersed in employment or having problems with employment related to the death? Were relationships in your family affected by your health problems or somebody else's related to the death or your grieving? Were there times when the death drew you closer together or pushed you farther apart?)

Did the loss affect your, or anybody else in the family's use of alcohol, drugs, or other chemicals? (If so, how? If there was a change in usage, how did that affect family relationships?) Did you or other family members use television watching, listening to music, sleep, work, or other things to dull the pain or to distract from the pain?

In what ways do you think there might have been misunderstandings in the family with regard to the loss, misunderstandings about feelings, how to grieve, how the loss happened, or anything else? How did that affect family relationships?

Did you and other family members feel the same way about the ways and amount to grieve? If not, what were the differences? How did the differences affect family relationships?

Other Possible Probes

Have you or other family members felt guilt about anything connecting to the death? (If so, what?) How has that guilt showed up in your family relationships?

Have you blamed yourself or somebody else about something connected to the death? Has any other family member blamed herself or himself or anyone else about something concerning the death? How has that blame showed up in your family relationships?

How, if at all, did you try to support family members following the loss? Was that support appreciated? How if at all did family members try to support you? Was it helpful?

Sometimes a person is affected by how others in the family grieve or what they say about a death and their feelings about it. Were you affected by how somebody else in the family reacted to the death? If you were, did that affect your relationship with that person or other family members? Did it affect your grieving?)

III. Questions About African American Grief

How, if at all, do you think racism or discrimination might be connected to the death? How, if at all, do you think racism or discrimination affected your grieving or the grieving of anyone else in your family? As you think back on the life of the deceased, do you ever think about how that life was affected by racism or discrimination? If so, what kinds of things do you think about?

Do you think there is something different about how African Americans grieve in comparison to how whites grieve?

IV. Concluding Question

What advice would you have for an African American going through what you have had to go through?

REFERENCES

Abrums, M. (2000). Death and meaning in a storefront church. *Public Health Nursing, 17,* 132–142.

Arias, E. (2002, December 19). United States life tables. *National Vital Statistics Reports, 51*(3).

Arias, E. (2004, February 18). United States life tables. *National Vital Statistics Reports, 52*(14).

Attig, T. (2001). Relearning the world: Making and finding meanings. In R. A. Neimeyer (Ed.), *Meaning reconstruction and the experience of loss* (pp. 33–53). Washington, DC: American Psychological Association.

Baer, H. A., & Singer, M. (1992). *African-American religion in the twentieth century: Varieties of protest and accommodation.* Knoxville: University of Tennessee Press.

Barrett, R. K. (1993). Psychocultural influences on African-American attitudes towards death, dying, and bereavement. In J. D. Morgan (Ed.), *Personal care in an impersonal world: A multidimensional look at bereavement* (pp. 213–230). Amityville, NY: Baywood.

Barrett, R. K. (1995). Contemporary African-American funeral rites and traditions. In L. A. DeSpelder & A. L. Strickland (Eds.), *The path ahead: Readings in death and dying* (pp. 80–92, 366–367). Mountain View, CA: Mayfield.

Barrett, R. K. (1997). Bereaved black children. In J. D. Morgan (Ed.), *Readings in thanatology* (pp. 403–419). Amityville, NY: Baywood.

Barrett, R. K. (1998). Sociocultural considerations for work with blacks experiencing loss and grief. In K. J. Doka & J. D. Davidson (Eds.), *Living with grief: Who we are, how we grieve* (pp. 83–96). Washington, DC: Hospice Foundation of America.

Barrett, R. K. (2003). Can we provide better aftercare services to blacks? Questioning the efficacy and cultural relevance of prevailing models and approaches of aftercare. In J. D. Morgan & P. Laungani (Eds.), *Death and bereavement around the world: Vol. 2. Death and bereavement in the Americas* (pp. 57–73). Amityville, NY: Baywood.

Bennett, G. (1999). *"Alas, poor ghost!" Traditions of belief in story and discourse.* Logan, Utah: Utah State University Press.

Billingsley, A. (1999). *Mighty like a river: The black church and social reform.* New York: Oxford University Press.

Black, H. K., & Rubinstein, R. L. (1998–1999). Narratives of three elderly African-American women living in poverty who have lost an adult child to horrendous death. *Omega, 38,* 143–161.

Bolling, J. L. (1995). Guinea across the water: The African-American approach to death and dying. In J. K. Parry & A. S. Ryan (Eds.), *A cross-cultural look at death, dying, and religion* (pp. 145–159). Chicago: Nelson-Hall.

Boyd-Franklin, N., Aleman, J. del C., Jean-Gilles, M. M., &Lewis, S. Y. (1995). Cultural sensitivity and competence: African-American, Latino, and Haitian families with HIV/AIDS. In N. Boyd-Franklin, G. L. Steiner, & M. Boland (Eds.), *Children, families, and HIV/AIDS: Psychosocial and therapeutic issues* (pp. 53–77). New York: Guilford

Boyd-Franklin, N., & Lockwood, T. W. (1999). Spirituality and religion: Implications for psychotherapy with African American clients and families. In F. Walsh (Ed.), *Spiritual resources in family therapy* (pp. 90–103). New York: Guilford.

Brice, C. (1999). *Lead me home: An African American's guide through the grief journey.* New York: Avon.

Brice, C. W. (1989). The relational essence of maternal mourning: An existential-psychoanalytic perspective. *Humanistic Psychologist, 17,* 22–40.

Brice, C. W. (1991a). Paradoxes of maternal mourning. *Psychiatry, 54,* 1–12.

Brice, C. W. (1991b). What forever means: An empirical existential-phenomenological investigation of maternal mourning. *Journal of Phenomenological Psychology, 22,* 16–38.

Bullard, R. D. (1990). *Dumping in Dixie: Race, class, and environmental quality.* Boulder, CO: Westview.

Bullard, R. D., & Wright, B. H. (1989–1990). Toxic waste and the African American community. *The Urban League Review, 13*(1–2), 67–75.

Burke, A. W. (1984). Racism and psychological disturbance among West Indians in Britain. *International Journal of Social Psychiatry, 30,* 50–68.

Christian, J. B., Lapane, K. L., & Toppa, R. S. (2003). Racial disparities in receipt of secondary stroke prevention agents among US nursing home residents. *Stroke, 34,* 2693–2697.

Clark, R., Anderson, N. B., Clark, V. R., & Williams, D. R. (1999). Racism as a stressor for African-Americans: A biopsychosocial model. *American Psychologist, 54,* 805–816.

Collins, C., Leondar-Wright, B., & Sklar, H. (1999). *Shifting fortunes: The perils of the growing wealth gap.* Boston: United for a Fair Economy.

Conant, R. D. (1996). Memories of the death and life of a spouse: The role of images and sense of presence in grief. In D. Klass, P. R. Silverman, & S. L. Nickman (Eds.), *Continuing bonds: New understandings of grief* (pp. 179–196). Washington, DC: Taylor & Francis.

Cooper, R. S. (2001). Social inequality, ethnicity and cardiovascular disease. *International Journal of Epidemiology, 30*(Suppl. 1), S48–S52.

Cooper-Lewter, N. C. (1999). *Black grief and soul therapy.* Richmond, VA: Harriet Tubman Press.

Cooper-Patrick, L., Gallo, J. J., Powe, N. R, Steinwachs, D. S., Eaton, W. W., & Ford, D. E. (1999). Mental health service utilization by African Americans and whites: The Baltimore Epidemiological Catchment Area Follow-Up. *Medical Care, 37,* 1034–1045.

Costen, M. W. (1993). *African American Christian worship.* Nashville, TN: Abingdon Press.

Crawford, A. E. B. (2002). *Hope in the holler: A womanist theology.* Louisville, KY: Westminster John Knox Press.

Davis, J. (2000). *The white image in the black mind: A study of African American literature.* Westport, CT: Greenwood.

Dennis, G. C. (2001). Racism in medicine: Planning for the future. *Journal of the National Medical Association, 93*(Suppl. 3), 1S–5S.

Devore, W. (1990). The experience of death: A black perspective. In J. K. Perry (Ed.), *Social work practices with the terminally ill: A transcultural perspective* (pp. 47–66). Springfield, IL: Charles C. Thomas.

Din-Dzietham, R., Nembhard, W. N., Collins, R., & Davis, S. K. (2004). Perceived stress following race-based discrimination at work is associated with hypertension in African-Americans: The metro Atlanta heart disease study, 1999–2001. *Social Science and Medicine, 58,* 449–461.

Dorsey, M. K. (1998). Race, poverty, and environment. *Legal Studies Forum, 22*(1–3), 501–518.

Early, K. E., & Akers, R. L. (1993). "It's a white thing"—An exploration of beliefs about suicide in the African-American community. *Deviant Behavior, 14,* 277–296.

Ellison, C. G., & Taylor, R. J. (1996). Turning to prayer: Religious coping among black Americans. *Review of Religious Research, 38,* 111–131.

Ellison, G. L., Coker, A. L., Hebert, J. R., Sanderson, M., Royal, C. D., & Weinrich, S. P. (2001). Psychosocial stress and prostate cancer: A theoretical model. *Ethnicity and Disease, 11,* 484–495.

Feagin, J. R., & McKinney, K. D. (2003). *The many costs of white racism.* Lanham, MD: Rowman & Littlefield.

Frantz, T. T., Trolley, B. C., & Johil, M. P. (1996). Religious aspects of bereavement. *Pastoral Psychology, 44,* 151–163.

Freeman, H. P., & Payne, R. (2000). Racial injustice in health care. *New England Journal of Medicine, 342,* 1045–1047.

Gilbert, K. R. (1992). Religion as a resource for bereaved parents. *Journal of Religion and Health, 31,* 19–30.

Gilbert, K. R. (1996). "We've had the same loss, why don't we have the same grief?' Loss and differential grief in families. *Death Studies, 20,* 269–283.

Gilbert, K. R. (2002). Taking a narrative approach to grief research: Finding meaning in stories. *Death Studies, 26,* 223–239.

Gunaratnam, Y. (1997). Culture is not enough: A critique of multi-culturalism in palliative care. In D. Field, J. Hockey, & N. Small (Eds.), *Death, gender, and ethnicity* (pp. 166–186). New York: Routledge.

Guyer, B., Freedman, M. A., Strobino, D. M., & Sondik, E. J. (2000). Annual summary of vital statistics: Trends in the health of Americans during the 20th century. *Pediatrics, 106,* 1307–1317.

Harvey, J. H. (1996). *Embracing their memory: Loss and the social psychology of storytelling.* Needham Heights, MA: Allyn & Bacon.

Herskovits, M. J. (1958). *The myth of the Negro past.* Boston: Beacon.

Hill, A. C. (1983–1984). The impact of urbanism on death and dying among black people in a rural community in middle Tennessee. *Omega, 14,* 171–186.

Hill, S. A. (1997). Ethnicity and the ethic of caring in African American families. *Journal of Personal and Interpersonal Loss, 2,* 109–128.

Hillemeier, M. M., Geronimus, A. T., & Bound, J. (2001). Widening black/white mortality differentials among U.S. children during the 1980s. *Ethnicity and Disease, 11,* 469–483.

Hines, P. M. (1986). Afro-American families. *Family Therapy Networker, 10* (6), 31–32.

Hines, P. M. (1991). Death and African-American culture. In F. Walsh & M. McGoldrick (Eds.), *Living beyond loss: Death in the family* (pp. 186–191). New York: Norton.

Ho, T., Snowden, L. R., Jerrell, J. M., & Nguyen, T. D. (1991). Ethnic populations in public mental health: Services choice and level of use. *American Journal of Public Health, 81,* 1429–1434.

Hobbs, F. B., & Danon, B. L. (1993). *65+ in the United States.* Washington, DC: U.S. Bureau of the Census, Economics and Statistics Administration, U.S. Department of Commerce, publication P23–190.

Holloway, K. F. C. (2002). *Passed on: African American mourning stories.* Durham, NC: Duke University Press.

Holstein, J. A., & Gubrium, J. F. (1995). *The active interview.* Thousand Oaks, CA: Sage.

hooks, b. (1992). Representations of whiteness in the black imagination. In b. hooks, *Black looks: Race and representation* (pp. 165–178). Boston: South End Press.

hooks, b. (1993a). *A woman's mourning song.* New York: Harlem River Press.

hooks, b. (1993b). *Sisters of the yam: Black women and self-recovery.* Cambridge, MA: South End Press.

Horner, R. D. (1998). Racial variation in cancer care: A case study of prostate cancer. *Cancer Treatment and Research, 97,* 99–114.

Jackson, M. (1972). The black experience with death: A brief analysis through black writings. *Omega, 3,* 203–209.

Johnson-Moore, P., & Phillips, L. J. (1994). Black American communities: Coping with death. In B. O. Dane & C. Levine (Eds.), *AIDS and the new orphans: Coping with death* (pp. 101–120). Westport, CT: Auburn House/Greenwood.

Jones, F. (1991). The African American psychologist as consultant and therapist. In R. L. Jones (Ed.), *Black psychology* (3rd ed., pp. 653–666). Berkeley, CA: Cobb & Henry.

Jones, J. M., & Block, C. B. (1984). Black cultural perspectives. *Clinical Psychologist 37*(2), 58–62.

Jones, W. R. (1998). *Is God a white racist?* Boston: Beacon.

Kalish, R. A., & Reynolds, D. K. (1973). Phenomenological reality and post-death contact. *Journal for the Scientific Study of Religion, 12,* 209–221.

Kalish, R. A., & Reynolds, D. K. (1981). *Death and ethnicity.* Amityville, NY: Baywood.

Kincheloe, J. L., & Steinberg, S. R. (1998). Addressing the crisis of whiteness: Reconfiguring white identity in a pedagogy of whiteness. In J. L. Kincheloe, S. R. Steinberg, N. M. Rodriguez, & R. E. Chennault (Eds.), *White reign: Deploying whiteness in America* (pp. 3–29). New York: St. Martin's Griffin.

Klass, D. (1988). *Parental grief: Solace and resolution.* New York: Springer.

Klass, D. (1993). Solace and immortality: Bereaved parents' continuing bond with their children. *Death Studies, 17,* 343–368.

Klass, D. (1996). The deceased child in the psychic and social worlds of bereaved parents during the resolution of grief. In D. Klass, P. R. Silverman, & S. L. Nickman (Eds.), *Continuing bonds: New understandings of grief* (pp. 199–215). Washington, DC: Taylor & Francis.

Klass, D. (1997). The deceased child in the psychic and social worlds of bereaved parents during the resolution of grief. *Death Studies, 21,* 147–175.

Klass, D. (1999). *The spiritual life of bereaved parents.* Philadelphia: Brunner/Mazel.

Klass, D., Silverman, P. R., & Nickman, S. L. (Eds.) (1996). *Continuing bonds: New understandings of grief.* Washington, DC: Taylor & Francis.

Klass, D., & Walter, T. (2001). Processes of grieving: How bonds are continued. In M. S. Stroebe, R. O. Hansson, W. Stroebe, & H. Schut (Eds.), *Handbook of bereavement research: Consequences, coping, and care* (pp. 431–448). Washington, DC: American Psychological Association.

Krakauer, E. L., Crenner, C., & Fox, K. (2002). Barriers to optimum end-of-life care for minority patients. *Journal of the American Geriatrics Society, 50,* 182–190.

Krieger, N. (2003). Does racism harm health? Did child abuse exist before 1961? On explicit questions, critical science, and current controversies: An ecosocial perspective. *American Journal of Public Health, 93,* 194–199.

Lamb, V. L. (2003). Historical and epidemiological trends in mortality in the United States. In C. D. Bryant (Ed.), *Handbook of death and dying* (Vol. 1, pp. 185–197). Thousand Oaks, CA: Sage.

Landrine, H., & Klonoff, E. A. (1996). Traditional African-American family practices: Prevalence and correlates. *Western Journal of Black Studies, 20,* 59–62.

Leach, M. S., & Braithwaite, D. O. (1996). A binding tie: Supportive communication of family kinkeepers. *Journal of Applied Communication Research, 24,* 200–216.

Lee, W., Jr. (1995). Behind smiles and laughter: African-American children's issues about bereavement. In E. A. Grollman (Ed.), *Bereaved children and teens: A support guide for parents and professionals* (pp. 93–112). Boston: Beacon.

Levine, R. S., Foster, J. E., Fullilove, R. E., Fullilove, M. T., Briggs, N. C., Hull, P. C., Husaini, B. A., & Hennekens, C. H. (2001). Black-white inequalities in mortality and life expectancy, 1933–1999: Implications for Healthy People 2010. *Public Health Reports, 116,* 474–483.

Lincoln, C. E., & Mamiya, L. H. (1990). *The black church in the African American experience.* Durham, NC: Duke University Press.

Lopata, H. Z. (1973). *Widowhood in an American city.* Cambridge, MA: Schenkman.

Mandelblatt, J. S., Kerner, J. F., Hadley, J., Hwang, Y., Eggert, L., Johnson, L. E., & Gold, K. (2002). Variations in breast carcinoma treatment in older Medicare beneficiaries: Is it black or white? *Cancer, 95,* 1401–1414.

Martin, E. P., & Martin, J. M. (1995). *Social work and the black experience.* Washington, DC: NASW Press.

Martin, T. L., & Doka, K. J. (2000). *Men don't cry . . . women do.* Philadelphia: Brunner/Mazel.

McDonald, J. M. (1987). Support systems for American black wives and widows. In H. Lopata (Ed.), *Widows: Vol 2. North America* (pp. 139–157). Durham, NC: Duke University Press.

McIlwain, C. D. (2003). *Death in black and white: Death ritual and family ecology.* Cresskill, NJ: Hampton Press.

McIntosh, P. (1988). *White privilege and male privilege: A personal account of coming to see correspondences through work in women's studie.* (Working Paper, No. 189). Wellesley College Center for Research on Women.

Meagher, D. K., & Bell, C. P. (1993). Perspectives on death in the African-American community. In K. J. Doka & J. D. Morgan (Eds.), *Death and spirituality* (pp. 113–130). Amityville, NY: Baywood.

Mills, R. J., & Bhandari, S. (2003, September). *Health insurance coverage in the United States, 2002. Current Population Reports.* Washington, DC: U.S. Bureau of the Census.

Minkler, M., Roe, K. M., & Robertson-Beckley, R. J. (1994). Raising grandchildren from crack-cocaine households: Effects on family and friendship ties of African-American women. *American Journal of Orthopsychiatry, 64,* 20–29.

Moon, D. (1999). White enculturation and bourgeois ideology: The discursive production of "Good (White) Girls." In T. K. Nakayama & J. N. Martin, (Eds.), *Whiteness: The communication of social identity.* (pp. 177–197) Thousand Oaks, CA: Sage.

Moore, J. L., III, & Bryant, C. D. (2003). Black funeralization and culturally grounded services. In C. D. Bryant (Ed.), *Handbook of death and dying* (Vol. 2, pp. 598–603). Thousand Oaks, CA: Sage.

Nadeau, J. W. (1998). *Families making sense of death.* Beverly Hills, CA: Sage.

Nadeau, J. W. (2001). Meaning making in family bereavement: A family systems approach. In M. S. Stroebe, R. O. Hansson, W. Stroebe, & H. Schut (Eds.), *Handbook of bereavement research: Consequences, coping, and care* (pp. 329–347). Washington, DC: American Psychological Association.

Nakayama, T. K., & Martin, J. N. (1999). *Whiteness: The communication of social identity.* Thousand Oaks, CA: Sage.

National Institute on Alcohol Abuse and Alcoholism (2003, May 28). *Databases.* Washington, DC: National Institutes of Health, United States Department of Health and Human Services.

Neighbors, H. W. (1985). Seeking professional help for personal problems: Black Americans' use of health and mental health services. *Community Mental Health Journal, 21,* 156–166.

Neimeyer, R. A. (2001). The language of loss: Grief therapy as a process of meaning reconstruction. In R. A. Neimeyer (Ed.), *Meaning reconstruction and the experience of loss* (pp. 261–292). Washington, DC: American Psychological Association.

Ofili, E. (2001). Ethnic disparities in cardiovascular health. *Ethnicity and Disease, 11,* 838–840.

Owen, J. E., Goode, K. T., & Haley, W. E. (2001). End of life care and reactions to death in African-American and white family caregivers of relatives with Alzheimer's disease. *Omega, 43,* 349–361.

Papacek, E. M., Collins, J. W., Jr., Schulte, N. F., Goergen, C., & Drolet, A. (2002). Differing postneonatal mortality rates of African-American and white infants in Chicago: An ecologic study. *Maternal and Child Health Journal, 6,* 99–105.

Perry, H. L. (1993). Mourning and funeral customs of African Americans. In D. P. Irish, K. F. Lundquist, & V. J. Nelsen (Eds.), *Ethnic variations in dying, death, and grief* (pp. 51–65). Washington, DC: Taylor & Francis.

Pine, J. C., Marx, B. D., & Lakshmanan, A. (2002). An examination of accidental-release scenarios from chemical-processing sites: The relation of race to distance. *Social Science Quarterly, 83,* 317–331.

Pleck, E. H. (2000). *Celebrating the family: Ethnicity, consumer culture, and family rituals.* Cambridge, MA: Harvard University Press.

Plumpp, S. (1972). *Black rituals.* Chicago: Third World Press.

Preston, S. H., Elo, I. T., Rosenwaike, I., & Hill, M. (1996). African-American mortality at older ages: Results of a matching study. *Demography, 33*(2), 193–209.

Prouty, E. N. (1983). *The impact of race, age, and other factors on the experience of bereavement.* Unpublished doctoral dissertation, Department of Psychology, Georgia State University.

Raider, M., & Pauline-Morand, M. B. (1998). *Social work practice with low-income, urban, African-American families.* Lewiston, NY: Edward Mellen Press.

Riches, G., & Dawson, P. (1996a). "An intimate loneliness": Evaluating the impact of a child's death on parental self-identity and marital relationship. *Journal of Family Therapy, 18,* 1–22.

Riches, G., & Dawson, P. (1996b). Making stories and taking stories: Methodological reflections on researching grief and marital tension following the death of a child. *British Journal of Guidance and Counseling, 24,* 357–365.

Rosen, R. (1994). Who gets polluted? The movement for environmental justice. *Dissent, 41,* 223–230.

Rosenblatt, P. C. (1983). *Bitter, bitter tears: Nineteenth century diarists and twentieth century grief theories.* Minneapolis: University of Minnesota Press.

Rosenblatt, P. C. (1993). Cross-cultural variation in the experience, expression, and understanding of grief. In D. P. Irish, K. F. Lundy, & V. J. Nelsen (Eds.), *Ethnic variations in dying, death, and grief: Diversity in universality* (pp. 13–19). Washington, DC: Taylor & Francis.

Rosenblatt, P. C. (1997). Grief in small scale societies. In C. M. Parkes, , P. Laungani, & B. Young (Eds.), *Death and bereavement across cultures* (pp. 27–51). London: Routledge.

Rosenblatt, P, C. (2000a). *Parent grief: Narratives of loss and relationship.* Philadelphia: Brunner/Mazel.

Rosenblatt, P. C. (2000b). *Help your marriage survive the death of a child.* Philadelphia: Temple University Press.

Rosenblatt, P. C. (2001). A social constructionist perspective on cultural differences in grief. In M. S. Stroebe, R. O. Hansson, W. Stroebe, & H. Schut (Eds.), *Handbook of bereavement research: Consequences, coping, and care* (pp. 285–300). Washington, DC: American Psychological Association Press.

Rosenblatt, P. C. (2003). Bereavement in cross-cultural perspective. In C. D. Bryant (Ed.), *Handbook of death and dying* (Vol. 2, pp. 855–861). Thousand Oaks, CA: Sage.

Rosenblatt, P. C., & Elde, C. (1990). Shared reminiscence about a deceased parent: Implications for grief education and grief counseling. *Family Relations, 39,* 206–210.

Rosenblatt, P. C., & Karis, T. A. (1993). Economics and family bereavement following a fatal farm accident. *Journal of Rural Community Psychology, 12* (2), 37–51.

Rosenblatt, P. C., Karis, T. A., & Powell, R. D. (1995). *Multiracial couples: Black and white voices.* Thousand Oaks, CA: Sage.

Rosenblatt, P. C., & Tubbs, C. Y. (1998). Loss in the experience of multiracial couples. In J. H. Harvey (Ed.), *Perspectives on loss: A sourcebook* (pp. 125–135). Philadelphia: Taylor & Francis.

Rosenblatt, P. C., Walsh, R. P., & Jackson, D. A. (1976). *Grief and mourning in cross-cultural perspective.* New Haven, CT: Human Relations Area Files Press.

Rosenthal, C. J. (1985). Kinkeeping in the familial division of labor. *Journal of Marriage and the Family, 47,* 965–974.

Ruiz, D. S., & Carlton-LaNey, I. (1999). The increase in intergenerational African American families headed by grandmothers. *Journal of Sociology and Social Welfare, 26,* 71–86.

Sandven, K., & Resnick, M. D. (1990). Informal adoption about black adolescent mothers. *American Journal of Orthopsychiatry, 60,* 210–224.

Shapiro, E. (1994). *Grief as a family process.* New York: Guilford.

Shenk, D. (2000). Views of aging African American women: Memories within the historical context. *Journal of Aging and Identity, 5,* 109–125.

Shrestha, L. B. (1997). *Racial differences in life expectancy among elder African Americans and whites: The surprising truth about comparisons.* New York: Garland.

Sims, M., & Rainge, Y. (2002). Urban poverty and infant-health disparities among African Americans and whites in Milwaukee. *Journal of the National Medical Association, 94,* 472–479.

Smedley, B. D., Stith, A. Y., & Nelson, A. R. (Eds.) (2003). *Unequal treatment: Confronting racial and ethnic disparities in health care.* Washington, DC: National Academies Press.

Smith, S. H. (2002). "Fret no more my child . . . for I'm all over heaven all day": Religious beliefs in the bereavement of African American, middle-aged daughters coping with the death of an elderly mother. *Death Studies, 26,* 309–323.

Snead, J. A. (2000). Repetition as a figure of black culture. In R. Ferguson, M. Gever, T. T. Minh-ha, & C. West (Ed.), *Out there: Marginalization and contemporary culture* (pp. 213–230). Cambridge, MA: MIT Press.

Sormanti, M., & August, J. (1997). Parental bereavement: Spiritual connections with deceased children. *American Journal of Orthopsychiatry, 67,* 460–469.

Spencer, J. M. (1996*). Re-searching black music.* Knoxville, TN: University of Tennessee Press.

Staples, R., & Johnson, L. B. (1993). *Black families at the crossroads.* San Francisco: Jossey-Bass.

Steffen, P. R., McNeilly, M., Anderson, N., & Sherwood, A. (2003). Effects of perceived racism and anger inhibition on ambulatory blood pressure in African Americans. *Psychosomatic Medicine, 65,* 746–750.

St. Jean, Y., & Feagin, J. R. (1998). The family costs of white racism: The case of African American families. *Journal of Comparative Family Studies, 29,* 297–312.

Stroebe, M. S., & Schut, H. (2001). Meaning making in the dual process model of coping with bereavement. In R. A. Neimeyer (Ed.), *Meaning reconstruction and the experience of loss* (pp. 55–73). Washington, DC: American Psychological Association.

Sullivan, M. A. (1995). May the circle be unbroken: The African-American experience of death, dying, and spirituality. In J. K. Parry & A. S. Ryan (Eds.), *A cross-cultural look at death, dying, and religion* (pp. 160–171). Chicago: Nelson-Hall.

Taylor, R. J., Chatters, L. J., & Levin, J. (2004). *Religion in the lives of African Americans: Social, psychological, and health perspectives.* Thousand Oaks, CA: Sage.

Thomas, H. N. (1988). *From folklore to fiction: A study of folk heroes and rituals in the black American novel.* New York: Greenwood.

Titus, S. L., Rosenblatt, P. C., & Anderson, R. M. (1979). Family conflict over inheritance of property. *Family Coordinator, 28,* 337–346.

Tully, M. A. (1999). Lifting our voices: African American cultural responses to trauma and loss. In K. Nader, N. Dubrow, & B. H. Stamm (Eds.), *Honoring differences: Cultural issues in the treatment of trauma and loss* (pp. 23–48). Philadelphia: Brunner/Mazel.

U.S. Bureau of the Census (1999, March). *Current Population Survey.* Washington, DC: Author.

U.S. Bureau of the Census (2000). Money income in the United States: 1998. *Current Population Reports,* P60–206.

U.S. Bureau of the Census (2002). *Statistical abstract of the United States, 2001.* Washington, DC: Author.

U.S. Bureau of the Census (2003, June 4). *Asset ownership of households, 1998.* http://www.census.gov/hhes/www/wealth/1998_2000/wlth98-2.html

U.S. Bureau of the Census (2004, May 13). *Median household income by race and Hispanic origin: 1967 to 1999.* http://www.census.gov/hhes/income/income99/incxrace.html

U.S. Centers for Disease Control (1995). *Morbidity and Mortality Weekly Report, 44*(01): 6–7, 13–14.

Van, P. (2001). Breaking the silence of African-American women: Healing after pregnancy loss. *Health Care for Women International, 22,* 229–243.

van Dijk, T. A. (1992). Discourse and the denial of racism. *Discourse & Society, 3,* 87–118.

Walker, W. T. (1979). *"Somebody's calling my name": Black sacred music and social change.* Valley Forge, PA: Judson.

Williams, D. R. (1999). Race, socioeconomic status, and health: The added effects of racism and discrimination. In N. E. Adler, M. Marmot, B. S. McEwen, & J. Stewart (Eds.), *Socioeconomic status and health in industrial nations: Social, psychological, and biological pathways. Annals of the New York Academy of Sciences, 896,* 173–188.

Williams, D. R., & Collins, C. (2001). Racial residential segregation: A fundamental cause of racial disparities in health. *Public Health Reports, 116,* 404–416.

Zane, N. (1997). Interrupting historical patterns: Bridging race and gender gaps between senior white men and other organizational groups. In M. Fine, L. Weis, L. C. Powell, & L. M. Wong (Eds.), *Off white* (pp. 343–353). New York: Routledge.

Author Index

Subject Index